TIM GENT

DARTMOOR WALKING AND CAMPING

First published in Great Britain 2022 by Pesda Press

Tan y Coed Canol

Ceunant

Caernarfon

Gwynedd

LL55 4RN

Maps by Bute Cartographics. Contains Ordnance Survey data © Crown copyright and database right 2022

ISBN: 9781906095833

Printed in Poland, www.lfbookservices.co.uk

For Lloyd, Otto and Ernest

Foreword

Upland areas are often likened to islands, yet none in Britain, with the exception perhaps of the Cairngorms, lives up to the comparison quite as successfully as Dartmoor. Lifting in dark metamorphic magnificence from a green pasture ocean, this rolling upsurge of granite and rough grass looms over the surrounding Devon landscape. Tideline strands of ancient oak woodland fringe a bracken-covered edge, lapped by an amorphous collection of small stone-bound fields and shaded sunken trackways.

From almost all points in Devon, Dartmoor has a very physical presence. It hovers at the edge of vision, in the thoughts of any keen fell walker. Travel almost anywhere in the county, even some way beyond, and the soft interlocking summits of High Willhays, Cosdon, Hangingstone and Ryder's Hill rise to break the horizon; cast red or gold under a clear autumn sky, sometimes purple against a midwinter yellow sunset, near black in spring, often capped, in any season, by a pale windswept crown of mist or cloud.

Like any true island, Dartmoor's unique character stems from contrasts. Yet where the Shetlands or Scillies lie distinct from their encircling ocean, the moor is set apart solely by its height and geology. That distinction is still very clear though, with the resultant climate, flora and fauna, human history and current land use each existing in stark difference to the lowlands spread beyond. Dartmoor is also surrounded by an ever busier sea of human activity, with farmland and coastal plains criss-crossed by roads, all slowly disappearing beneath housing estates, out-of-town business parks and shopping malls. By contrast, the moor offers a desert island, almost devoid of modern development. Admittedly, a rather damp desert island.

That's not to say that Dartmoor is uninhabited, far from it. Farms, hamlets and modest villages are very much part of the makeup of the moor. On the whole though, these settlements lie strung out along the infrequent roads, or manage to edge their way only a short distance up flanking valleys, bound by radiating fields. As with many real islands, the population of this oval volcanic upcast have their homes mostly around the fringe. People cluster in the moorland edge towns of Okehampton, Tavistock and Ashburton, or in villages with evocative names such as Chagford, Mary Tavy, Widecombe-in-the-Moor. Only a few hardy souls live in the interior, drawn deep into the moorland outback either by work or the lure of a very real solitude. Step only a few hundred yards from one of those rare, high moor roads, away from the picnickers with their tartan rugs, busy photographing crisp-eating ponies, and the population density plummets. Head deeper into the interior of Dartmoor and you might not speak to another person all day.

Matchless in southern England as a substantial body of true upland, and situated less than one hundred miles from Bristol or Southampton, only a few short hours in fact from the capital, Dartmoor is a very special place. For those caught amidst the increasingly hectic human shipping lanes of the lowlands, tired of breasting the tide of deadlines and targets, Dartmoor offers an opportunity to pull ashore, to climb in search of space, open skies and countless restorative possibilities. Eyes can now gaze out unhindered to a far slope, to follow the line of a galloping herd of ponies, the shadows of a seemingly unending flock of gale driven clouds. Ears catch the raven's chuckle, the mew of a buzzard, the run of a stream heard tinkling yet unseen, deep beneath a tumbled slew of moss-covered boulders.

Without apology, this book will celebrate all this, revelling in the tors, the valleys, the rivers and the bogs that combine to make up Dartmoor's intriguing whole. At its heart though lies a key aim; to provide an introduction and guide to exploring the moor on foot, the wooded fringe and the high invigorating centre. As this upland also offers another opportunity, unique in England and Wales, in fact much of Europe, a chapter will also give advice to those who, having found this compelling space, decide to tarry a while, pitch a tent and create a temporary home amongst its glorious folds.

Welcome then to walking and camping on Dartmoor.

Dartmoor.

Contents

Contents

About the Author

Tim lives in Devon, not far from the north edge of Dartmoor. He has also lived on the moor, working at various interesting locations up there over the years. On almost every walk across Dartmoor, and further afield, Tim has been accompanied by his wife Susannah, which is why she appears in so many photographs in this book. If Tim is in view, Susannah was behind the camera.

Devon: looking south from Exmoor, with Dartmoor on the far horizon.

Introduction

Mention where I live, and it sometimes feels as if almost everyone and their aunt once took a holiday within Dartmoor's welcoming shadow. Fond recollections abound, in which any rain is conveniently forgotten and a warm summer sun shines unbroken over thatched cob barns and Devon cream teas. Then there's the moor itself, and few it seems who retain those happy childhood memories of a holiday in the West Country, fail to recall the inevitable visit to the upland itself.

In a corner of southern England blessed with rugged upland, Dartmoor still manages to stand out. Exmoor and Bodmin Moor each have their qualities, very clear qualities at that, yet the upcast of granite planted solid at the centre of Devon remains preeminent. Head up along one of the deep shadowed lanes that flank the moor, onto the high, tor studded ground, and even if your visit involves no more than making friends with a pony and a sunlit afternoon in a pub garden, the memory is set. Bound up with legend, folklore and an almost tangible sense of a very deep history, the moor takes a hold on the imagination and remains in the thoughts. The magic is done. This is a place where experiences stick.

Dartmoor by horse, in this case with a spare.

You can drive across Dartmoor of course, heading along the smooth undulating roads beyond Moretonhampstead, Ashburton or Tavistock, windows down, weaving between the ponies and sheep sunning themselves against the verge. There are some extremely fine views to be had from the B3357 or B3212.

The moor is ideal for exploration on horseback too. With stables dotted around the edge there are numerous opportunities to go riding for the day, to imagine you are traveling across some empty quarter of Montana or Mongolia.

With developments in cycle design and technology, a mountain bike could also take you just about anywhere on the moor. The many miners' or old army tracks provide almost perfect cycle avenues to the interior.

All that said, you won't be surprised when I suggest it is on foot that Dartmoor is best encountered; up close, right underfoot and at a slow pace. On two legs you can weave through the shattered granite spread wide beneath a mighty tor, leap from waterworn stone to waterworn stone across a bright foam-flecked stream, before climbing to piece together a dry route through a peat-covered and often

It's a fine place for a drive.

A good flat bit.

Walking country.

Dartmoor wild camping.

waterlogged ridge. Free from many of the hazards of upland travel found elsewhere, and brim full of interest, whether from archaeological remains, rare bog plants or contorted geology, Dartmoor is ideal wild walking country.

A central aim of this book is to enhance that experience and try to ensure that the best can be obtained from the many walking opportunities on offer. Advice is given on various aspects: when and where to go, what to wear and what to take with you. Various safety concerns are also considered. A large chunk at the end of this book then provides details of specific walking routes, with thirty descriptions, that offer a range in length from just a few kilometres to a couple covering over 50.

While the moor offers a plethora of beneficial prospects to the traveller on foot, it also possesses another very special quality, one that's unique in England and Wales, in fact unique across much of mainland Europe. For after a day of satisfying exploration, a walker is allowed to stop, pitch a tent, and to spend a night under canvas. It's often called wild camping, and I'll describe this wonderful facet of Dartmoor travel later; looking at kit, and the best places to make camp. Other opportunities, such as swimming, will also be considered, but not until after I've dealt with matters connected to that all-important walking.

Before heading out though, I want to introduce the moor itself. What is it exactly that makes up this rare southern English upland? How did it end up looking the way it does? What and who still consider the moor home?

We can also look at the changing relationship we humans have had with the moor over the years. Dartmoor is a living and evolving space after all, an upland space in which nature and people have coexisted for millennia.

Unlike just about any other place in England south of the Lakes, this dome of time-ravaged granite provides something else of significant merit. Home to tough flora, stubborn fauna and thinly scattered and equally resilient residents, it also represents one of the last strongholds of that rarest and most valuable of resources… emptiness, or at least a healthy absence of us.

One important clarification though, before we take a closer look. Amongst the many ways any area can be categorised, Dartmoor exists in two distinct forms, the National Park, and the smaller extent of the high moor. Many of the statistics given for Dartmoor online and in books relate to the National Park, which extends over a roughly circular area, approximately 32km (20 miles) across. This designated, and legally protected, National Park extends beyond the open moor to include a significant area of farmland and woodland, particularly to the east. Although extremely pretty, it falls outside the focus of this book. It is the upland, the largely unenclosed and elevated ground, that will be considered in the following chapters: the high moor.

Dartmoor.

The height above sea level around the periphery of the moor at which this high moor area begins is arbitrary of course. To a large degree, it will depend on your point of view. With regard to the definition employed for this book, it also varies quite a bit. Very roughly, however, it includes the land that extends above about 200–250m above sea level on the south side of the moor, and at elevations greater than 300–350m to the north. Look at an Ordnance Survey 1:25,000 map, and it is the yellow bit, the access land enclosed by an orange line, that pretty much represents the area we'll be looking at. We will stray at times into the surrounding enclosed farmland, it is very pretty after all. On the whole, however, this will only be visited in order to gain access to an isolated outlier of that glorious high ground.

So having defined our area of interest, and leaving the bustling lowlands behind, let's take a closer look at Dartmoor.

Dartmoor.

The Moor

We have our mode of transport, walking, and we've defined Dartmoor as our area. It's an alluring mix, together offering access to high, wide and open spaces, dramatic views and fresh Atlantic air. Stand at any point on the edge of this exuberant upwelling of Devon granite and countless routes spread out in every direction, each rich with possibilities, every one peppered with interest. Yet before we leap to plant a boot on that pony cropped turf, we should take some time to look more closely at this very special place, the moorland those wandering herds of stocky wild horses think of as home.

Where is it?

Like a plump frog on a bright green lily pad, Dartmoor sits almost at the centre of the ancient county of Devon; the shire itself forming the broader, eastern half of the South West peninsula. Rising high and slightly austere above this rolling patchwork of Devon meadow and woodland, Dartmoor dominates views from almost every corner. For travellers arriving from 'up country', Dartmoor is the defining feature on the horizon as they descend from the Blackdown Hills that form the border with Somerset. From Exmoor and the Quantocks in the north, to the high ground around the cities, towns and fishing villages on the south coast, even from Bodmin Moor in Cornwall, Dartmoor fills the distant skyline.

Set out on foot across the high moor on a bright day, and the elevation soon makes it easy to place yourself within this setting. Across much of the south side of the moor, the sun reflects off the not-so-distant waves of the English Channel. Plymouth Sound fills a low gap on the coast, while the iron bow of Isambard Kingdom Brunel's famous bridge can be made out, crossing the River Tamar just inland. On the far edge of Dartmoor, at the moor's highest point, High Willhays offers coastal views in both directions; a more distant sighting of the shimmering English Channel to the south, but also the edge of the Atlantic Ocean to the north-west, at least on a clear day, if you know where to look.

Eleven rivers fall into that sea to the south of the moor, two more in the other direction, where they meet the Atlantic surf along the cliff-bound northern coast. All but two of these rivers start life at the sodden centre of the moor, or at least have tributaries that rise here, as moisture oozes from the waterlogged peat to form the tiniest of infant streams. Falling from this vast elevated sponge, these moorland streams ensure a steady and reliable supply of water for the lowlands beyond, helping to make Devon one of the finest and most verdant pasture lands in Europe. It might be damp, and often cool, but Dartmoor is very much the heart of Devon.

What is it?

Dartmoor forms an oval area of upland, rising to a maximum height of 621m. Not high, even by British standards, but still elevated enough to represent the highest ground in southern England. It's true that some of the hills sharing the border with Wales rise a little higher, but you need to reach Kinder Scout in Derbyshire before the rest of England exceeds this elevation.

A view across the centre of the moor.

The loftiest spot on the moor, fittingly named High Willhays, sits close to the northern edge, and as a rough rule Dartmoor is angled towards the sun, falling gently to the south. Each of the three ridges on the moor that poke their heads above the 600m mark are situated in the northern third. There are exceptions, but on the whole, the craggiest ground also lies north of a diagonal line drawn across Dartmoor by the B3212, one of only two 'main' roads that cross the high moor.

Almost the whole of Dartmoor, and certainly all the high ground, has been part of a National Park since 1951. It was one of the first areas in Britain to gain this designation, pipped to the post earlier the same year, only by the Peak District, Eryri (or Snowdonia) and the Lake District. The current version of this designated area, protected by the Dartmoor National Park Authority, or DNPA, covers an area of 954km^2, which equates to 368 square miles.

Measuring 32km (20 miles) across, the Park includes four nature reserves, 25 Conservation Areas, 2,750 Listed Buildings, 1,082 Scheduled Monuments and over 40 Sites of Special Scientific Interest (SSSI), although, as mentioned in the introduction, it should be noted that the Park extends quite a way beyond the high moor, particularly to the east.

Depending how you define it, the high moor, the bit that forms the geographic focus for this book, covers an area of a touch over 50,00 hectares, or nearly 200 square miles. Again, far from massive when compared to other upland areas, even in the UK, but still a place, and this is its crowning glory, in which it is very easy to feel miles from anywhere.

The only significant settlement situated within the high moor, at least in terms of size, is Princetown, with a population of roughly 1,500. After this large village, built to serve the famous Georgian prison, only relatively small hamlets dot the two main roads that cross the high ground. The major conurbations of Okehampton to the north, Tavistock to the west, Mortonhampstead and Ashburton lying to the east and Ivybridge on the southern edge, are all situated below the unenclosed moor. In brief, the high moor is largely free of people.

Geology

Much of southern England is dominated by chalk or gravel. These geological deposits form either the vast rolling downland, spread out between Dorset and Kent, or the alluvial floodplains of the venerable Thames and its many smaller cousins. Head west however, and not far beyond the Devon border all this soft rock gives way to something much less forgiving.

Granite, the signature rock of the South West, started life with fire. Once part of the molten core of our planet, granite, like other igneous rocks such as basalt and gneiss, was formed when some of that superheated geology escaped through a fissure in the earth's otherwise rock-tight mantle. Here, this infant rock cooled and hardened, the individual elements, including feldspar and quartz, often forming sizeable crystals that characterise this material today. Tough, and extremely resistant to erosion, granite forms not only Dartmoor, but Exmoor, the moors around Bodmin and long stretches of the South West coastline.

There are other rock types in Devon and Cornwall, and sedimentary versions such as sandstone surround Dartmoor. There's even a small outcrop of limestone at the north-west corner of the high moor itself, and a little more on the western fringe, but much of this high plateau is granite, representing the geology underlying at least 65% of the National Park, and almost all of the high unenclosed area.

Formed almost 300 million years ago, it pushed up beneath the crumpled shales, slates, mudstones and sandstones of an ancient seabed. Once exposed, it was weathered by successive waves of frozen Arctic conditions. Fissured and shattered,

Classic Dartmoor granite, with visible lumps of quartz and feldspar.

all this granite eventually produced a very distinctive landscape, far removed from the soft curves of Salisbury Plain or the Sussex Downs.

As the emerging granite cooled all those millions of years ago, and with the surrounding rocks subjected to the superheated gasses, not only feldspar formed, but also a varied range of minerals including metals such as copper, zinc, lead and silver. One mineral was formed in significant quantities, and later, a lot later, this cassiterite, or tin ore, would have significant bearing on human activity on the moor.

Mineral-rich and tough, granite is also what geologists refer to as impervious, meaning that unlike porous chalk or soluble limestone, it presents a complete barrier to water. The upshot is that while rainfall might drain away into chalk or gravel, or through gaps that develop over time in limestone, any precipitation falling on granite stays there, on the surface. Put simply, granite landscapes are wet landscapes. Rather than sinking into the ground, any rain runs across the surface. Where it meets a slight dip, it pools and loiters.

In stark contrast to that neighbouring sedimentary chalk, with its plant-sustaining alkaline chemistry, granite is pretty acidic. This inbuilt chemistry, with its resultant thin soils, tends to restrict the range of flora that grows at the surface. Put simply, far fewer plants can cope with the nutrient poor conditions up there on the moor. With a limited range of plant life comes a corresponding limit on the number of insect and other animal species.

All this water and acidity has another consequence, one that ultimately dominates the character of much of Dartmoor and similar uplands. When vegetation dies here, falling to that saturated ground, instead of rotting as it might elsewhere, fading away and releasing any nutrients, the stems and leaves of the moorland plants often end up in all that surface water. Here, in a weak acid bath, with almost no oxygen, the fibres remain almost intact, decomposing very slowly over many centuries. As more dead vegetation falls on top, the layer deepens until eventually a great wodge of peat is formed, waterlogged, and with only the most resilient bog and marsh plants able to grow at the surface. Of course, the right wetland plants love it, and Dartmoor is home to an impressive collection of mosses, sedges and reeds.

Cassiterite, the dark crystalline bit.

Water pools and loiters.

This abundance of wetland, combined with that less than fertile soil, is not very conducive to farming. Not that this has stopped us trying. We're a very stubborn lot after all, or perhaps just desperate, and I'll return to our agricultural endeavours up on the high moor in a few pages.

High, cool and damp, and subject to much human intervention in the past, some continuing today, the moor isn't the best spot for trees either. That's not to say that the moor doesn't have trees, the native ones just tend to cluster in impressive contorted bunches around the edges.

Weather

Sat high, and representing one of the first obstructions to an endless succession of squalls, gales and storms that sweep in from the nearby Atlantic Ocean, it should come as no surprise to read that Dartmoor can be pretty wet and windy. In stark terms, the high moor is one of the wettest spots in Britain, experiencing over 2,000mm of rain in an average year. Up to 250mm can often fall in any winter month, and even in summer the monthly fall is often in excess of 100mm.

Sooner or later it's going to rain.

As the relatively warm, and very wet, Atlantic air meets Dartmoor it is pushed up suddenly, causing it to cool rapidly. The result is a lot of rain, and the tors, bogs and mires of Dartmoor are also subject to a high number of misty and foggy days.

On the plus side, and although freezing weather is far from unknown, the average annual low temperature is still just over 5°C, with freezing conditions on the moor limited by its southerly location. That said, the British record for snowfall in any one day, is still held by Huntingdon Warren, where 173cm, that's a whopping 68 inches, fell in only 15 hours on the 16th February 1929.

It can snow too.

An unofficial weather record made by Will Hand, Chief Meteorologist at Haytor Weather Station, provides a useful window into the weather conditions on the moor. Recorded over the 16 years running up to 2018, Will identified the following averages:
    Annual rainfall, 1,614mm (and this is on the much drier east side of the moor)
    Maximum temp, 13.1°C
    Minimum temp, 6.2°C
    Number of days with significant snow lying, 9.2
    Days of sleet or snow falling, 23.8
    Days with air frost, 33

The same records produced the following extremes:
    Warmest day (July), 29.8°C
    Coldest day (Dec), -8.4°C
    Greatest snow depth (Jan), 22cm
    Windiest day (Jan), 59mph (although even in July, on one day, the wind managed 42mph)
    Most ice days in a month (January), 8
    Most clear sunny days in a month (June), 2.4

Generally the wettest month on Dartmoor is November, the driest being September and June.

Unfortunately, Will didn't record the number of foggy days. Perhaps there were too many to count.

Looking out towards Cranmere Pool, over boggy ground and water destined for the River Taw.

A dipper.

Rivers

There's a rather special spot on the moor, not far to the west of Hangingstone Hill. Here, surrounding a particularly soggy area known as Cranmere Pool, lies a Westcountry river maternity unit.

Circling the edge of what was once a small lake, the rivers Taw, West Okement and East Dart all start life as clean, bright water oozes from the peat. The East Okement emerges from a shallow cleft just to the north, while the River Teign and main tributaries of both the Tavy and West Dart ease into existence a little to the south. Of all the major Devon rivers, only the Axe and Otter have no connection with the moor. Even the Exe, whose main course begins life, unsurprisingly, on Exmoor, has a tributary, the Creedy, that emerges from the peat on the east edge of Dartmoor. Both the Torridge and Tamar also have sizable side arms that make a start up here.

Having first swum and fished in these rivers in the early 70s, I'm probably biased, but I've rarely known a watercourse with such vigour and exuberance. They might not hold the bulging, wild brown trout, or deep beds of weed found in a Wessex chalkstream, and few grow to any real size, but they're boisterous becks, seemingly eager to meet the sea, the peat tainted water often falling over huge waterworn granite boulders, tumbling beneath twisted oak limbs swathed in green moss. At each season in turn, these adjacent oak woodlands burst with snowdrops, wild daffodils, primroses, bluebells and foxgloves, the air thick with bumblebees, dragonflies and butterflies.

Brown trout do live here, suitably dainty versions that is, with improbably bright flanks, speckled with vivid scarlet spots. Sea trout and salmon also run, far up implausibly insubstantial stretches of water, hurling themselves from pool to seemingly bottomless pool as dippers and kingfishers flash overhead.

Most Dartmoor streams are pretty small, but even the most modest up there has the ability to grow quite significantly in times of high rainfall. Known as spate rivers, these watercourses can make this dramatic jump from small tumbling stream to raging torrent with surprising speed, making these streams one of the few significant dangers to walkers on the moor, and an important subject that's revisited on page 74.

Bridges, fords and other river crossings

Although Dartmoor streams rarely exceed a few metres in width, this is still too far to jump. A couple even manage to grow quite large before they leave the high moor, the Dart being the most notable. In all cases some form of practical crossing is required.

These are often provided by no more than a ford: a shallow, and therefore often relatively wide section of river. Care, experience and good dollop of luck are needed to negotiate these crossings successfully, with dry feet that is.

The upper Taw.

The Tavy.

Fording the River Lyd below Arms Tor.

Left: some form of natural crossing will need to be found.

Right: stepping-stones on the East Dart.

A clapper bridge on the North Teign river.

Fortunately, quite a few of these wide shallow sections have been augmented with stepping-stones, sometimes covering quite impressive bank to bank distances.

Where the high moor rivers run deep, and those stepping-stones fail to breast the flow, some form of bridge is needed. With many miles of river and stream up there, flowing over wide expanses of moor holding no other manmade feature than the odd standing stone, the chance of a proper bridge is slim, and some form of natural crossing will need to be found.

Occasionally a proper bridge will turn up, including the standard arched versions, dating back to the medieval period or later. The classic Dartmoor bridge however, is a clapper. These are very simple, with wide, flat slabs of granite resting either directly on stone uprights, or sometimes just propped on opposing banks. Although almost impossible to date, it is suspected that some may even have been built before the Roman invasion.

Lakes

In brief, and despite that impermeable granite geology, there are very few bodies of still water on the high moor. Any sizeable areas that do exist are all artificial, usually the result of industry, such as the abandoned granite quarry pit at Merrivale or the Red Lake clay pit. The rest are dammed rivers.

Five reservoirs, Meldon, Fernworthy, Venford, Burrator and Avon, each lie pretty close to the edge of the high ground. Burrator, on the western edge is the largest, surrounded by woodland.

Cranmere Pool, with a name possibly meaning the lake of the cranes, or herons, was once a true pool, but has since been lost as blanket peat has risen above surface water levels. As far back as 1912, William Crossing wrote that it might have been 100 years since it last existed as a permanent feature. The pool does reappear occasionally, but only after particularly heavy and sustained rainfall, and even then it would need a very generous observer to refer to it as impressive.

All this said, and just to confuse the issue, a quick look at a map will show that Dartmoor is in fact covered in features referred to as a Lake. However, these lake names are attached not to bodies of standing water, but small watercourses.

Debate surrounding the use of lake as a description for a stream on the moor continues, although it is likely the term is simply a derivation of the original local word for a small river. After all, streams are known elsewhere in Britain by names as diverse as beck, burn, rill and linn.

Some of the origins for individual lake names are pretty clear. Red Lake and Dark Lake probably refer to discoloration for example, possibly the result of mining, some of which started long ago. Dead Lake and various Dry Lakes on the moor are also likely to have names that originate in this industry. Tin extraction often resulted in stream diversions, causing the flow in the original streambeds to fail.

The Avon Dam Reservoir.

Dry Lake.

Left: Devonport Leat.

Right: following Mine Leat into Tavy Cleave.

Leats

Along with its many rivers and 'lakes', Dartmoor possesses another healthy collection of watercourses, in this case made by man. Leats are ingenious mini canals that follow hillside contours, over routes that sometimes cover tens of kilometres.

Designed to provide fresh water to sites as far off as Plymouth, these leats emerge from the dammed edge of Dartmoor rivers, often constrained within stone-walled channels. Although most lost their original purpose long ago, many still run deep and clear, sometimes proving quite a challenge to cross. Occasionally, you will find two flat slabs of granite jutting out from opposing banks. These are designed to allow sheep to jump the gap.

Woodland

As mentioned already, the high moor isn't known for its woodland. What it does have is pretty special though.

In fact, Dartmoor was once covered with trees. These had crept back gradually to recolonize the high ground about 12,000 years ago, following the retreat of the last ice age. As the glaciers, depending who you talk to, either never quite made it this far south (petering out along the edge of what is now the south coast of Wales), or only extended occasionally onto the very northern edge of the moor, a few hardy trees may even have held on here. By the time temperatures had returned to something like the levels seen today, the area would have held a fairly dense mix of indigenous species such as birch, willow, hazel, alder and oak. It was only with the advent of agriculture, during the Neolithic period, that the felling of this forest began, to make way for animals and crops. Very roughly, this started to take place about 5–6,000 years ago (or 3–4,000 BC).

What it does have is pretty special though.

Black-a-tor Copse.

Wistman's Wood in winter.

A wooded tributary of the Dart, and another fine clapper bridge.

By the time the use of metal had appeared on these shores, during a period now called the Bronze Age, much of the woodland on the high ground had gone. A mix of high elevations and grazing pressure held back any potential recolonisation, as it still holds it at bay today. Only a few strips of the original forest were left, lying close to streams in the deeper valleys.

Today, these remaining ancient woodlands, dominated by oak, are extremely special, with fully grown, but weather-stunted mature trees growing tight amidst huge moss-covered boulders. Black-a-tor Copse, spread along the east slope of the West Okement valley, Wistman's Wood close to the West Dart and Piles Copse in the Erme Valley are the three rare survivals of high oak woodland left on the moor.

These may well represent some of the only patches of untouched forest left in Britain, and each is visited by a route later in the book on pages 205, 127 and 221 respectively. The tricky terrain formed by the boulders seems to have made felling not worth the considerable effort, or at least that's one suggested reason for their survival.

Other woodland also persists along the banks of many of the streams and rivers as they leave the high ground, particularly on the southern half of the moor along the valleys of the larger watercourses such as the Dart. Although probably regenerated, these oak, rowan and willow growths still represent some of the prettiest woodlands you'll see, especially in April and May when bluebells cover the forest floor.

The only other woodland you'll see up on the high moor will be the grim swathes of commercial coniferous plantations. These dingy monoculture deserts are only of any value to walkers as windbreaks, although occasionally fairly useful as navigation aids.

Tors

Along with ponies, and the prison, there's another aspect of Dartmoor that evidently resonates with people, even those who've never paid a visit. In fact, after the imagined horrors of the bogs, tors are often the major topic of conversation when Dartmoor is discussed. People do seem to hold them in a certain regard. But then should we be surprised?

For a start, tor is a very good name: short, rather noble sounding and evidently memorable. Besides, hardly a photo taken of Dartmoor fails to depict at least one of these outcrops, sat brooding and megalithic on the horizon. Granite appears at almost every peak, even the most vague of moorland eminences, where it seems to have burst from the soggy ground, dark and convoluted.

In reality, and despite geological appearances, the creation of Dartmoor's tors wasn't anything near as exciting as that. I won't bore you with the details, if only because I don't fully understand them, but about 280 million years ago molten granite seems to have done little more than ooze about deeply. There then followed a complex collection of odd geological events, all taking place deep underground, culminating in eventual exposure and an awful lot of weathering.

Great Staple Tor.

Great Links Tor.

Yes Tor, from an unusual angle.

Stenga Tor.

And the result? Well, some sort of elevated plutonic wonderland; a natural stone sculpture park, high, surreal and sublime. One minute you stride out across open moorland, the heather, cotton grass and sedge spread far in every direction, the next you enter a towering upland exhibition, nature's precursor to Henry Moore or Barbara Hepworth: age-carved stone, wind moulded, frost pecked, patinated by countless years.

On some days the stone is bathed warm by the sun, on others it's glazed with ice, but the granite is always tactile and approachable (and pretty much irresistible to anyone with a tendency to climb). Each granite edifice has its own character, some friendly and inviting, others, at least in certain lights, dark and brooding. No visit is ever dull though, and like any meeting with good art, you leave the encounter changed.

Hundreds of tors spread out across the moor, ranging in size from exuberant mini mountains to discreet piles of sometimes teetering slabs. Ok, perhaps I exaggerate a little here, at least about the big tors. In reality, few of these outcrops stand more than 5 or 6 metres high. Hardly mountainous at all, they just look a lot bigger as you approach. They have a presence that exceeds their mass. They demand attention.

Some of these tors seem almost untouched, their hard folded sides standing high and proud, their defences seemingly unbreached by wind, frost or time. As the weather deteriorates (and it often does up there), ponies, sheep, belted Galloway cattle (and the odd hillwalker or two), cluster, sheltered in the lee of these gale-battered bastions.

Other tors appear to be on almost their last legs, the remaining rickety stands of teetering granite surrounded by a sea of shattered fragments. This disintegrated spread of ex tor, or 'clitter' as it's known on the moor, can cover whole hillsides, a fact that's even more impressive when it's realised just how much of this convenient stuff has been removed over the centuries, carted away to build barns, bridges, houses and roads.

Many of the tors have names that fit their lumpy magnificence – Great Mis, Beardown, Steeperton, Great Staple. Others, such as Lints Tor, Kitty or Little Kneeset are rather less imposing, and more than a little baffling. Then there's the splendidly named Laughter Tor or the intriguing Honeybag. I could carry on like this for pages.

And if many of the names are a bit peculiar, so too are some of the tors. Branscombe's Loaf is one of my favourites, and not just because of the odd label (there's more on this subject on page 123). This really is a strange stone lump. Prehistoric inhabitants of the moor certainly thought it was special, and ringed it with a ditch and bank. It's easy to see why they felt drawn to this natural monument, and their need to encircle it in ritual significance.

Occasionally tors have the same name. I can think of at least three Black Tors for example. One of these, overlooking the twisted oak splendour of Black-a-tor Copse, is home to the increasingly rare ring ouzle. We saw a pair the last time we visited. Then there are two Fox Tors, and, as a seeming balance, a couple of Hounds too. Ironically, some quite impressive tumbles of stone appear to have no name at all, or at least none listed on any modern map. One of my favourite tors, like the famous Lakeland tarn, seems to be innominate.

Part of Kitty Tor.

Branscombe's Loaf.

Yes Tor, and yes this is in colour.

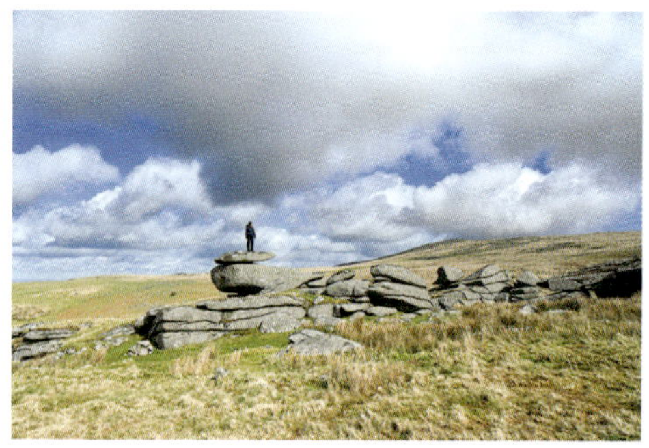

Shelstone Tor.

Wild Tor, with Yes Tor on the horizon.

Even after over three decades spent working or wandering around on the moor, as well as living up there for a while, there are still many tors I've not visited. As there are said to be about 170 in total, and that's just the ones with 'tor' in their name, I suppose this isn't surprising. On the other hand, and often simply because they lie on a favourite route, there are some I've encountered many times. I can only begin to guess the number of occasions I've visited Belstone Tor for example, or nearby Higher or Oke Tors (there's a route guide on page 213 if you want to see them for yourself). Even the famous Yes Tor, visible from where I'm typing now, and almost the highest point up there, has provided a very fine observation point on dozens of occasions. The views out across northern Devon from here are spectacular.

Turning from here to look into the heart of the moor, they're pretty good in that direction too. Tors dot the long undulating horizon, monstrous and modest, graceful and grotesque. If you visit the moor only in search of its tors, that's excuse enough to set out on foot.

Bogs and mires

With its impervious granite geology and high rainfall, it's not surprising that water hangs about on the moor. Even after prolonged dry weather, the ground is often wet underfoot.

A Dartmoor mire, and another bit to avoid.

These wetlands provide a perfect environment for the growth of sphagnum mosses, of which at least twelve species are known to live on the moor. In turn, the acidic and poorly oxygenated water around and over which this moss grows, severely inhibits the decay of dead plant material, and as the deposits of fallen organic material build up, they turn to peat which itself further increases the waterlogged nature of the area, perpetuating the process. Much of the blanket bog area has deposits of peat over 0.5m (nearly 2 feet) deep, and in places many times that depth.

Dartmoor holds about 120 square kilometres of blanket bog. Compared to some areas of British upland, this isn't actually a particularly large amount, although it can sometimes feel like it. There are few of these natural carbon 'sinks' situated further south in Europe. It's not only moss that grows in these bogs, they are also the home for deer grass, cotton grass and such wetland specialists as the insectivorous sundew.

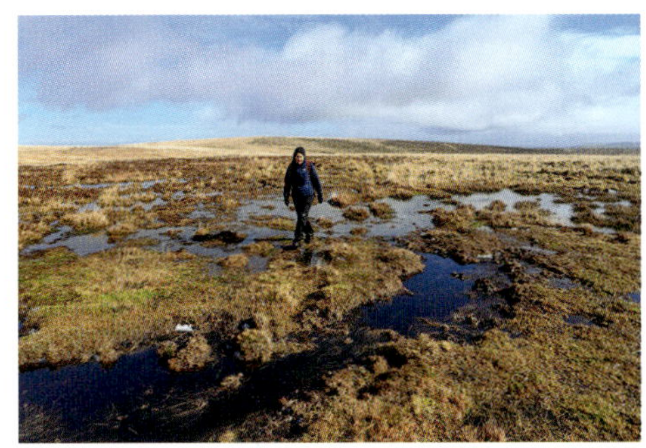
Blanket bog.

Much of this blanket was initially formed in the late Bronze Age. After soils had been impoverished by early farming, the climate altered a touch, part of the normal changes that took place over centuries; temperatures dropped slightly and rainfall increased. Peat formation continues even today, although it is slow, with perhaps a depth of only 1mm added each year.

There's also a lot less peat on the moor than there used to be, with extraction forming an ancient, and at times significant, industry. Most peat digging took place to provide fuel, either to heat homes or power various industries, on and off the moor. These could be hungry, and in the mid 1800s it's said that gangs from the famous Dartmoor prison, alone, removed as much as 2,400 tons a year. Some peat was distilled to produce gas for lighting, and naphtha was extracted for use, amongst other things, in the production of mothballs. A little peat was even employed to make paper. A walk described later (page 163) starts from a peat distillation works near Shipley Bridge.

An impressive amount of work could accompany these endeavours. Only a year after a license to extract peat near Dartmoor's Great Links Tor was issued by the Duchy of Cornwall in 1878, The Rattlebrook Peat Works had installed a standard gauge railway, which climbed the 300 metres from Bridestowe. Peat-drying kilns were constructed at the head of Rattlebrook itself, and a home, Bleak House, was built for the mine manager.

Interestingly, the sheer scale of this industry prompted one of the earliest outbreaks of conservation interest anywhere in the world. Worries over the amount of peat being removed, and valid concerns regarding the potential impact this might have on the flow characteristics of Devon's rivers, led to concerns being raised as early as the 1880s. In the end, the prevalence of cheap coal put a natural halt to the practice.

Today, many of the peat bogs on the moor are relatively dry, and some, particularly those that have been harvested, are quite well drained. This certainly can't be said of the mires that rest soggily in valley bottoms and natural dips in the ground. These can be very wet indeed. Not so good for walkers, these rare conditions are havens for a wide range of flora and fauna, ranging from the relatively common cotton grasses, bog beans, bog asphodel and water crowfoot, to rarities such as white beak sedge, bog myrtle and marsh lousewort.

Not surprisingly, these generous wetlands provide homes for a whole swathe of insect life, in turn providing food for numerous frogs, dragonflies and damselflies, as well as snipe, lapwing and curlew.

I'll return to a more detailed consideration of these charming damp locations on page 35.

Wildlife

Having read about the cold, damp and windy weather, the exposed land, the unforgiving geology and waterlogged acidic soils, it may not come as a great surprise to find that the range of birds, animals and plants able to cope on the high moor is not great. That said, Dartmoor is certainly not devoid of life.

The surrounding lowland is remarkably diverse, with thickly wooded stream valleys, unimproved heathland and meadows that have often not been touched for decades, even centuries. Farming practice at these margins is also often of a far less intensive nature, with fewer sprays and less physical disturbance. The corresponding diversity in wildlife does creep up onto higher ground, or along the numerous watercourses that run off the moor, and these lower margins can be surprisingly rich in plant, bird and animal life, particularly were woodland scrub has started to work its way back uphill. Great flocks of fieldfare and redwings feeding on thorn berries can be quite a sight for example, and almost all woodland birds can be seen at these moorland edges.

A Wistman's Wood robin.

A flock of golden plover scoot off across the moor.

With a drop of a degree centigrade for every 100m in elevation, however, along with the increased wind and precipitation, many creatures and a swathe of softer vegetation just can't manage up there. Some birds are very happy though, including golden plover and dunlin, which are often seen on open ground, along with woodcock, snipe and a whole range of other waders. Various duck species are also often encountered, and a number nest up here in spring.

Smaller birds such as stonechats and stone, meadow and wood pipits are common, as are skylarks, the air alive with their song over some parts of the moor in spring and summer. Cuckoos can creep quite a long way uphill in spring, seeming to be happy, so long as some form of post or standing stone can be found from which to call. I usually first hear them each year along one Dartmoor edge valley or another. A much rarer cry is the call of the ring ouzel, a slightly metallic blackbird-like call that can be heard sometimes at certain favoured tors.

While buzzards are common, hopping through the grass in their hunt for food in winter, circling high on summer thermal uplifts, it is the raven that rules the roost on the moor, often sat proud on a favoured granite outcrop, providing unbroken views over their domain. All Dartmoor walkers will be familiar with the vocal accompaniment, as a pair of ravens seem to chat to each other about your progress, often lifting from their roost to drift over on the breeze for a closer check. I doubt that many miles are walked on the moor without at least one pair of intelligent eyes fixed on the journey.

Left: a Dartmoor ring ouzel.

Right: a Dartmoor raven keeps watch.

Up here in their kingdom, the vegetation may look fairly uniform, but although the high moor is dominated by what looks, at first glance, like an unvarying spread of grass, there is good variety. A range of tough sedges, reeds and, yes, grasses have adapted over thousands of years to this seemingly inhospitable landscape, so while molinia certainly provides the main cover, a closer look will find little hidden gems such as the flower of the lesser pond sedge or lousewort.

Of course, this little sedge, like many Dartmoor plants, favours damp ground. The peat wetlands, whether mire or bog, are undoubtably special, providing a home for many rare bogland plants, including the likes of stag's clubmoss and black bog-rush. Minerals exposed by mining in some areas have even resulted in the proliferation of lichens unable to grow elsewhere. Other lichens thrive in the almost pollution-free surrounding of the rare patches of native woodland. Black-a-tor Copse, for example, contains a nationally important collection.

Roe deer can often be seen at the edges of the high moor, tending not to care for the larger, open expanses at the centre. Until relatively recently, red deer were the preserve of Exmoor, which now holds quite a sizable population. For this reason perhaps, these deer, the largest in Britain, are now often spotted on land between the moors, and increasingly on Dartmoor itself. During the Perambulation walk (page 257), we spotted about a dozen not far from Fernworthy reservoir.

Foxes are present, but not in high numbers. Badgers though, can be quite numerous in places, and are often seen in the evening, particularly in areas frequented

Left: lesser pond sedge, growing close to Cranmere Pool.

Centre: Lousewort, enjoying a boggy stretch alongside the Dart.

Right: Cotton Grass near the West Okement River.

English stonecrop, cropping from a stone, in this case Black-a-tor.

Frogspawn laid in a mire.

A common lizard, near the source of the Taw.

by rabbits. Many of these bunnies are likely to be ancestors of those that escaped in the past from a healthy collection of now abandoned warrens (rabbit farms) scattered around the moor. One of my favourite colonies lives in a sandy mound alongside an upper section of the River Taw. As with the rest of Devon, hares are often present, usually at a distance.

One mammal that is reasonably common, but not so often seen, is the otter. Utilising watercourses, they can roam over large territories from estuary to high moor. Polecats, not so long ago absent from the moor, are also making a return after reintroduction, although I've yet to see one.

Bats, mice and even dormice are present, the bats sometimes particularly numerous alongside Dartmoor streams on a summer evening.

The high moor also contains a pretty healthy population of adders and common lizards, often found sunning themselves on bare ground in the summer.

Dartmoor ponies.

Ponies

Take almost any walk on the high moor, and it won't be too long before you come across ponies. This is as it should be, because these rugged little horses represent an integral part of the area's cultural and economic heritage.

There have almost certainly been ponies on the moor since prehistoric times, either wandering in under their own steam, or introduced a few thousand years ago, when farming first took hold. Horse remains have certainly been found in Neolithic burial monuments.

Considering their natural habitat, and seemingly uninhibited life, I could have included these ponies in the wildlife section above. After all, their herds are evidently free to do pretty much as they please. Each pony is, however, owned by someone, even if that Dartmoor commoner may never have actually laid a hand on its flanks.

Each autumn the ponies are rounded up in what are called 'drifts'. This is the time it's decided which will be sold, and which lucky ponies will remain 'wild' on the moor.

Some of the lucky ones.

There's a lot of Shetland in this lot.

Hardy beasts, Dartmoor ponies.

Unlike the Exmoor pony, which displays a pretty uniform shape and colouration, the Dartmoor pony is quite varied, although they do all share the characteristics of relatively small size, combined with large chunks of grit. These are tough individuals, able to survive on thin pickings, in some of England's worst weather.

The Dartmoor pony, or perhaps more accurately, the ponies on Dartmoor, for there are strict breed standards for the registered animal, is a bit of a mix. This is the result of different requirements over the centuries, including light draught animals and riding mounts. Some of the particularly small ponies you'll see on the moor originate from animals shipped in from Shetland, supplied as suitably tiny pit ponies for mining use. There is even a little Arab in the mix, as a result of Victorian 'improvement'. Piebald (black and white) and skewbald (brown and white) ponies are quite numerous, even if the Dartmoor Pony Society doesn't recognise them as part of the accepted breed.

Although you will see ponies, particularly in some of their favoured haunts, you certainly won't see as many as you once could. Records from the 1950s cite as many as 30,000 roaming the moor at the time. The most alarming estimates today suggest there may be as few as 850, the result of a distinct drop in demand, with a consequent collapse in value. Whatever the figures, I don't see nearly as many as I did in the 1970s.

For the record, and depending where on the moor they're encountered, I've found the ponies on Dartmoor tend to fall into two camps. Those found close to the road, especially near a road with a layby or pub, can be very friendly. Many will have grown used to a diet supplemented regularly by various forms of holiday snack. They don't know the damage this will do after all. Further into the moor, ponies will behave like any other moorland animal, usually keeping their distance, although I have encountered numerous occasions on which curiosity gets the better of them, especially if you choose to camp in their patch. Sharing a campsite with half a dozen inquisitive ponies can be an entertaining business.

Whatever the circumstance, please note that these mares, foals and stallions are as wild as a pony comes. People do occasionally get bitten and kicked if they take liberties. On the whole though, these rare interactions tend to occur away from roads and regular contact with humans, especially when they have young foals. It's also worth noting that while animals may often seem to be spread at random across the hills, each pony is part of a discrete herd, and an ever-watchful stallion can occasionally display his disapproval if he considers too many liberties are being taken. This is often more a case of high drama than any actual threat, with plenty of rushing around and loud whinnying, but it is always best to take the hint and move gently away.

Cattle and sheep

It may seem slightly odd to mention farm animals, but due to the harsh conditions, the range of cattle and sheep breeds seen on the moor is far from ordinary.

One of the more common breeds of sheep is still the Greyface Dartmoor, a relative rarity off the moor. You might also see White Dartmoors, and it's suggested that both breeds are direct descendants of the original sheep brought onto the moor in prehistory. That makes sense.

Not a good idea.

A Dartmoor mix.

A flock coping with winter.

Belted Galloways.

A herd of Galloway cattle with their calves; best given a wide berth.

Breeds brought in from more distant and even more testing environments include the Scotch Blackface and the tough Herdwick sheep, familiar to any Lakeland fellwalker.

Undoubtedly the most visible breed of cattle on the moor is the belted Galloway, with its broad white cummerbund. These black and white cattle are hard to miss, and sometimes found in surprisingly large herds. Unbelted Galloways are also pretty common. Like these small and rugged cows, Highland cattle, with their long coats, are also perfectly suited to the 'dreich' Dartmoor conditions. While never numerous, they frequent various spots around the high moor.

With rather more ancient links to the moor, the South Devon cow, with its curly red coat, is a more common sight. While renowned for being a very gentle breed, a characteristic you can't really apply to Galloways for example, they are extremely tough, and quite at home on the high moor.

At the end of this section, and as this is a walking guide, a couple of comments for those Dartmoor visitors unfamiliar with sheep and cattle:

Firstly, all sheep, and most cattle, will move out of your way as you approach. Even those cattle that will stand their ground are usually only lazy or inquisitive, perhaps both. The only exception is when they have calves in spring and summer, when maternal instincts can prevail. Bear in mind that you may not be able to see the calf, perhaps resting in long grass or bracken. If you approach a herd and you spot young, it is probably best to deviate slightly. Certainly, for their sake as much as yours, try to ensure that you don't come between a mother and its calf.

The other problem can arise with dogs. As natural prey animals, dogs are feared by both cattle and sheep. Sheep will run, a problem in itself. A cow with a calf may occasionally decide to stand its ground. Where there are a few cattle mothers, they might, and it is rare, work together. If you do find yourself in a threatening situation, and this is the only time it's advised, let your dog free, even if this means just dropping the lead. The dog will almost certainly be fast enough to evade trouble, and once your canine companion has left your side, you cease to be of concern or interest. You can reunite with your hound further down the trail, providing any required sympathy or reassurance.

Otherwise, unless 100% certain you can maintain control by voice command (and this is a very rare situation, believe me), please keep your dog on a lead. Even the best behaved hound can get carried away when faced with a big open space, especially one brought up in a town or village. Add a few panicking sheep, and they will panic at times when confronted by a dog, and your otherwise perfectly behaved companion can sometimes lose its composure. Even a very brief chase can result in aborted lambs. Some encounters end up being even more serious. And a last thought on this matter: if faced with a dog worrying his flock or herd, a farmer is entitled, by law, to shoot... and every now and again they do.

Human use

While the moor today may seem largely devoid of humans, and that's a pretty accurate assessment, this certainly hasn't always been the case. In fact, at times, large areas of the moor would have heaved with activity.

Some of that past human activity on the moor has been touched upon already. What needs to be stressed here, is both the extent and scale of human goings on up there. The impact this has had on the moor itself can be profound. For those used to the present near emptiness, this may well come as quite a surprise.

First off then, let's take a step back to that distant point when we first made an appearance on the moor, or at least a proper reappearance.

Prehistory

Along with the rest of the globe, the area we now call Dartmoor has been subject to a repeated sequence of warmings and coolings, the colder bits often known as

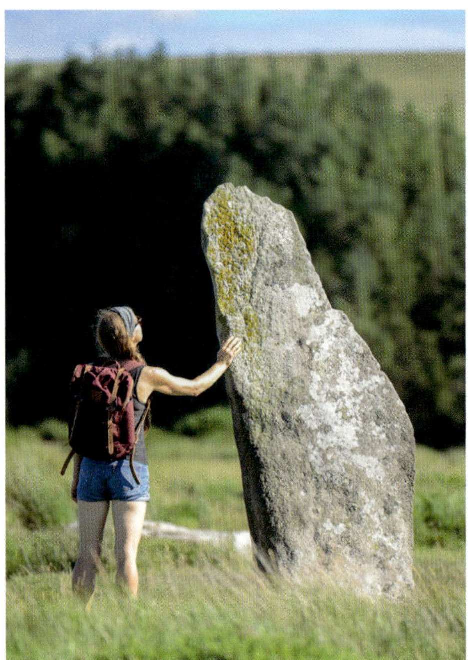
A prehistoric standing stone.

ice ages. During the warm spells, at least the later ones, early humans must have done things up on the moor, some hunting and a little gathering, but in reality we know next to nothing about what went on during the many thousand years known as the Palaeolithic, or old stone age.

The last ice age ended approximately 12,000 years ago, and as the glaciers retreated, and the frozen high ground at its southern edge, including Dartmoor, finally thawed, trees started to move back in, and with them came us humans. For the next few thousand years, during what archaeologists call the Mesolithic, or middle stone age, those trees flourished and we carried on hunting, foraging and gathering. We may have cleared a few areas with fire to encourage wildlife to move in and feed, and pay a price for the experience, but that was probably the extent of our impact.

At a point about six thousand years ago (and that's a very approximate about), something extremely profound occurred, with farming hitting our shores. It won't have been long before animal and plant domestication reared its head on the moor. To cut a rather long story short (this is a walking guide after all), a lot of a rather different sort of cutting took place up there, first using flint axes, and then ones made from copper, bronze and finally iron. Before long, those early farmers had altered the moor completely by chopping down almost all of the trees.

In their place they left the moor pretty much as we know it today, with thin acidic soils, a very meagre fringe of oak-dominated woodland, and blanket bogs that formed on the exposed slopes. Those Neolithic and Bronze Age farmers also left numerous burial mounds (or cairns), hut circles, field boundaries and an impressive collection of carefully arranged standing stones. Their Iron Age descendants also added a few hilltop enclosures.

The long and the short of all this, is that the moor is almost alive with prehistoric remains, ranging in size from the heaped stones of sometimes tiny burial mounds to almost untouched Bronze Age field systems, with banks, or reaves, covering whole hillsides. Sometimes entire valleys are swathed in these reaves, the boundary banks best seen when highlighted by the shadow from a low winter sun.

Once your eye is in, it's rarely a distance of more than a few hundred yards on the moor before another standing stone, stone row, stone circle, or almost untouched prehistoric village is found. Some of the circular stone walls to these huts survive to such a height, you could almost roof them again and move straight in.

Much of this prehistoric bounty is the result of the relatively light agricultural use the moor has experienced in the intervening period. It's true that some areas of the high moor experienced damage from the plough, but very few, and although many archaeological features have been plundered, this will have been more for the removal of convenient building stone than any hope of treasure (although that did happen too). The level of archaeological survival up there is sometimes breathtaking. It's often very easy to imagine yourself living in one of those once busy villages, or witness to the spectacle of a late Neolithic or early Bronze Age burial, the light from torches and fires flickering across the flanks of the many standing stones.

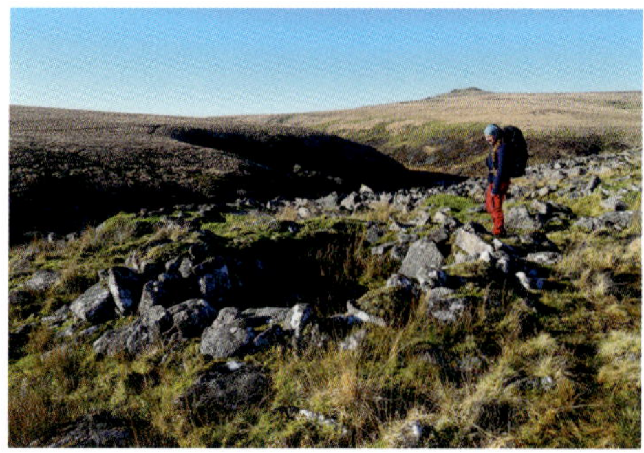

The remains of a prehistoric hut.

A large Bronze Age burial cairn on Corndon Down.

The Manga Rock, a medieval Dartmoor Forest boundary marker.

The remains of a medieval house.

History

With the arrival in Britain of the Romans, and their tendency to write things down, prehistory came to an end.

From the outset, a particular interest of that Mediterranean empire was tin, a valuable metal they knew was present in large quantities in neighbouring Cornwall; and a fact that may well have played a significant part in their decision to pay a visit. Although tin was also present on the moor, and almost certainly exploited at the time, it doesn't look as if this was a fact that much influenced the Romans. Evidence of their presence on the moor exists, although the record is surprisingly thin.

Making a sweeping and somewhat dismissive statement, the next real event, in Dartmoor terms, was the arrival of the Normans. Apart from cathedral building and a penchant for stocktaking, this impressively efficient band of Viking descendants and European mercenaries loved to hunt. As a result, Dartmoor was soon designated a Forest; a term that had little to do with trees, but was instead used to describe areas, including the New Forest, set aside for Royalty and their chums to enjoy this mounted sport. Dartmoor Forest remained in Royal hands until the 1240s when it was given as a gift to the then Duke of Cornwall. This is relevant today, as the current Duke, Prince Charles, still owns much of the moor. In addition, because of that 13th-century act of generosity, we have an excuse for a very fine extended walk, described on page 257.

Following the moor's designation as a hunting ground, little changed through the medieval and early post-medieval period. A few farming villages crept up onto the edge during a period of slight climatic warming in the 14th and 15th centuries, soon to be abandoned as temperatures fell again. The remains of a couple of these villages are visited later (pages 225 and 231).

Before the late 18th century, farming had continued in a limited upland way on the moor, with no great impact on the land itself. This all changed with the attempts to 'improve' agricultural practice, coinciding with the legalised theft of land associated with various Enclosure Acts. On Dartmoor, much of this loss of common land was the responsibility of Duchy steward Sir Thomas Trywhitt, resulting in the founding of Princetown and the enclosure of significant swathes of the central moor. These fields represent one of the biggest changes to land use on the moor, and this intake land stands in stark contrast to the open moor on either side. Not only did the Dartmoor commoners lose out in a big way, but all those fields have hardly been a boon to walkers here either.

There was one activity of significance however, that had already started in earnest during the mediaeval period. It's already been mentioned; the ground-shifting events, quite literally, involved in the extraction of tin.

Industry

It's quite likely, if not a running certainty, that tin mining began in a small way on the moor in the late Bronze Age. Excavations at a site of this age on Dean Moor in the South Hams produced a fragment of tin slag. Sediments found in the Erme Valley, dated loosely to the Romano-British period, are also believed to have their origins in tin mining on the moor.

At the risk of a long drawn account, it is important to stress the importance of this industry. Come across almost any stream on Dartmoor and the surrounding ground, sometimes to impressive distances from the present banks, will be rucked up in linear piles. Even at the very top of hills, acres of ground will have been turned, the spoil left in heaps, sometimes metres high. It will look as if a JCB has spent days up there moving gravel and stone. In reality, and at any time over a period covering hundreds of years, many thousands of men will have been at work with picks and shovels. They moved almost unimaginable amounts of soil, peat and underlying degraded granite gravel, or growan as it's known locally, all to get at buried tin deposits.

Many miles of stone-metalled tracks were created, to bring equipment in and to ship tin out to the stannary towns of Tavistock, Chagford and Ashburton that

Intake fields near the River Taw.

The tinners have been here, almost at the top of a hill.

The remains of a tinner's hut.

Even small streams were exploited.

Split and ready for removal (only, for some reason, that didn't happen).

surround the moor. Given the right by the crown to control the tin industry, these urban developments, and various sizeable monastic establishments on the moorland fringe, were founded almost solely on the wealth from this metal.

As a result, whole stream and river courses were shifted, either to gain access to the deposits below, or in order to use the flow to scour out fresh exposures. Individual buildings, in fact whole villages, were built to house the workers and those attracted to these rough settlements to provide for their various needs. Some corners of the moor, or more accurately whole swathes, would have been covered in busy humanity, interested only in what lay below the surface.

Mining also took place for lead, zinc, arsenic, silver and copper, the latter drawing some of my ancestors across the border from Cornwall.

Then there's stone and clay. Granite may be tough to work, but it's also an extremely durable building stone. Early endeavours with the material can still be seen in late Neolithic stone rows and Bronze Age round house walls. The material for these early constructions would have been pulled from what would have seemed almost inexhaustible scatters of granite 'moorstones', the shattered and weathered remains, found around most Dartmoor tors. This 'clitter' will have been raided right up to the present day, the stone now seen in farm walls, bridges and churches all over and around the moor. Local farmers and builders won't have been averse to reusing earlier construction efforts, and many a farm will have a floor or fireplace formed from what had once been a Bronze Age cist lining or stone circle constituent.

Often whole stones will have been lifted from their resting place on the moor and carted (quite literally) away. Where the resting granite lump was too big, they would be split, and the characteristic marks left by 'feather and tare' and later 'flat wedge' stone reduction methods can be seen across the moor.

Some time in the 17th or 18th century, it was felt that this surface source was not quite keeping up with demand. Quarries were opened up, dotted across the moor. In the Victorian period, some of these grew to quite astonishing proportions,

A granite piece, abandoned where it was worked on Lee Moor.

with a railway even built to haul material out to cater for construction demand in Plymouth. Perhaps the easiest of these quarries to see lies just off the road at Merrivale, the area still heaped with granite fragments. This quarry was open until as recently as 1997.

Meldon quarry, on the north-west corner of the moor, not far from Okehampton, was opened in 1897, providing ballast for railway construction. Working the local limestone outcrop, it represents a rare Dartmoor quarry extracting a stone other than granite.

Clay is also a stone of sorts, and Dartmoor is renowned for its china clay deposits, with small pits once dotted across the southern edge of the moor. The abandoned clay works at Red Lake, not far from the Avon Reservoir, still provide a dramatic view, with a conical spoil heap looking like a mini volcano. Today, this activity is restricted to the south-west corner, resulting in a more concentrated, if still very substantial, assault on the body of the moor.

The Red Lake spoil heap.

Something old: the tallest of the Drizzlecombe stones, often called the Bone Stone.

Something new: a Two Moors Way marker.

Standing stones

Those who know a little of the moor might wonder why this section isn't slotted in under the prehistory banner, and it's true that Dartmoor is covered in Neolithic and Bronze Age standing stones, either set up singly, or in some form of pattern. Look closely though, or sometimes not so closely, and there's usually something that gives a younger origin away. Stones have been set up on the moor for a whole range of reasons, and carved letters, occasionally whole words, indicate a historic or even quite recent date.

Over the centuries, stones have been used for a variety of reasons, to mark incidents or locations of unknown prehistoric importance, Saxon land ownership, parish boundaries (with say GB, for Gidleigh bounds, carved into a side) and the edges of quarry rights, to name but a few. Some have even been set up to show where quarrying isn't allowed. A ring of stubby uprights with the letter B carved into a face encircles Roos Tor for example. These demarcate the area where locals weren't permitted to remove stones. We can be thankful to B, in this case the Duke of Bedford, for that bit of early conservation endeavour. The most recent stones show the line of modern walking routes such as the Two Moors Way. Put simply, you're unlikely to walk far on the moor before you come across a monolith trying to tell you something.

The Army

The British Army has used large swathes of the moor for training since about 1800, but it was not until the 1870s that a dedicated range was opened near Okehampton. This area grew, with the purchase or lease of land resulting in much of the northern half of the moor eventually falling under military control.

In reality, as far as walkers are concerned, this isn't the problem you might assume. With shrinking armed forces, the periods when red flags fly to show that the area is out of bounds are relatively few. That said, the closure of camps in Germany and elsewhere abroad, may mean that closures become more frequent and extended again.

One very positive spin off from the military involvement on the moor is the annual Ten Tors Challenge. Started in 1960 as a training programme for cadets, the event now sees 2,500 youngsters, aged between 14 and 19, setting out over two days each May, attempting to walk one of a collection of 35, 45 and 55 mile courses, and that's a distance as the crow flies. I'm certain the experience remains a vivid memory for all who take part.

Left: Ten Tors.

Right: welcome to the range.

The Army road where it splits just to the south-east of Rowtor.

The outer edge of the Army road, now just bare granite slabs, as it approaches Hangingstone Hill.

A former Army road, now providing a reasonably sound route along the Belstone ridge.

Tracks

Although the high moor might seem rather barren today, its industrial and military past provides one surviving legacy to the walker, a reasonably significant number of tracks. These can vary enormously in quality, with many of the early tinners' and army tracks being very rough indeed. Quite a few sections, even when marked on an OS map, bear little resemblance to what many of us would even think of as a track at all, some surviving as little more than a shallow linear gulley. Even so, they still offer a much easier route across the interior than the often boggy and lumpy going close alongside.

Occasionally, the tracks up there are really quite good. What the locals call the 'ring road', heads up and away from Okehampton Camp, before splitting to take you out to a couple of spots a fair way into the moor. A stretch around Row Tor even has a tarmac surface. These army 'roads' slowly deteriorate, but even at their outer extent provide firm and reasonably level footing.

The Willsworthy Range track.

Another short section of tarmacked Army track leads up onto the western side of the moor at the Willsworthy Range, and at the south-east corner, a civilian road runs some five to six kilometres from Shipley Bridge to the Avon Dam to the north. Each of these provides a very useful route into the moor for those less able to deal with the usual rugged ground.

Crushed stone miner's tracks, or paths, are also reasonably common across the high moor. Some, such as the route south and then south-west from Princetown to Nattor, provide a good walking surface the whole way.

The other transport system to provide easy going for the walker is the railway, and former rail lines offer good, level routes over some considerable distances. Examples include the old Princetown line, that runs from the central moorland settlement to Burrator Reservoir, the former clay industry route that heads north into the centre of the moor from Ivybridge, and the former London and South Western Railway line that skirts the edge of the Moor between Okehampton and Lydford. The latter is now tarmacked the whole way. While this route never impinges on

Part of the miners' track between Princetown and Nattor.

the high moor itself, it does provide wonderful views for anyone unable to set out across the less forgiving ground nearby.

Further into the moor, the rail line cut to extract peat from close to Great Links Tor, provides a very useful route over what would otherwise be quite testing ground. The rails from this Rattlebrook works line were removed in the 1930s.

Around the edge of the moor, a healthy collection of very ancient trackways still work their way up onto high ground, often bounded by tumbled, dry-stone, granite walls. I say very ancient, as many of these 'hollow' ways are certainly medieval at the latest, literally worn into the ground by the feet of ages, but I suspect most have origins even earlier than this.

Last mention should go to the many ad hoc tracks, formed by no more than the repeated tramp of countless walkers' boots. Many a ridge route, or the best line from one side of a valley to another, is marked for anyone with even the most untrained eye to see. If a little lost, sticking to a bearing will almost always bring you a across a route to follow.

Anyway, enough of the preamble; let's get out onto that moor.

A medieval, or earlier, track, heading up onto the north-east corner of the moor.

The walkers' routes here near Bellever Tor are pretty obvious.

You'll soon have the place to yourself.

Walking

When to go

Bearing in mind its deserved reputation for rain, wind and heavy mist, the weather is always going to be a key consideration when deciding on the best time for a walking visit to Dartmoor. If you want to avoid the worst, as with anywhere else in Britain, there's no doubt that summer is going to offer the best bet. Strike lucky through the lighter months and you might see weeks of fine weather; you also have those wonderfully long summer days.

On the whole though, any time from May to the end of October will carry a reasonable chance of blue skies. In recent years, and this is just my opinion, March and April have seemed to offer fine weather with surprising regularity. September, and even October, can do the same. If you have a long way to travel, November through to the end of February are probably not the best months to pay a visit.

For those looking to avoid the crowds, school term times are inevitably quieter, although it does bear stressing, that many moorland visitors rarely venture more than a few hundred yards from the road. While established car parks, such as the one at Postbridge, will soon be filled in the 'season', what from the verge can seem to be quite a throng, will soon be left far behind as you head away over the tufty grass.

Unlike the highlands of Scotland, and even parts of northern England and Wales, Dartmoor is largely free of flying summer pests. Sure, there will be a few gnats and the odd, surprisingly painful, horsefly, but although the insect life may grow a little wearisome next to a stream on a still summer evening, the moor doesn't see the clouds of assaulting midges associated with many wilder spaces.

The woodlands fringing the moor are quite spectacular in April and early May, many filled with bluebells. Later in the year, at their peak in July and August, stone banks bristle with foxgloves.

Winter is wet on the moor, there's no denying it. The wind can also blow, day after day at times, between October and March. That said, some of the most wonderful walking days can be found up on the moor in the colder months, with still air and bright, pale blue skies eventually turning up somewhere between the often tailgating successions of low pressure. And when it does freeze, the ground, so often soggy and hard to cross, is turned overnight into a hard flat expanse. Going that may be a soggy slog in June, sometimes just about impossible to cross, now stretches out, firm to a well-insulated walking boot. Just be sure it is all truly frozen.

How to go

For those with their own transport, the high moor is easily reached, either leaving your vehicle in a fringe village or town, or using one of the car parks on the moor itself. There are many of these, strung along the main roads (B3212 and B3357), and quite a few on the more minor ones too, with a fair number shown on OS maps. Most though are very small, and will soon fill on a sunny, summer day, so try to arrive early.

One request here on the subject of parking, made on behalf of those that live and work on the moor; please try very hard not to leave vehicles in gateways. The last thing a farmer needs on a busy day, is to find a Volvo or Mitsubishi blocking the way to his field.

It's also important to recognise that what may look like a string of convenient parking spots, laid out along the edge of a narrow road, will almost certainly represent essential passing places, allowing vehicles to slip by on the moor's many single-track roads and lanes. It wasn't that long ago, when, if in any doubt about your chosen parking space, you would leave your car keys in the ignition, allowing a farmer to shift your vehicle temporarily if it was in the way. I wouldn't advise that now.

Public transport in these parts isn't what it was, alas, but the train connections are still pretty good to Exeter and Plymouth, with a bus service that should get you to the major moorland edge towns. From there, the provision of bus transport across the moor is far less extensive, but should still be found, especially in summer. As the situation seems to change almost monthly, I won't risk mentioning any details.

Cycling across the moor is fun, with any traffic, at least in principle, restricted to 40mph. You may also be pleased to know that the main effort for cyclists is found in getting up on top of the moor. Once the steep climb at the edge is achieved, pedalling around the interior is relatively easy.

Heading towards Princetown on two wheels.

Fine for a short stroll.

Clothing

Experienced fell and hill walkers will know the clothing drill, and can disregard this bit, but if your visit to Dartmoor marks the start of what, I hope, will be a very satisfying relationship with upland walking, this section offers some basic advice. That said, it would be impossible in the space available to deal with every clothing matter, but fortunately help is at hand, and any good outdoor kit shop should be able to provide answers. Few, for example, know Dartmoor conditions as well as Taunton Leisure.

Planning your first walk on Dartmoor, you may well feel that the clothes you usually wear will do, and this is probably true, for short walks, in good weather. On slightly longer routes however, the inbuilt deficiencies will begin to emerge. Jeans, for example, will soon start rub. A little rain, and they're quickly wet, and will stay that way for hours, rubbing even more. Standard socks will slip and slide about inside your footwear, almost certainly resulting in blisters. A cotton t-shirt, which might feel wonderfully comfortable in sunny weather, will take on rather less pleasing qualities when the sun dips behind a cloud, soon feeling sweaty, clammy and cold. A keen breeze, that might not have been apparent at the start of the journey, now seems to cut right through your coat. And is that rain you see on the horizon?

Waterproofs

On that important subject... even on a seemingly good day, conditions can change fast. Opportunities for waterproofs to be left behind safely are few and far between. The best bet, even if the weather forecast looks good, is to pack at least a light set of good waterproofs: jacket and leggings. By good, I mean a coat and overtrousers that both keep the rain at bay, and, importantly, let any perspiration out too. A decent retailer can advise on the plethora of breathable membranes and water management systems available today.

Some of these waterproofs will seem shockingly expensive, but can turn wet weather from a grim and trying experience, to something you might even enjoy.

It won't be long before a decent waterproof coat is needed.

Walking leggings are gaining in popularity.

Just don't allow yourself to be taken in too much by the cost. While the expensive garments do often merit the price (well almost), some of the rainwear at the cheaper end of the range can still be very effective, and a good outdoor shop will be happy to point you in the right direction.

Walking trousers

Having decided to take the plunge, and spend a little money, modern walking trousers are also a sound initial investment. Unlike jeans, these will stretch a little, and carry no raised seams to rub. They will also block the bulk of any cold wind, and dry quickly if caught unprotected by a sudden shower. If you need to watch the pennies, and already own a pair of tracksuit bottoms, these will often perform pretty well. With weather in summer and winter so very different, it is also worth looking at walking trousers that suit the conditions. Many now choose thin leggings for warmer conditions.

Some walking trousers can even be turned into shorts.

Socks

Proper walking socks are just wonderful, and a good pair, matched to the conditions and time of year, will even be worth what can often look like crazy prices. Stretchy where they need to be stretchy, firmer where they don't, and cushioned in just the right places, good walking socks are soon likely to represent your favourite outdoor gear. Not surprisingly, dedicated walking sock manufacturers also offer versions that suit the conditions, ranging from light summer pairs, to cozy items almost guaranteed to keep your feet warm when trudging through the snow.

Base layers

Good walking base layers (the clothes next to your skin) are made from either fancy man-made fibres, or my favourite, merino wool. Quite a few today also use bamboo in the mix, which can be surprisingly soft and comfortable. Unlike cotton t-shirts and underwear, these base-layer garments will 'wick', or draw away, any perspiration from your skin, helping to keep you dry and warm. They really will make a big difference.

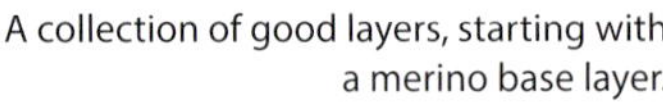

A collection of good layers, starting with a merino base layer.

Insulation

Don't forget to take along at least one extra layer, just in case, even in summer; you just never know. A long evening wait with a twisted ankle, watching for help to arrive as the wind picks up, will be made much easier if there's something extra to pull from your rucksack. In winter, Dartmoor can feel as cold and inhospitable as just about anywhere. Here I will champion wool again, not least for its amazing thermal qualities, even when damp, but because as it breaks down, or is washed, it won't be adding millions of tiny, and damaging, plastic fibres to the environment.

Footwear

Footwear is a very personal thing of course, and the heavy leather boot, loved by many, may be something you wouldn't go near. All I will do here is remind anyone heading up onto Dartmoor that it will always be wet somewhere on your route, and that's even after a protracted hot spell in summer. In winter, you might not place a foot on a dry spot for miles. Boots that can keep the worst of the damp out are a good idea, and the advice of a good outdoor clothing store, especially one with local knowledge, is of particular value here. This advice is also vital when it comes to fit, and well-fitted footwear is essential. Even the best boot will do you no good at all if it just doesn't suit your foot.

A good store will also have a dedicated footwear advisor, who understands the local walking conditions and can identify your needs, matching them to a selection of suitable boots or shoes. That selection should also be large, offering options for particular foot shapes (yes, really) and sizes, including half sizes. They can also advise on the use of special footbeds (the removable liners between foot sole and boot), some of which can make a huge difference to foot health and comfort.

Good leather boots, with proper walking socks, worn below walking tights.

A decent cold weather hat, teamed up with a few other good winter warmers.

Hats, gloves and other peripherals

Whether it's particularly cold (not uncommon) or particularly sunny (it does happen), the right hat can make a big difference. When temperatures drop, or the wind picks up, some form of fleecy head covering, either in wool, a manmade material, or a mix of the two, can be very welcome. Something that can also be pulled down over the ears when conditions really deteriorate is even better.

At the other end of the extreme, a hat with a proper brim can avoid all sorts of problems when the sun burns bright. There are many dedicated summer walking hats on the market, the best with some form of cord to either keep it in place on your head should the wind also blow, or to help secure it in place on your rucksack when not in use. I've long had a high regard for versions made by the Canadian company, Tilley.

A good summer hat.

Left: a summer Buff.

Right: a Polar Buff, accompanies a whole swathe of good winter clothing, including a warm hat.

Another product that I'm rarely seen on the moor without is some form of tubular neck scarf, of the sort produced by Buff. These can keep the chill out in cold weather, and the sun from your neck when it's warm. When really hot, a quick dip of your Buff in a stream provides a cooling neck collar. Specially designed Polar versions, that are both thicker and longer, are almost essential items of clothing in more Arctic conditions, in my opinion.

Gloves are a tricky things to get right, but some form of hand protection is essential in really cold weather, when it may be sensible to wear two layers: a heavy insulated outer pair, and some thin linings to offer protection when these need to be taken off to adjust laces or open a packet to get at food. For the outer layer, in really chilly conditions, I prefer mittens. As with all clothing considerations, and I don't mind repeating myself on this important topic, it is nearly always best to take advice from an experienced outdoor kit shop.

Time for some decent gloves.

Two Ordnance Survey OL28 maps.

Kit

It's hard to know quite how to pitch this bit. Weigh in with the sort of comprehensive list needed by a beginner, and many readers will be bored rigid after the first couple of lines. Once again though, if you are an experienced fell walker, you can always skip this bit.

Maps

First off, you really must carry a map. Some corners of the moor feel as familiar to me as my garden, but I still carry a map, even if only to remind myself of local names and hidden corners. Once away to some of the less visited corners, a map is vital.

There are two particular maps that spring to mind, the Ordnance Survey (OS), double-sided Outdoor Leisure Map (or OL) 28, and the Harvey's Dartmoor sheet. The former is printed at a very pleasant 1:25,000 scale, and my favourite version is laminated. Even if this does make it a little bulky, it will last many times longer in the wet conditions I keep banging on about. The Harvey Mountain Map (Dartmoor) goes one better, with the graphics printed directly onto a polythene sheet. This makes a neat, light and almost indestructible map, and the 1:40,000 scale is a useful compromise between the two usual scales used by the OS. The coloured contours are another particularly pleasing addition.

Compass

A decent compass.

With that map should go a decent compass, and by that I mean the sort of walker's model with a baseplate from which bearings can be taken. Silva makes a great range, with 3NL-360 or Ranger models being a good balance between performance and cost. And if you don't know how to obtain and walk on a bearing, then I strongly recommend that you find out, and Kevin Walker's book *Mountain and Moorland Navigation* will help. Dartmoor is notorious for its many wide, and sometimes almost featureless stretches, and without the ability to use a map and compass to walk on a bearing, you really do run the risk of getting into difficulty.

Digital navigation

You may have noticed that I haven't yet mentioned digital navigation devices. This isn't because I don't recognise their value, which can be huge, but because effective and efficient as they often are, I want them to be seen as backups to essential map and compass use skills, even if the smartphone is often pulled out first.

That mobile phone might also make a useful safety feature in its primary role, although the signal is so poor up there, that the chances are that when you may need to make 'that' call, nobody will hear it. Further discussion on the use of a mobile found can be found on page 78.

Whistle

Last mention here of safety essentials is a good, loud whistle. These are used to call for help (the internationally recognised signal is six blasts every minute), and the signal that your emergency call has been heard and help is on the way (three blasts every minute). You can also use a torch, using the same number of flashes. I carry both on all walks, even short ones in daylight.

Left: using a phone to get a location fix.

Right: a good loud whistle.

A 38-litre rucksack.

A good camping rucksack of 65-litre capacity.

Rucksacks

Before moving on to other essentials, it might be best to mention the way you will carry it all, which will be a good rucksack. Again, preferences vary, but at the very least, this glorified bag should have a hip belt and chest strap, and be big enough to carry everything. In practice, this will be a rucksack of somewhere around 15–25 litres capacity for short walks in the best summer conditions, through to 25–40 litres in winter, when you will need to carry a good selection of spare, warm clothing, and more food. These sizes don't consider camping, and as this glorious activity is an option on the moor, summer rucksacks will need to rise to around 50 litres in size, and winter ones to 60 or 70, possibly a little more. As with all kit, advice is always available from – yes, you're ahead of me now – that good outdoor kit shop.

On the subject of rucksacks, some people swear by waterproof covers that envelop the whole thing in light, impermeable fabric. Considering the weather up there on the moor this does seem to be a good idea, as most rucksacks aren't designed to repel water completely. I have my doubts however, prompted by the number of covers I see billowing and flapping in windy weather, often torn right off and blown away. Instead, my response is to pack everything vulnerable into a selection of dry bags. These come in a range of sizes, weights and colours, and are worth every penny. Colours are important, if only to allow packed items to be found easily, assuming of course that you remember what item went in which coloured bag.

Food and drink

To fill your bag, and after your spare clothes, map and compass have been dropped in (the clothes in their own dry bag), you should add a healthy supply of drinking water, in a light but sturdy container. If stored on the outside of your rucksack, this will need some form of clip or other secure attachment to ensure it doesn't disappear. You then need a good supply of food, with a decent reserve to cover any eventuality in which you might find yourself out on the moor a little longer than

Left: don't forget to carry water.

Right: my First Aid kit.

expected. Unforeseen problems aside, high energy snacks, particularly those that use ingredients that release energy slowly, such as oats, are the best option.

First Aid kit

While it doesn't need to be huge, some form of First Aid kit is also a must, even if it only holds blister protection, in the form of plasters or specialist tape, and a bandage to support a lightly sprained ankle. I also try to carry a few good painkillers and some antihistamine tablets. Everything then goes in a dedicated dry bag (green in my coding system).

Head torch

Finally, except perhaps in the middle of summer, a good head torch, accompanied by a spare battery, are items I deem close to essential in my rucksack. In reality, even in August, you'll probably find one in there.

Walking poles

Walking poles are a very personal thing. Some walkers swear by them, others are more likely to swear at these supposed walking aids. I'll comment only by saying that while much of Dartmoor is relatively easy and safe to traverse, significant problems can often arise in the form of the many streams and small rivers that

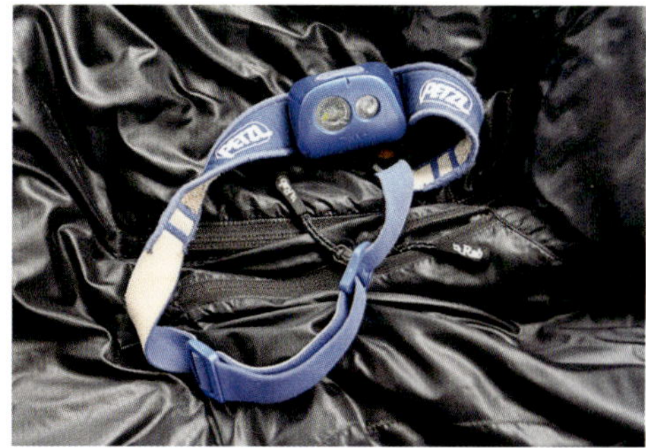

A good head torch.

My hazel stick.

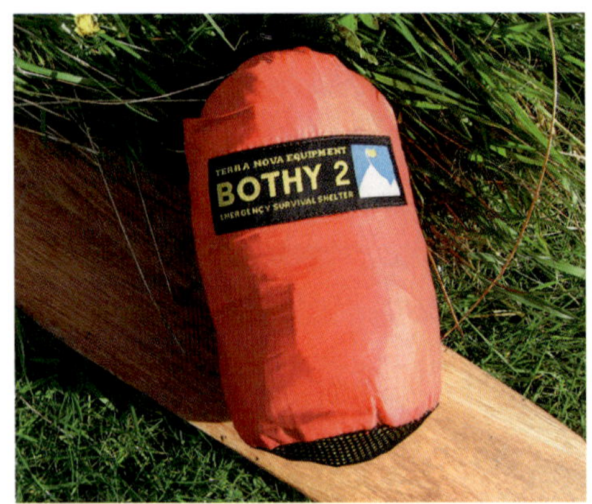

A bothy bag for two.

work their way across the hills, removing the copious amount of rain that falls each month. Depending on precipitation levels, Dartmoor streams can run low at one moment, high and foaming the next, and will be discussed a few pages on as one of the moor's very rare, but significant threats. In short, crossing these streams, their flow often broken only by rounded and moss-covered boulders, can require some very nimble footwork. A walking pole, while considered by many to be redundant over much of the journey, might suddenly take on a very new light as a stream is met. I often carry a hazel thumbstick that's really only ever brought into play at these critical moments. I've often been extremely grateful for its added support, and remember much of the high moor is treeless, so finding a stick when you do eventually need one is unlikely.

Bothy bag

My last suggestion concerns colder and wetter weather, and it is to carry a bothy bag. These are small emergency shelters, designed to be deployed very quickly and easily, and used to keep the worst of cold and windy conditions at bay. Little more than a large waterproof and windproof bag, they are often made of brightly coloured rip-stop nylon, so are easily seen in the murk of a snow or rainstorm.

Different sized bothy bags are made to cater for one, two or more people, so can be selected to suit the party heading out. In bad conditions, when cold can be a real danger, and if a stop is required for whatever reason, they can make things a lot more comfortable. When things go badly wrong they can save lives. Packing down small, and weighing very little, everyone is advised to carry one through early autumn to late spring.

Safety

Specialist kit, including navigation aids, mobile phones and head torches aside, there are several other safety considerations to contemplate, some general to upland walking, a couple particular to the moor itself.

In reality, and in a situation dissimilar to many upland regions, Dartmoor is relatively free of physical dangers. It's one of the truly wonderful things about this place. Unlike the Lake District or Eryri (Snowdonia) for example, the moor possesses no exposed, narrow ridges. Even steep slopes are confined to a few spots such as Tavy Cleave or the West Okement valley, and even these can still be negotiated easily with a little care. There are a couple of proper drops, but again, restricted to very limited locations, such as the edge of Merrivale Quarry. In essence, the high moor can be walked with relatively few of the usual upland walker's concerns. This makes wandering about on Dartmoor both possible, and one of its greatest assets.

Of course a walk across the middle of the moor is not completely without risk. There are still plenty of gulleys to fall into, or rocks to fall off, but most of pretty modest size.

Tors

On the subject of rocks, some care does need to be taken on the tors. Along with almost every walker who will visit Dartmoor, I often succumb to the allure of climbing one of the many stunning piles of granite. The views from the top are often superb, and many are relatively easy to ascend.

Like many piles of geology, they are also often surprisingly difficult to get down from. In fact, I'd argue that Dartmoor tors are worse than most. All rock climbers know that going up is invariably easier than getting back down again, abseiling aside, but granite tors do seem to exaggerate that phenomenon. A pleasingly rounded outcrop might be fairly easy to shimmy up and over, but all those smoothed edges, each one dropping away ever more steeply, are also surprisingly awkward to negotiate in reverse. Whatever the reason, a surprisingly large number of people end up having to call on the ever-patient Dartmoor Rescue teams to help them down from what can be really quite modest granite lumps.

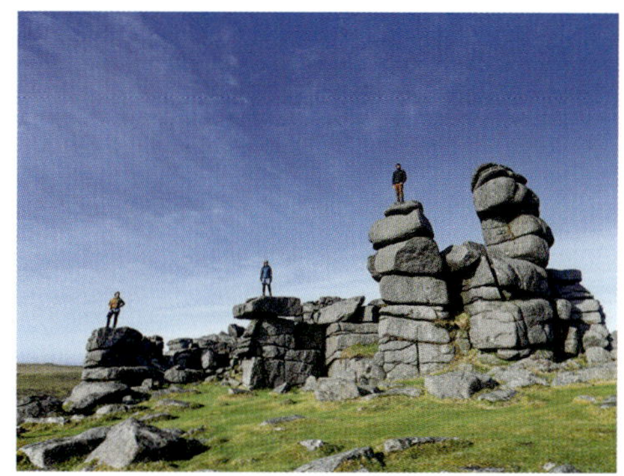

Everyone wants to climb a tor.

It also needs mentioning that many of these lumps are also far from modest. They're certainly big enough to make any unplanned and therefore rapid descent a very serious matter indeed. So, in summary, go carefully on those tors.

Left: a red flag.

Centre: a Dartmoor range marker.

Right: the military have an extensive presence on the moor.

Best left where it is.

Ranges

A safety subject that's fairly particular to Dartmoor relates to its use as a firing range. While there is definitely less activity up there than was seen in the past, the military still maintain very large areas of northern Dartmoor for training. Range boundaries are marked on OS and Harvey maps, and on the ground by red and white posts (which, while a bit of an eyesore, can be very useful for navigation).

Anyone can walk these ranges on public holidays, throughout August, or whenever they're not in use. While this might sound inconvenient, in practice the red flags (by day) and red lights (at night), shown at various prominent points to demonstrate that the ranges are in action, are rarely seen these days. To save a wasted trip though, you can call 0800 4584868 to check.

While on the subject, the military do still 'lob things about' that can go bang. It seems a less common event these days, but if you do come across anything suspicious, give it a wide berth and call the Okehampton Camp Commandant on 01837 650010 to let him know where you found it.

Bogs and Mires

A subject almost of fable, in reality the wetlands of the high moor are usually more of a trial than a true danger. Find yourself in the wrong place, and you will end up with wet legs, very wet legs. Walk long enough on the moor, and it's a certainty that this cloying, peaty dampness will one day extend even to your middle, but the whole experience will rarely result in any real danger.

Perhaps the only exception is Foxtor Mire, situated not far to the south-east of the now abandoned Whiteworks Tin Mine, near Princetown. This reasonably large expanse of boggy ground is said to be dangerously deep in places. As a direct result of this reputation I've only skirted this mire, and therefore can't comment myself. I have, though, heard some pretty concerning reports, and advise its avoidance. And yes, Conan Doyles' Grimpen Mire in his *Hound of the Baskervilles* tale is this very spot.

Almost anywhere on the moor can catch you out, and even seemingly sound paths or stretches of ground can hide a surprise. In general though, the presence of reeds will indicate damp ground, and the rougher an area of reed or grass, the wetter it often turns out to be. While it may be found that in many upland areas the

Another wet bit.

Childe's Tomb and a distant view (probably the best sort) of Foxtor Mire.

higher and steeper ground is often dry, this certainly isn't the case on Dartmoor, where quite extensive and trying patches of blanket bog can languish. Just try to approach Cranmere Pool from the east.

To cross poor, boggy ground, the obvious advice is to do so slowly and carefully, trying each potential footfall before committing any weight. In these situations a walking pole or stick can be invaluable, not only helping you to stay upright on what can become very unstable ground, but also allowing you to test a patch of seemingly sound ground before taking that next step.

If walking in groups in soft areas, ensure that you are not too close together. It's bad enough having one person in difficulty. Two could be disastrous. A companion on firm ground, or at least ground that is reasonably secure, can make all the difference when things do go a little awry.

Should you find yourself in trouble... stop. Things are unlikely to get better by proceeding. The next step, presuming you're not still sinking, is to retreat. After all, the ground you've covered has demonstrated that it can support your weight. This is often easier said than done mind you, particularly the initial turn. If you're carrying a stick, things will be a lot easier.

If you do find yourself in the nasty position of being stuck, and particularly if you are beginning to sink, don't struggle. Any movement is only likely to loosen the ground further. If things are really serious, try to throw yourself backwards. The idea of lying on wet ground may not appeal, but by spreading out your weight you are much less likely to sink, particularly if you do land on ground that held you so recently. Besides, your rucksack should take the brunt of the damp.

If you're travelling with others, and if it hasn't been a reflex reaction, shout out for help. While avoiding getting too close, and using say a walking pole, a belt, even a rucksack, your companions should be able to provide you with something to hold onto, helping to drag you clear.

On your own, you should be able to unclip your rucksack, leaving it in place to allow you to turn, and use it as a raft or knee/foot support – a springboard to drier ground. A walking pole can also be used, placed flat on the ground as a support.

Ticks

Ticks never seemed to be a problem when I was a lad. Perhaps we just didn't recognise the dangers, although a well fed parasitic arachnid attached to your body should be pretty hard to miss. I suspect it's simply the case that ticks weren't that common, having increased significantly in numbers in recent years, perhaps as a result, in part, of global warming.

Apart from being just plain unpleasant, the risks from having a tick dig its mandibles into your skin include Lyme disease. This much misunderstood ailment seems to be on the increase. I've known a few sufferers personally, although not people, I admit, who have picked it up on the moor. What I have seen of Lyme isn't pleasant, with a range of symptoms, some long-lasting and potentially very serious.

The best way to avoid ticks is to reduce their chance of reaching you in the first place. Ticks literally hang about at the end of vegetation, favouring the tips of reeds, grasses and ferns. When they detect heat they jump, trying to find bare skin. Keeping skin covered, especially legs, can make a big difference.

It's then a case of checking yourself at the end of the day, or to ask a companion, if you're on very friendly terms. Ticks tend to go for warm soft areas. I'll leave that to your imagination!

Removal is slightly tricky, with the key aim of not squeezing the body, which increases the chance of infection significantly. Special tools can be bought from good chemists or outdoor stores. I still use something from the vet, originally intended for use on a retriever.

Finally, be reassured that not all ticks carry anything nasty, far from it. And even if they do, rapid and careful removal may very well avoid infection anyway.

Tick removers.

A Dartmoor stream in spate, and not worth the risk.

Making the most of a natural boulder crossing.

Rivers

I've left rivers until almost the end of this safety section, not because they represent the least concern, but for exactly the opposite reason. By mentioning them near the end, I hope they gain the most attention.

Barring a fall from a tor, or perhaps hypothermia during a very cold spell in winter, rivers represent the most significant risk on Dartmoor, or more specifically, river crossings. Attempts to ford moorland rivers in the wrong place, at the wrong time, really do result in drownings, and the most obvious wrong time is when the river is in spate.

With high catchments on impervious granite rock, and where the thin peaty soils are often already soaked to saturation point, any rain will quickly run across the ground. This water then falls straight into the countless feeder streams that criss-cross the moor. If it rains on the moor, the rivers rise. If it rains hard, and this happens often on Dartmoor, those rivers rise fast, often breaking free from their channel. What might have been a fairly modest stream will look very different after just an hour or so of protracted rain.

Even at fairly normal levels, Dartmoor streams and rivers still provide a hazard. Only a few, near the top ends of their course, are narrow enough to jump. In most situations, some form of safer crossing will need to be found. This will often be a natural stone bridge. Fortunately, the bed of Dartmoor rivers are invariably littered with rounded, waterworn boulders, and a bit of a search will usually find a spot where they have collected naturally to provide a crossing. Regularly used spots are often betrayed by the stones themselves, often worn free of lichens and moss.

Natural fords are also relatively common, their presence often revealed by eroded banks, with visible paths or animal tracks approaching from each side. Wide and shallow, the going can still be a little precarious, and some form of walking stick, as with the boulder bridge crossings, can be particularly helpful.

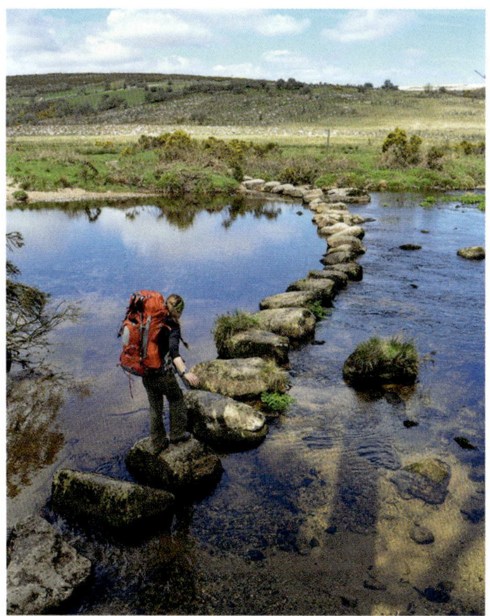

Left: using a stick to assist the fording of a Dartmoor stream.

Right: using a convenient set of stepping stones.

Rudimentary bridges and stepping stones fringe the high moor, and at normal river levels provide reasonably safe crossing points. A close look at a map may throw something up.

Even here though, a modest rise can cause problems. Stepping stones soon disappear beneath the flow, and even bridges can be covered. It's not unknown for them to be swept away, and I can think of at least two occasions when the bridge I've been heading for wasn't there when I arrived. During one recent visit, the clapper bridge still stood proud of the water, but only just, and burst channels to either side had left it as a distant and completely useless island.

Not surprisingly, there are very few bridges on the high ground across the centre of the moor. A river crossing here, teetering from one exposed and mossy boulder to another, or walking straight across, becomes much more difficult, and risk-laden, as levels rise and flows increase. After a day or two of rain, moorland rivers, even the small streams, will surge through their deep, narrow channel at an alarming rate, carrying substantial volumes of peat-stained water.

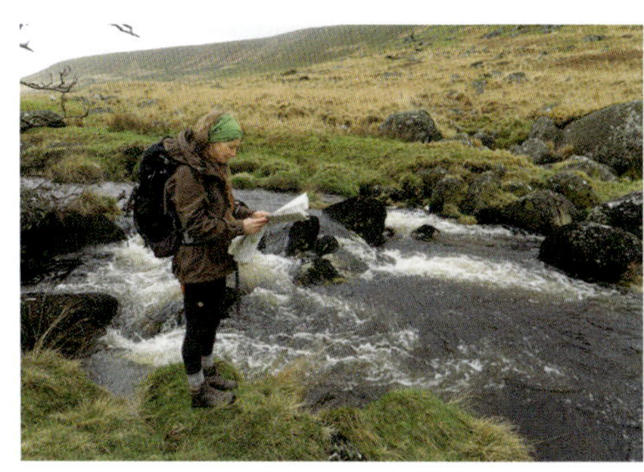

In drier conditions, there's a good crossing point here.

In these situations, even the most experienced moorland walker should avoid them. In fact, those that know Dartmoor rivers will do anything they can to avoid making a crossing, even if a detour to find either a bridge or a narrow section far upstream may take them miles out of their way.

And that is the answer when a river in spate is met. Turn and walk along its bank to find a safe crossing, either a bridge marked on the map for example, or uphill to find a point where a secure crossing is guaranteed at a narrower point. Even if you have to travel a considerable distance, it will be worth it. Where tempted to make a crossing please pause a while to consider the implications.

There are, of course, ways to lessen the risk of a crossing, but in what may seem an unreasonable manner, I don't intend to offer them here. Were this a guide to walking in Mongolia or Alsaka, where, when faced with a river crossing, options are often few and far between, then some form of instruction would indeed be required. However, on Dartmoor that opportunity to turn and walk upstream is almost always there, and any diversion really shouldn't be that long before somewhere much safer can be found. I'll stick then with the advice just given.

Faced with a moorland river in true spate, only a team of very experienced moorland walkers, equipped with ropes, and I'm thinking here of one of Dartmoor's rescue teams, would ever consider heading straight across, and even then, only when there was a very pressing reason to do so, without delay. After all, some will have witnessed the awful results of a walker getting it wrong.

Cold

Many of the potential dangers on the moor described here are tangible, often very visible. You can spot the drop from the edge of a tor, the boggy ground or the swollen river. One danger, however, a very real danger, isn't visible at all, but arrives unseen with a clear sky or the slow build of a northerly breeze.

The results of cold, or at least the results once the situation has become dangerous, are known as hypothermia. Contrary to most people's expectations, it

Left: Dartmoor can produce some truly cold conditions.

Right: a cold day on the moor.

doesn't actually need to be that chilly for hypothermia to set in. Even when the thermometer might read above 0°C, the damp of a constant drizzle can combine with a stiff breeze, to make the risk of hypothermia very real. Of course there are many days on the high moor when the temperature falls much lower.

The clinical definition of hypothermia is a body core temperature that drops from its normal 37°C or so, to below 35°C. In fact, any sustained drop in body temperature can result in this very dangerous condition. In the field, the first thing is to ensure that you are able to spot the symptoms.

The first signs are any impairment to normal coordination or cognitive functions. This might include slurred speech, stumbling or loss of dexterity. Walkers suffering from the beginnings of hypothermia tend to go quiet. Some can get grouchy, or perhaps more grouchy. And remember, in cold miserable conditions, it's not only important to keep an eye on companions, you need to make a critical judgement of your own behaviour too.

Shivering may be a sign of mild hypothermia, but as things deteriorate this can stop, as heart rates and breathing slow. Pupils may become dilated as hypothermia

A bothy bag can make a huge difference when the conditions take their toll.

becomes more severe. At its worst, casualties will simply grind to a halt, eventually losing consciousness. Sadly, heart failure can occur in severe cases.

Of course, the aim is to have stepped in to do something long before this.

If you or a companion starts to show any signs of hypothermia, even mild hypothermia, call a stop and try to implement actions to halt, and hopefully reverse, the situation. Add clothing, particularly windproof and insulating layers. If you're not already wearing a hat, put one on.

Find some shelter, even if only the lee of a tor; cutting out the wind can make a big difference. If you have one, use a bothy bag. Take on fuel (food) and hydration (drink). If you have warm drinks, or the ability to make them, this is the time to bring them out. Sugary food is ideal.

If a casualty still shows no sign of improvement, add more clothing, and make sure they have an insulated layer between them and the ground. Importantly, make sure you don't go without adequate protection yourself. You won't be of much help if you're hypothermic too.

If things still don't improve, call up some help.

Before an emergency

On a safety note, it's worth stressing that the mobile phone signal isn't great on Dartmoor. It's often non-existent. That said, a phone still represents an extremely important aid in an emergency, so try to ensure it is fully charged before setting out.

The poor signal up there, as I understand it, makes keeping that important charge all the more tricky, as a phone on the moor is constantly working hard in an attempt to find what signal there is. For this reason, it is often best to either turn your phone off while walking, or to place it in 'aeroplane mode' until needed. It might also be a good idea, especially when setting out on longer trips, to carry an additional power pack.

One last suggestion; while it's always preferable in the case of an emergency to make a standard 999 'voice' call, since 2009 it has been possible to send a text to call the emergency services. This might even be possible when the signal is poor. Introduced primarily to assist those with hearing or speech impairments, the service is not restricted, and could be very useful for any walker when weather and signal conditions make a standard call difficult or impossible.

To register your phone with emergencySMS

Send the word 'register' to 999.

After reading the message received, reply 'yes'.

You will receive a further message, either confirming registration, or identifying any problems with registration.

At any time, you can check that your phone is registered by texting 'register' to 999.

To use, and only if you can't place a 'voice' call, send a text describing your emergency to 999, and await a reply (this should arrive in two to three minutes).

In case of an emergency

Should things go wrong, Dartmoor walkers are fortunate to have a very experienced mountain rescue team, The Dartmoor Rescue Group, based at four locations around the moor.

Should genuine difficulties arise, call 999 or 112, and ask first for the 'Police', and then 'Mountain Rescue'.

The Dartmoor Recue Group will want the following details:

*   Your location (preferably with a grid reference)

*   The name, gender and age of any casualty

*   The nature of the injuries or emergency

*   The number of people in your party

*   Your mobile phone number

Weather conditions, while not essential, would also be helpful

Any text sent to emergencySMS should provide the same information.

The Dartmoor Rescue Group advice is then to stay where you are until contacted by the rescue team.

Kit checklist

Worth a quick check before setting out, with asterisks used to indicate essential items (this list doesn't include clothing or boots):

*   Rucksack* (suited to the journey and time of year)

*   Map* (OS or Harvey)

*   Compass* (a good model you can use to take a bearing)

*   Whistle*

*   Water container* (that can be clipped to your rucksack for safety)

- Food* (enough to cater for the journey in mind, plus a few high-energy snacks as back-up)

- A dry bag for your food

- Waterproof coat*

- Waterproof overtrousers (almost essential, and worth a * in colder months)

- Spare insulating layer (again, almost essential, and worth a * in colder months)

- Warm hat (and again)

- Gloves (ditto)

- Dry bag for spare clothing

- First aid kit* (even if fairly basic)

- Mobile phone* (as almost everyone has one these days, I suggest you take it)

- Bothy bag* (You may disagree about the essential nature of this bag, until you, or somebody else for that matter, actually needs it. Even an apparently warm summer evening can soon start to feel cold if you are incapacitated for a few hours on an open hillside. And besides, they make a very visible target for a rescue team)

- Headtorch (up to you, but I always carry one, just in case)

- Walking stick or sticks

All this may sound like quite a lot, but it should still slip into a modest rucksack, leaving plenty of space.

Where to go

By British standards, Dartmoor is certainly pretty big. Viewed on a map from the comfort of home, it can also look worryingly feature free. A few patches of woodland cling around the edges, and a couple of roads head through the middle, flanked by a few fields, but the rest can appear disconcertingly uniform; a broad expanse of high ground, peppered with just a few small, rocky outcrops. A handful of tracks wander here and there, often seeming to fade away to nothing as they climb. Even the river valleys appear only vaguely distinct, particularly on the highest ground. This isn't an easy place across which to identify obvious routes.

To help, the final section of this book offers a range of routes, with distances, way-marks and directions, laid out in the detail you'd expect of any walking guide. These walks vary in length from very short, some only a couple of kilometres long, to a few that will take two or three days to cover. There should be something for just about everyone, with each route chosen and designed to take you along some of the most impressive and interesting trails on the moor.

There's plenty of space to wander.

Meandering

Fixed routes aren't for everyone though, and for experienced walkers Dartmoor offers something particularly special; the chance to just wander.

With very little in the way of truly hazardous ground, and in good weather conditions, it is quite possible for those who feel confident in wilder and emptier places, to take a map and compass, and to just set out and see where they end up. To many this may seem rather reckless, and for those with limited fellwalking experience it would be, but a competent and seasoned hiker really can take advantage of the rare conditions offered by the moor; to embark without a fixed route, and to meander.

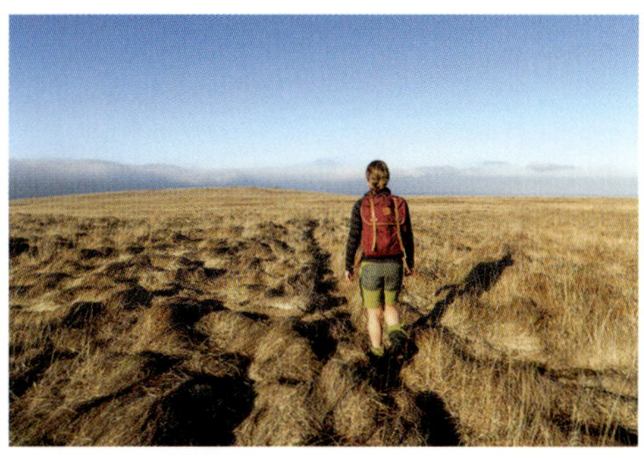

Just following your nose.

Without set destinations, this form of travel may also seem unstructured. In some ways it is, but this is deliberate. A form of travel that at first glance may appear to be without an aim, is in fact anything but aimless.

All too often, a fixed and preordained route will take us very successfully from point A to point B, and over terrain with very steep slopes, scree or narrow ridges, and certainly across any ground with cliffs and sheer drops, the only safe option will be to follow a known and well-documented route. This makes absolute sense. However, following a fixed route means the chance to see something new is inevitably limited. With experience, it's true that you can wander a little across the high ground of the Eryri Glyders for example, or Helvelyn and Fairfield in the Lakes, but the risks are there, sometimes quite significant risks. Wandering about is not a prospect to be taken lightly in these areas. Head 'off-piste' on Dartmoor on the other hand, even completely 'off-piste', and those dangers are few. You have a much greater chance of enjoying the experience and returning in one happy piece. Not only is Dartmoor meandering fun, it also offers the only real chance to experience the place fully. Seemingly purposeless, this approach to travel is in fact packed with intention, and that intention is to explore.

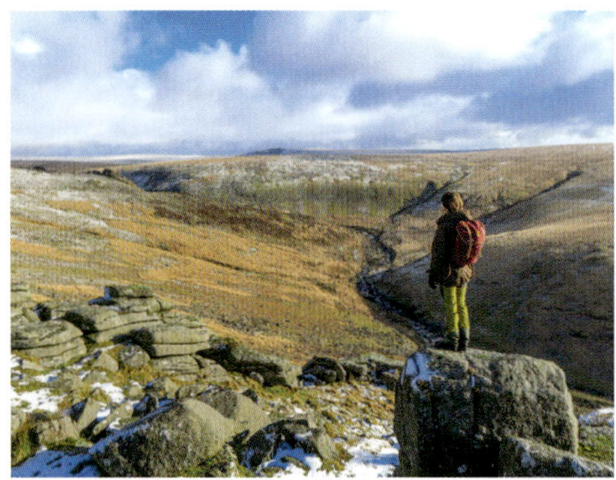

... with opportunities that swell to encompass a whole moor.

Broad ridges.

This uplifting practice suits a single day on the moor, when a surprising amount of new land can be seen. It is even more fun if camping gear and food is packed, and a long weekend is set aside for the experience. Setting out from Belstone for example, not knowing whether the next night will be spent at a spot to the west of Fur Tor, amongst the sheep of Hew Down or beside Sandy Hole Pass on the East Dart River, the very essence of the walk is transformed. By meandering, we take what might normally be a narrow and prescribed line on a map, replacing this unnecessary restriction with opportunities that swell to encompass a whole moor. This is heady stuff.

A description of just such a walk starts on page 245.

On one meandered outing, Susannah and I set out from the northern edge of the moor, camping no further south than Lints Tor, a few miles from the car park and still in sight of High Willhays. On another, we ended up way down in the south-east corner, alongside a river below Eastern White Barrow. On journeys like these, stripped of limiting and preordained routes, new burial mounds and abandoned farms are found, previously unmet herds of ponies become neighbours for a night, the song of a nightingale may fill our thoughts in a remote dell as we drift off to sleep. Home might be a tiny stream valley, the air thick with the heady smell of meadowsweet. It's amazing what you can find when you have no idea where you're going.

While acknowledging that the division fails to include all of Dartmoor's land, the high moor, at least away from the central enclosed section, can be split for the meandering walker into two key blocks: ridges and valleys. On the whole, the former are broad and often relatively featureless, the latter usually fairly wide and open. There are exceptions, of course, at least with the valleys, and both the Tavy and the West Okement flow through reasonably tight clefts, or 'cleaves', as they're known here. Tavy Cleave is particularly narrow, and particularly pretty. Both valleys possess sides that require some care to traverse. More typical is the valley holding the Taw, a wide bowl.

The result of all this, and again I am generalising, is that upland routes provide plenty of sky and distant prospects, but can sometimes be tricky to navigate, while

Left: wide open river valleys. This one holds the Taw.

Right: and the occasional narrow one. This is Tavy Cleave.

The path here is pretty clear, even though nothing appears on a map.

Tavy Cleave.

the valleys offer less spectacular long views, yet should be somewhere in which it is far harder to get lost. You have that ever-reliable watercourse to follow after all. This natural aid can be particularly useful on those frequent days when mist and low cloud settles over the moor.

That said, while many of the open expanses of grassland between one tor and another may not have much in the way of prominent features, they will often possess a clear path. Frequently, this will be pretty wide and visible, a route over which walkers have worked their way, dodging the many soggy pits, thick with soupy black peat stirred up by countless Vibram-soled boots. A valid and reliable path should be easy to see.

These boot-worn paths can be very helpful, especially in those murky conditions. They allow walkers to chart a safe, and usually very visible, route along the moors, many being wide and relatively featureless tracts of high ground. They can be equally useful when looking for the right place to leave the ridge and an eye kept open for a trodden diversion can often take you down safely, to a river crossing point, or through the worst of a bog or mire. The other very useful informal track is the result of farmer's quad bikes. Again, even if they don't head quite where you had in mind, the route will be easy to follow, and likely to take the line of least resistance. Those quad bike riders will know exactly where they're going after all.

There are also narrow tracks caused by animals, 'trods' as they're known in the Lakes. Over tough ground, these seemingly insignificant and sometimes quite ephemeral paths, no more than a pair of hooves wide, can be a real boon, even if they're not heading quite where you thought you were going.

Occasionally, however, boot-worn paths can cause a few difficulties; ironically, this tends to occur where a right of way is marked on a map. This isn't a situation unique to Dartmoor, and maps of many upland areas in Britain show marked routes that don't necessarily match those found on the ground. The confluence of marked paths to the south of the Red Lake quarry is an example, where the line indicating the rights of way on the map, diverges from reality just enough to confuse even experienced walkers. The last time we swung off the Two Moors Way there, heading for the ridge route past Western White Tor, we were followed by two walkers who were convinced they were still on route to meet the River Avon. That would make sense, if you trusted the map.

Another very good example lies just to the south of Little Hound Tor. Approach this point along a clear trodden path from Wild Tor to the south, and the map marks two footpaths, one heading slightly west towards the Taw valley, the other north-east in the direction of South Zeal. In reality, the most visible path will take you straight on up to the top of Cosdon Beacon. By contrast, and illustrating the nub of this point, the marked path to Taw Marsh is all but invisible. In brief, don't trust every dashed green line on the map.

Following a stream, while not always the best course of action in steep mountain country, should reduce the chance of getting lost considerably, although even here on the moor this tactic may well come at a price. Dartmoor watercourse edges abound with marshy stretches, where side streams ooze in across extensive and often very boggy mini deltas.

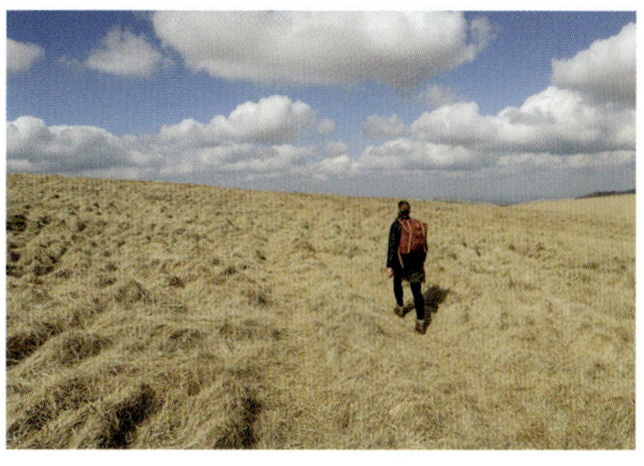

A quad bike track, providing a very easy route across rough ground.

A good path through tinners' spoil heaps, close to the bank.

Babies' heads.

The other bar to easy valley-bottom travel is present as the result of tinners, who left the spoil from their enthusiastic and very widespread workings scattered with no regard for future walkers. That said, a good dry route can sometimes be found that might run for a considerable distance along a ridge of spoil, laid out parallel to the stream, and possibly once flanking its diverted flow, but that sort of assistance certainly can't be relied upon. Past manipulation of the river often leaves relics in the form of side streams and channels. Annoyingly, these are often just too wide and deep to cross. If you do choose to follow a valley bottom, and if a path can't be found right alongside the bank, or along the top of one of those linear spoil ridges, it may be best to work your way along the edge of the slightly raised ground where it begins to lift at the valley side.

Returning to those ridges, and if a path of some sort is found that doesn't quite seem to be heading the way you want to go, it may still be worth following. The slight deviation from your desired course may be preferable to a direct line across broken ground. Once off a path on the high moor, every mile through the lumpy vegetation-swathed ground can soon feel like three or four, and that's in the rare case when you don't hit a bog or mire; often identified by dense swathes of club and spike rush, or the pale wisps of common cotton grass seed heads.

The upland can also be divided broadly, giving us the central high ground, characterised by peak bogs, rushes and moss, and the drier periphery. Here, vast areas of gently sloping hillside are covered with short, cropped grass (the good bits, which always feel quite small in area) or purple moor grass (the not so good bits, which can sometimes feel huge). These rough grasslands, with acres of long leaves waving in the breeze, can be surprisingly tough to weave through. The thick cover of long leaves hides a sometimes hideously lumpy terrain, known famously by the army as babies' heads. As you stumble, and sometimes fall, through this unremitting prairie, the tor ahead just not seeming to grow any closer, a Dartmoor mile can start to feel more like ten.

Don't be put off. Adopting a meandering style, in which predetermined destinations are unimportant, means that should a bad patch be met, and you just don't

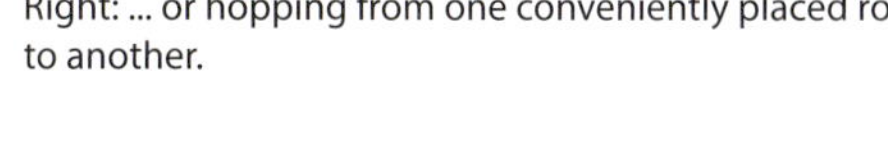

Left: tiptoeing through the shallows of a ford.

Right: ... or hopping from one conveniently placed rock to another.

fancy the effort, you can simply look to either side, pick a new objective, and set off afresh. You never know what you might find over the next brow.

And despite the warnings given about Dartmoor rivers, these should be considered in context. It needs to be stressed that the risks, within reason, only relate to spate conditions. At normal heights and flows, most watercourses on the moor can be crossed pretty easily, either by tiptoeing through the shallows of a ford, or hopping from one conveniently placed rock to another. A blue line on the map is rarely a restriction to travel.

Little is, in fact, and while a bog might need to be skirted, a riverbank tramped a short way before a natural set of steeping stones can be found, if you decide to travel in a certain direction, you almost always can. For someone happy to leave a pre-set route, to let the day unfold as it will, Dartmoor can be a very accommodating and fulfilling place.

Named routes

Not surprisingly, Dartmoor has attracted a number of named routes, some devised by local authority tourism offices to promote the area. A fair proportion skirt the moor, covering ground located more in the National Park than up on the high moor. These include the West Devon Way, Mariner's Way, Templar Way, Drakes Trail and the main circuit of the Dartmoor Way itself. Each has its own website.

A few routes do cut right across high ground, wending their way over the area covered by this book. A route known as the Perambulation has its origins in a medieval survey. It runs right round the high moor, covering a route of over 80km (50 miles), and is described in detail on page 257.

Another medieval route, often known as the Monk's Path is much shorter, but this is all relative. The path, or lack of it, which runs right across the middle of the moor, about a third of the way up, is described on page 250, with part of the walk set out in detail on page 201.

Left: a medieval cross on the Monk's Path.

Right: part of the Perambulation.

All sorts of theories surround the formation of the Abbot's Way, some even based on historical fact. What's almost certain is that the precarious route between Buckfast Abbey to the east of the moor and Tavistock Abbey to the west, meant that some form of markers were required to avoid various churchmen getting lost. As a result, a series of stone crosses were set up. Part of the route is included in the Monk's Path that runs, for the same reason, between Buckfast and Buckfastleigh. The route, which runs through Princetown, makes a fine walk.

It was once a requirement to bury all dead in the local parish church. Easy enough you might imagine, unless you lived within Dartmoor Forest in early medieval times, when your parish church was in Lydford. The Lych Way is the route those parishioners are alleged to have followed as they carried their deceased family members off the moor. It cuts right through the middle of the high moor, at one point crossing a bridge lying only a few yards from where Susannah and I once lived.

A marker on the Two Moor's Way.

Blackwood Path enters the moor at Wrangton Moor Gate and heads up onto high ground, reaching Stony Bottom in Hook Lake. This was almost certainly set out and used by peat cutters, tinners and other moorland folk accessing the head of the Erme valley.

The Two Moor's Way has a much more modern origin. Opened in 1976, It travels over 115 miles across Devon, from coast to coast, taking in, as the name suggests, both Exmoor and Dartmoor. It cuts through the latter on a route that runs along the eastern edge of the northern high moor, and pretty much through the centre of the southern half.

The Dartmoor Way also shares a modern origin. The main body of the route encircles the high moor on a 173km (108 mile) circuit, but a central section runs across the centre of Dartmoor, with Hexworthy roughly marking the central point.

Each of these routes is described in detail on various websites.

Getting lost

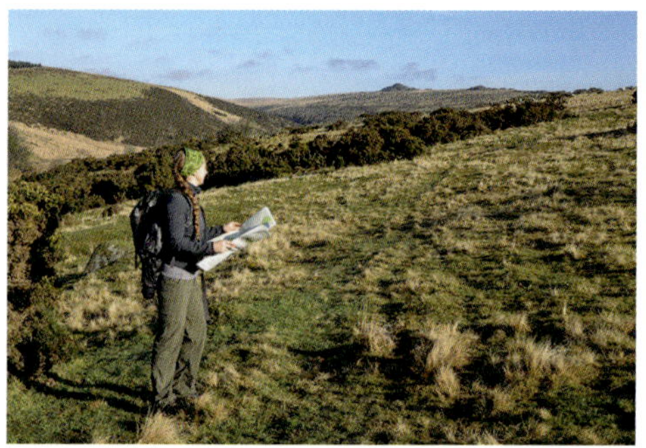

Where exactly am I?

A walker might travel for years on Dartmoor without losing their way. Then, one day, the clouds drop, the drizzle increases, and certainties begin to fray. Is that the first stream valley on the left, or have I passed one already? Did I miss the wall, or is it still somewhere up ahead in the mist? Is that a tor on the horizon? Where exactly am I?

Despite what novices might imagine, this can happen to walking beginners and veterans alike, although one would hope less often with the latter, a lot less often. The response will also differ. The experienced walker has, in a manner of speaking, been here before. They'll react to the situation, not with any sense of panic, but with something that's probably closer to a mix of mild resignation and amusement. They'll probably know where they went wrong anyway, or at least can make a pretty good guess, and they'll be well versed in the methods of putting themselves back on track. A combination of heightened observation and more diligent attention to their map, will soon have the situation remedied.

As this book is intended as guide to walking on Dartmoor, and not a guide to walking in general, I'm going to avoid the temptation to run through those methods. I'd soon run out of space after all, and besides, there are plenty of very good guides on navigation out there already, including Kevin Walker's *Mountain and Moorland Navigation*.

What I am keen to do however, especially as this section follows the one on meandering, is to emphasise the generosity of Dartmoor to the truly lost walker. This is a key reason why a veteran walker here, might seem so relaxed at the prospect. While they might harbour a few concerns if properly lost somewhere in the Torridon range, and some quite serious ones if in the Cuillins of Skye, experience of Dartmoor will have told them that the situation isn't actually that worrying at all, even if they continue, for some time, to be unsure exactly where they are.

All this might come as a surprise to those that have heard lurid tales of the ease with which a walker might get lost, amid Dartmoor's featureless boggy hills. And here it should be acknowledged that when the clouds descend, much of the centre of the high moor can be a tricky place from a navigational perspective, especially in poor weather. What also needs to be stressed though, is that even if really quite lost, the situation is really not that much of a problem. It's certainly nothing to get concerned about.

The reason for all this goes back to that relative lack of physical dangers. For while a wrong turn in many upland regions could be anything from distinctly unpleasant to deadly, and I think here of the summit of Ben Nevis for example, a little confused wandering on Dartmoor should risk little more than tired feet, and maybe a good peaty poultice for your legs.

I certainly don't want to downplay the threat completely, and Dartmoor walking can never be risk free, but the absence of cliffs, gullies, or even of any very steep slopes, means that a walker can travel over nearly all unknown ground on the moor, safe in the knowledge that it shouldn't throw up any more nasty surprise than a swollen river, a fast flowing leat or a particularly soggy marsh (the sudden and deep drop, close to the edge of a waterfall on Shavercombe Brook marks almost the only exception during my walks on the moor, and even here, the acute danger is extended over perhaps only a twenty metre length of riverbank).

The going might not always be easy. In fact, it certainly won't always be easy. A vast patch of thick gorse or scattered granite rubble, for example, can make for tedious and slow progress, but head in one direction, and before long, a river will be found, a wall, a track, a forest edge or a line of those very useful red and white military range makers. The relatively feature-free nature of the moor should mean that whatever change in the landscape you have just encountered can be identified easily. Before long, you'll be back to a position where a finger can be placed with confidence on the map. "I'm here."

As the light begins to fail, you can look for a campsite.

Camping

Making the most of Dartmoor's welcoming and generous landscape, a traveller on foot can wander happily in a deliberately aimless, and distinctly positive fashion. They can climb modest hillocks to inspect appropriately modest tors, wend their way along bright bubbling streams, discovering a small setting of Bronze Age stones here, a cluster of bog edge flowers there. Then, as the sun begins to drop towards a darkening purple horizon, Dartmoor walkers are blessed with something very special. Up here amidst the pony herds, watched by a pair of wheeling ravens, they can think about staying.

Instead of retracing those many steps on the long walk back to the car park, a Dartmoor explorer can carry on, turning thoughts to other matters. As the light begins to fail, you can look for a campsite.

To be fair, the ability to camp for the night exists in many upland areas of England and Wales, where a walker or climber can pitch a shelter high in the fells. This is not a legal right, however, but more a case of everyone turning a blind eye. In theory every camper, in the Lake District or Snowdonia for example, should ask permission from the landowner before making camp. On Dartmoor, in a situation found nowhere else south of the Scottish border, the right to camp does exist. A walker on the moor can think differently.

Campsite found.

Dartmoor dawn.

For lovers of space and freedom, this is where Dartmoor really shines. It may not be the biggest upland area in Britain, far from it in fact. It certainly isn't the highest, the most rugged, or perhaps even the most dramatic, but here you really are allowed to just wander in and put up a tent. You can pitch it almost anywhere you like. You can then carry on exploring the next day.

There are a few restrictions of course, and these are discussed below, but in brief, and as long as you leave your chosen campsite looking just as it did when you arrived, you can pitch a small tent in the evening, breaking camp in the morning before setting out again. This wonderfully flexible approach offers an extraordinary and almost unique sense of freedom. The ability to wild camp transforms exploration, turning a day on the moor into the possibility for a true journey; two days, three, perhaps even a week of discovery and escape from the rest of busy southern England spread out down below. There's something very special about a Dartmoor dawn, the moor to yourself, the choice to head in almost any direction.

One of our many camps within an army range.

One of the most civilised and uplifting outdoor privileges in the whole country.

Where and when

Although wild camping is allowed on Dartmoor, you'll not be surprised to learn that you can't just pitch a tent anywhere, not quite anyway. Camping on much of the Common Land on the moor is allowed though, and the good news is that there's a lot of it. Other than the intake fields at the centre, much of the high ground described in this book is included, and the Dartmoor National Park Authority (DNPA) website carries a page with details of the areas involved.

Camping is also allowed within the Army firing ranges, so long as they're not in use of course. The way you can tell, which includes checking that no red flag is flying from various prominent positions, is detailed on page 70.

It's then simply a case of ensuring that you don't overstep your rights, which are the use of a small tent, for a single night in any one place. This is much the same as the informal arrangements at play in the high areas of the Lake District or Eryri

Some walkers will love the sense of remote space offered by a campsite placed high and close to a tor.

(Snowdonia), only here it's sanctioned officially. I'd go as far as suggesting that this is one of the most civilised and uplifting outdoor privileges in the whole country (and one that should be adopted more widely).

Offering advice on particular camping spots is tricky, in large part because the range of options available is truly vast. There really is a lot of land to choose from. We then have personal preference. Some walkers, for example, will love the sense of remote space offered by a campsite placed high and close to a tor. The views up here are likely to be spectacular. Others will prefer the convenience of water nearby (which should be boiled well before drinking), the opportunity to swim (more on that later) or just the chance to lie awake for a while under canvas, listening to the song of the stream. Riverbanks are usually a grand choice, spoilt only slightly in warmer months by evening fly hatches.

Often it's enjoyable, and quite feasible, to simply stop for the night where sore feet or an aching back suggest. It's amazing how often you will stumble across a

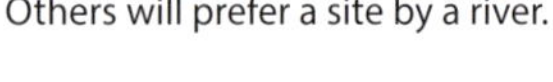

Others will prefer a site by a river.

little lawn, sprinkled with wild flowers, where the grazing ponies and sheep have maintained an almost perfect plot. Sometimes these are just too perfect to pass by.

While the tinners of the past have transformed the valley bottoms of even the tiniest Dartmoor streams, and not necessarily with the best aesthetic outcome, their efforts often provide very good camping spots. Numerous level plots lie between many of the ridges and banks, where machinery once stood perhaps, or a track ran between huts. These make fine places to pitch a tent, often protected from intrusive winds by those shoulder-high adjoining strands of deposited spoil. Once off the tops, and their upstanding granite guardians, I imagine nine out of ten of our camps on the moor will have sat, tight in amongst these industrial remains. The stony ground isn't particularly kind to tent pegs mind you, or hands trying to push them in.

Use the right kit, in some months this might include good four-season sleeping bags and true mountain tents, and you can happily camp on Dartmoor at any time of the year. It's really all down to how enthusiastic you are. There's no doubt though, that late spring through to autumn provides the golden period for a Dartmoor camper, with long days, warmer temperatures and at least a reasonable chance of dry weather.

Kit

Wild camping on Dartmoor is intended as an aid to walkers and explorers, and as such, should be a low-key affair. No basecamp tents and deckchairs here.

Tents

Besides, walking on Dartmoor can be pretty hard going at the best of times, so for this reason alone it's best to carry a tent that's as small and light as conditions and the number of occupants will allow. To ease the burden, if two or three of you plan to share a shelter, the individual tent components can be split between rucksacks, the poles and pegs in one for example, the rest in another. Three walkers? Then put any separate flysheet in a third.

The stony ground isn't particularly kind to tent pegs, or hands trying to push them in.

Dusk by the Taw.

Susannah and I often sleep under a tarp in summer.

A small, three-season Hilleberg tent.

This is a Terra Nova tent, built to take anything the weather might throw at it, yet still small and light enough to carry packed in a rucksack.

In summer, tents can be relatively insubstantial, as weather conditions, while often still a touch damp, are rarely extreme. As long as your tent is intended for more than just festival use it should be fine. Susannah and I often sleep under a tarp in summer, propped up by a couple of walking poles. Sometimes, when the weather is particularly fine, we dispense even with this.

If you plan to head out in late autumn or early spring however, that laid back approach needs to change. A good solid three-season tent is now a must, that is a tent suited to all but winter use. Once winter arrives with force, another step up is required. This might be southern England, but the moor sits high, with winds arriving fresh from a long and unhindered Atlantic run. Combined with frequent heavy rain, even snow, these conditions will soon test even the best tents, and not all are up to the challenge.

Winter is when a genuine, four-season mountain tent is required, a shelter designed and built by a reputable maker to cope at any time of the year. Not surprisingly, these tents will almost certainly be slightly heavier and bulkier than a three-season model, and the best advice, as with almost all camping kit, is to take

guidance from a good outdoor store and pay as much as you can. Very expensive three or four-season tents, from the likes of Terra Nova or Hilleberg, can still be really quite dainty.

Sleeping bags

You may be a seasoned camper and own a sleeping bag already. If you do, and it has your full confidence, you probably don't need to read further. If you do need to buy a sleeping bag, and while there are decisions to be made with regard to expected temperature ranges and conditions, the principal choice is going to be between two forms of insulation: down or synthetic.

Put simply, down filled bags are usually far lighter than their synthetic stuffed counterparts, and importantly, pack much smaller, therefore taking up less room in your rucksack. On the other hand, a down bag will cost a lot more than one with man-made insulation. Down filled sleeping bags also have a worrying tendency to not work at all well if they get wet (all the light fluffy heat-trapping feathery filaments collapse and stick together).

I still prefer a down filling. Despite significant advances in synthetic insulations, with impressive reductions in packed size and weight, down-filled bags are still much lighter, and store very small. Besides, if packed properly, and we'll come back to that, and used in a dependable tent, the problems from damp are reduced considerably. Manufacturers have also made significant advances with damp-repellent coatings, both for the overall bags and their contents. Some of the more expensive examples are fully waterproof, and yet still breath properly. Various water resistant coatings are almost as good, and a fair bit cheaper. My current down bag, made by the renowned British company Mountain Equipment, has a Pertex shell (outer fabric), and shrugs off the odd encounter with a little rain. Then there are treatments that literally coat each feather and deter water take-up. I've not tried these expensive 'hydrophobic' fillings yet myself, but reviews are encouraging.

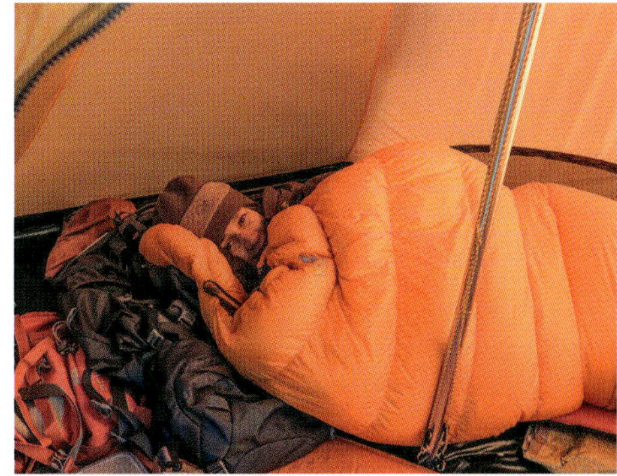

It's hard to beat a good sleeping bag.

Next up when making a decision about a new sleeping bag is the temperature in which you are likely to be camping. These bags have to cater for trips into every environment from the jungle to one of the two poles, and a bag designed to keep you alive amongst the ice flows at -30˚C, is not going to be much fun on the flank of Fur Tor in July. Neither will that skimpy jungle bag do much for a night's sleep anywhere in Britain just after New Year.

If you pick up a sleeping bag in a shop, a label is usually attached somewhere with a great swathe of additional temperature related information. This is the industry standard info, resulting from strict lab tests. The prevailing system in Europe (using what is called the EN13537 standard) is a little odd, and provides the following information (which I reproduce only in an attempt to reduce confusion):

- an **upper limit**, which is the highest temperature at which a 'standard' adult male is considered able to have a comfortable night's sleep

- a **comfort rating**, based on the lowest temperature at which it is thought a 'standard' adult female will have a contented night's sleep

- a **lower limit**, based on the lowest temperature at which a 'standard' adult male is deemed able to have a comfy night's sleep, and

- an **extreme rating**, or survival rating for a 'standard' adult male. This is an extreme survival temperature rating only. It is way below the point at which any comfort can be expected.

Still confused? I'm not surprised.

As an initial guide, something that caters for an expected minimum temperature between the comfort and lower limit, is a good purchase.

Fortunately, most sleeping bag retailers recognise the need for campers to be able to identify the right bag for the job. They are probably also aware that the industry standard information isn't always of much help. Catalogues, shops and online outlets often divide their wares into sensible, almost universally recognised, groups. These, as with many tents, use a season-based system, resulting in:

- One-season bags (summer only)

- Two-season (late spring, summer and early autumn)

- Three-season (anything but winter use), and

- Four-season (as the name suggests, designed for action all year).

You may also come across bags described as ready for 4+ season use, but unless you plan on heading up onto the moor during a prolonged Arctic spell, these probably aren't for you.

When it comes to sleeping preferences, and tolerances to discomfort, everyone is different. Specific advice is made yet more tricky by recognised variations, even if only slight, in the way manufacturers present their ratings, but here goes. For most British winter use, even on Dartmoor, a four-season bag will do (with an EN13537 'lower limit' of perhaps -9°C to -12°C). Women should note that the industry recognises that they usually need a warmer bag. Some may find this offering a little warm in all but the harshest conditions, but will certainly welcome the benefits when the temperatures really drop. For British summer Dartmoor use a two-season bag will cater for the odd chilly night. A lower rating of perhaps 0°C will suffice. Three-season bags make good all-rounders, with lower limits at about -7°C (please note the about) catering for all but the coldest months.

I said I'd return to sleeping-bag storage, and to cater for Dartmoor's, or in fact north-west-Europe's damp tendencies, my down sleeping bag is always stored in my rucksack within its own dry bag.

The information attached to my sleeping bag.

Some of the better manufacturers try to help further, and Mountain Equipment for example, include a 'recommended sleepzone' on the label for each bag. My winter bag reads +10°C to -9°C, while my all-purpose choice suggests +20°C to -5°C. Very helpful.

A good down-filled bag, stored in a dry bag.

Camping kit, much of it stored in various dry bags.

Dry bags

As they've cropped up, I'll mention these small and seemingly insignificant items of kit here. As the name implies, these are bags that keep their contents dry, using waterproof materials in a range of colours and sizes, sealed with tightly folded openings. Along with my sleeping bag, my spare clothes and food also travel in their own dry bag, each watertight container colour coded to make identification easier. I also have a separate dry bag for my first aid kit, one for electrical and photographic kit, and another for toiletries. In brief, everything is packed in its own waterproof container.

As a result of this precaution, and for reasons mentioned already, I don't use a waterproof cover for my rucksack.

Sleeping mats

Returning to the important matter of a good night's sleep, a sleeping mat is a must, with the initial choice between a dependable closed-cell foam roll, and a lighter, more comfortable, but much more expensive inflated mat. Not only are the latter costly, but also potentially puncturable, although carrying a repair kit (small and very light) should ensure you avoid any problems.

Left: rolling up a good sleeping mat.

Right: good, modern sleeping mats.

Some of the latest inflatable mats are extremely light, and pack down very small indeed. Not surprisingly, these are also even more pricey. It is worth stressing here though, that if you can afford a very tough but small and light tent, combining it with a down sleeping bag and a modern inflatable sleeping mat from one of the premier manufacturers, the space left in even a relatively small rucksack will be impressive. After a few miles on the moor, you really will be very thankful for that superlight load. I can head out for a camping trip these days, and often forget I'm carrying anything at all. Certainly not something I could claim in the past.

Cooking

Lighting fires is not allowed on Dartmoor, and to be fair, except in a couple of tiny wooded spots, where the trees are heavily protected by law (as they should be), there's very little fuel available anyway. As a result, if you want a warm drink and hot food, you'll need a stove. These can be fuelled in a variety of ways, including cheap and cheerful solid fuel blocks, of the type used by the Army, or liquid burning setups ranging from the traditional Trangia type, to the pressurized setups used by global explorers. Each have their merits, but I find a canister of butane, propane, or perhaps best, a mixture of the two, offers the best system... for me anyway. Reasonably well priced, a stove and screw-in canister is small, light, clean and dependable. I have to admit, as a traveller who usually cooks over a small wood fire, burning a modest collection of windfall twigs and branches, I really don't much like the idea of burning fossil fuels out there, or ending up with yet another empty can after a few meals, but this method suits this environment. I'll keep my usual wood-fuelled cooking methods for somewhere more appropriate.

A good, gas camping stove.

Gas stove choices, once again, are numerous, but within reason, small and light are the qualities to aim for in a stove. The best setup, at least in my opinion, is a stove and gas bottle that will, together, fit inside your cooking vessel. I usually carry a small pot, with the stove and gas container snug inside, and also a light kettle. It's nice to be able to pop this on for a brew after a meal without having to clean your sole cooking vessel first.

Matches, stored in waterproof containers.

A modern fire-steel, also known as ferro rod.

Most of these watercourses on the high ground carry water that is probably fine to drink.

Last mention here, is a reminder to ensure you have something to light that gas. Matches, stowed in a waterproof container, are good, with a spare box stored somewhere else being a sensible backup strategy. I like to carry a modern spark striking fire-steel system, often called a ferro rod. These are utterly dependable, even if they do get wet.

While on the subject of cooking, make sure to carry enough fuel to boil all the water you lift from a Dartmoor stream. Most of these watercourses on the high ground carry water that is probably fine to drink, but you can never be completely sure what lies unseen, just around that upstream bend.

Last comment, make sure you have something to cut into food packaging, help with food preparation and possibly even assist in mending a broken stove. I always carry a Swiss Army knife. As I've mentioned mending things, and although not strictly related to cooking, a small roll of strong tape, insulating or the duct type, can be very useful at times. I've even repaired tent poles with just tape before now.

Eating

Eating and cooking utensils are also up to you, with the same considerations of size and weight. I like to carry a Spork, made by the Swedish company Light My Fire. To this I add a plastic bowl (so much better when camping than a plate) and if I was sensible, I'd also carry a light plastic mug. Mine is made of wood, is quite heavy, but I'm not about to replace it.

Food

This is a matter of choice. The key aim is to ensure you have enough for each camper, plus a little extra, just to be sure. Weight, as with everything else that ends up on your back, is a principal consideration. Also bear in mind the limited cooking facilities. Pre-dried meals are available from any camping outlets, and help a lot in keeping the weight down, but the contents do vary a lot in quality. Our response to this is to dry our own meals using an Excalibur food dehydrator. Packed small and light we just need to add water and heat, to provide a meal we can enjoy.

Sundries

You should already be carrying a head torch and spare batteries, but even if you don't normally do so, now, when heading out to camp, is the time to change that habit.

I mentioned ticks earlier and carrying something that can remove one of these safely if it attacks is a very good idea. While on this subject, recalling my comments about avoiding bare skin, take particular care when getting up at night to answer a call of nature. If you can, try to avoid contact with grass or reeds, and particularly bracken fronds, which, in my experience, seem to provide favourite tick launching points. I'm sure the ticks I've attracted on the moor resulted from lightly clad nocturnal blunderings amongst the undergrowth.

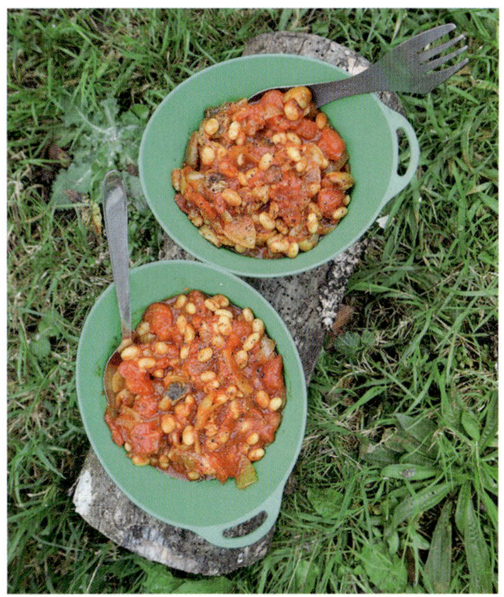

Plastic bowls and two forks, one a titanium Spork.

Dehydrated food, packed for a camping trip.

Classic tick country; they just love bracken.

I've mentioned toiletries, and you may well hope to keep clean while on the moor, especially if out for a few days. If you do choose to wash using river or stream water, please carry it away from the watercourse, try to use a biodegradable soap and use as little as you can. Throw any dirty water away a good distance from the flow.

Finally, there's the matter of what bears get up to in the woods, and while any ursine population on the moor is now long gone, and with them most of the trees, the subject still stands. The answer is to head as far from any watercourse as possible, to dig deep, and to refill your excavation in such a way that even you can't spot where you've been. Some will state that you need to carry any 'paperwork' out with you, I'd suggest that if all you use is a few sheets from a standard, undyed roll, and it's buried deep, that will be fine. After all, it should soon degrade in that particularly bacteria rich environment. Anything beyond a few loo-roll sheets should, however, be bagged and taken with you.

Checklist

Just to be on the safe side, here is a quick camping kit checklist, the essentials marked with an asterisk. I've not included walking kit:

- Tent*

- Sleeping bag (per person)*

- Dry bag for sleeping bag

- Sleeping mat (per person)*

- Cooking Stove*

- Gas (or other fuel)*

- Method of lighting cooking fuel (matches, lighter or ferro rod)*

- Fuel lighting spares

- Cooking pot*

- Food* (enough for each person, plus a little extra)

- Dry bag for the food

- Plastic bowl*

- Plastic mug*

- Spork (or other eating utensil/s)*

- Water container*

- Head-torch (* in my opinion), and spare batteries.

- Swiss Army knife (highly recommended)

- Loo roll* (in its own dry bag)

- A small amount of duct tape, perhaps wrapped around a walking pole or water bottle (also very much worth taking)

What other option can there be?

Swimming

It's a hot summer day, and you've just spent the last two hours stumbling across a vast swathe of Dartmoor's classic lumpy grassland, the parched fronds limp under a wide cloudless sky. Making your way carefully amongst the granite clitter scattered wide across a broad south facing slope, weaving amidst the larger boulders, you finally reach the valley floor. A typical Dartmoor stream tumbles amidst the exposed stones, the clear amber water (the colour nothing more than harmless peat staining) falling in rushing cataracts from one deep pool to the next. You haven't seen another person in hours. What other option can there be?

There's something special about swimming in any wild spot, river, lake or sea, but a pool on a Dartmoor stream, a stunted rowan or oak leaning out over the sky-reflecting water, is very special indeed. These pools seem purpose-built for a cooling dip.

Submerged, with just your sweaty head above the surface, the moor vanishes. Distant sun-soaked views are replaced by little more than the rounded flanks of a few granite boulders, their tops warm in the sun, their stream-facing flanks dark, cool and mossy. The air here, shadowed and still, seems almost held in place by the tree leaves hung low overhead. The bright green of a fern, almost lurid in the shade, bursts like a foliar firework from between two rocks.

An evening swim.

Perhaps my favourite time for a
dip is once the tent is up.

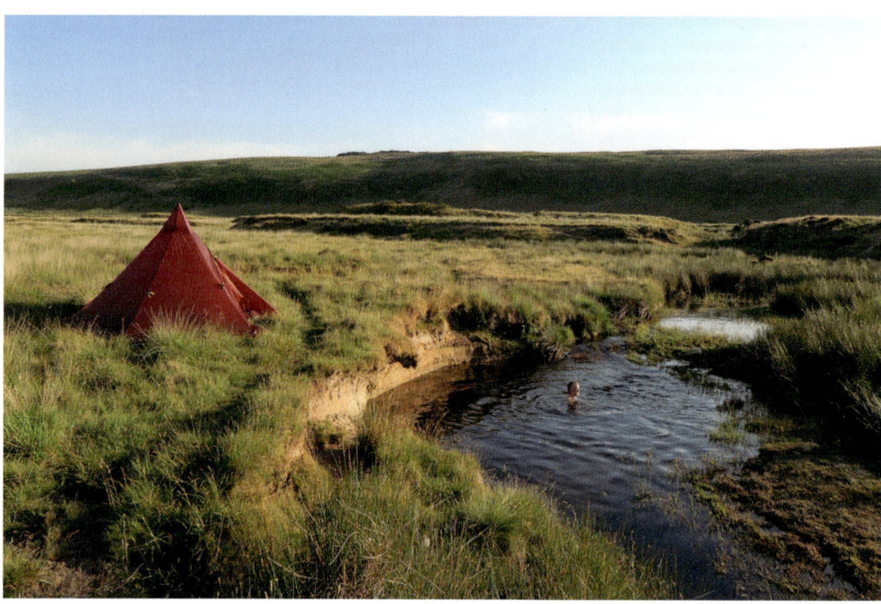

Watched perhaps by an inquisitive robin or bottom-jigging wagtail, the intimacy of these often astoundingly pretty spots is unique, exaggerated no doubt by the contrast with the open and somewhat unremitting moorland expanse experienced over the last few hours. With just a short slide over a grassy lip, far views across thousands of acres of waving yellow grass are replaced by cool shade, and a prospect extending little more than a few feet. Only a narrow slot downstream now provides any view, the outlook no more than a jumble of fractured sunlight, cast amongst the cool, almost impenetrable, shadow.

Perhaps my favourite time for a dip is once the tent is up. At the end of a long day, with many miles covered, and once camp is made and shelter pitched, clothing can be discarded. The next stage of your Dartmoor adventure takes place to the accompaniment of tinkling shallows, the caress of water crowfoot, the feel of fine, cool growan (granite shingle) between tired toes. Tiny trout rise upstream to take freshly hatched blue-winged olives, a kingfisher flashes overhead. Lounge there long enough, and a herd of black Galloway cattle might arrive, to peer at you suspiciously, before thirst encourages them to accept this recent arrival, to spread

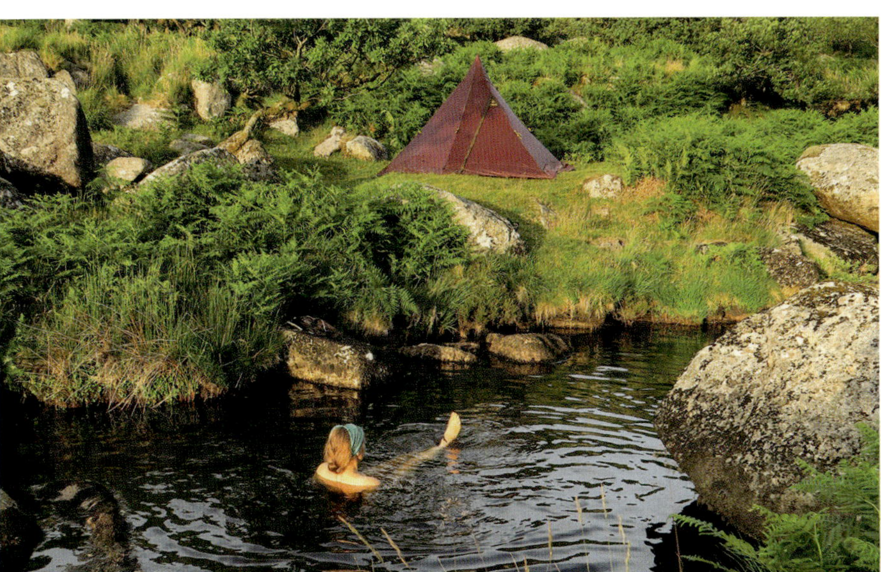

their legs, hooves planted splayed in the mud at the water's edge, to suck noisily at the fresh flow.

There's something extra special about sleeping next to a stream you've seen from below the surface.

Kit

Take a swimming costume if you wish, but it's rarely necessary. Besides, if you swim with the least water resistance, you've nothing to dry when you re-emerge but yourself, and I find the warmth in which I like to swim will soon do the trick.

Now, here I will admit that most of my swimming is done in the warmer months, the much warmer months. Drying off after a dip at this time of year takes little more than sitting on the bank for a few minutes. Susannah, on the other hand, seems unable to resist the allure, even in the depths of winter, and I've seen her swim on the

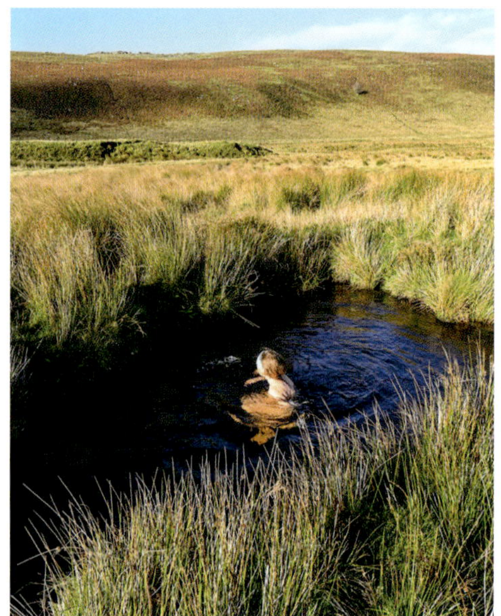

Even the smallest pool can be very welcome.

A broad section of the Dart, and somewhere for a proper swim, once summer arrives anyway.

moor with snow on the banks. Even in these situations though, she does little more than choose a warm, fleecy layer from her rucksack, or will that be mine, to dry off.

In short, I suspect you can often manage without any kit whatsoever, although please don't feel that this is advice you must take. If you suspect that a dip will be part of your day on the moor, some of the travel towels available today pack pretty small, and may well be worth taking.

One item of clothing that may be worth considering is shoes, or at least some sort of sandal that's happy with a dunking. It may seem an extra burden, but sandals can be pretty small and light, even the more substantial models best for this activity. Besides, they can also usually be clipped to the outside of a rucksack. While good for a dip, not many Dartmoor rivers or streams offer what most would class as true swimming opportunities, and the bottom, often stony, may not be very far down. Sandals with some form of toe protection may avoid unwanted, and sometimes very painful, contact. If planning to sleep out under canvas, this sort of light footwear can also make a welcome replacement around camp anyway, allowing you to lose those clumpy walking boots.

Where

I suspect I'm not going to be of much more help here. The thing is, the opportunities up there are almost endless, and even the smallest of Dartmoor streams, due to the often rocky nature of the valley bottoms through which they run, is likely to offer numerous opportunities. Characterised by a succession of pools, often separated by a cheery water chute or fall, they are perfect for a mid- or post-walk dip.

It's true that many of these pools are tiny, but some, even in streams of only a couple of yards in width are quite big, and deep enough for a plunge, if not an actual swim. Besides, even the smallest pool can be very welcome. I treat them as a welcome and cooling bath. As the streams widen slightly, the opportunity for putting in a few tentative strokes is there, although, unless you've adopted my sandal suggestion, I'd advise against too enthusiastic a use of your legs, as toes and granite boulders don't meet well at speed.

Put another way, I doubt there's a stream on the moor in which we haven't swum somewhere... or perhaps that should be dipped in somewhere. A list of potential spots would be very long.

The moor, even the high moor, does have some watercourses that can grow quite wide, and I think here of the Dart for example. You might even have a chance to kick those feet safely for a few yards.

Although lakes are few and far between on the moor, ponds can certainly be found, sometimes right out in the middle of an otherwise dry spot. These are often big enough for a dip, although being diminutive in size, they don't tend to appear on maps, even those at smaller scales. An example that springs to mind (no pun intended) sits on high ground to the east of Sharp Tor. The mine remains here are marked on the OS OL28 map, along with the track running to them, but not the

A small water-filled mining excavation on Holne Ridge.

very pleasant bathing pool. Former mine and quarry sites often carry a pool or two (there's another fine little example on Holne Ridge), and there are plenty of these scattered across the moor. You never know when an opportunity for a dip might appear over the next brow.

Pond and lake opportunities that do appear on a map include, Crazy Well Pool (SX 582 705), the abandoned pits at Haytor Quarry (760 775), Leftlake Mires (648 635) and the generously sized Red Lake Clay Works lakes (SX 646 669). The latter offers plenty of room for a proper swim, although due to their depth they do stay pretty chilly.

Watery stretches of mire and bog can occasionally offer a dip opportunity, but beware, the bottom and edges of these mini tarns can be very soft. Apart from making the pool tricky to enter and exit, one moment of contact between a swept leg and the bottom can, in an instant, turn a clear expanse of water into peat broth. Not such a pleasant experience.

One of the Red Lake pools.

Unless in spate, and I've hopefully stressed the related risks sufficiently already, almost all Dartmoor streams, at usual height and flows at least, are safe for a swim. There are a few dwellings and farms on the moor however, even on the high ground, and it is worth avoiding watercourses downstream. All sorts of things from farms end up in rivers, alas, and isolated houses on the moor are unlikely to possess the most modern and efficient of waste management systems. A quick look at a map will show you what may lurk unseen above the next bend in the river.

One last comment, and it concerns those cattle I mentioned just now, along with the moor's sheep and ponies. The rivers and streams we love so much also provide the animals up there with almost their only source of drinking water. Sometimes the spot you've found, where it's easy to get into the stream is, for exactly those reasons, the only place for quite some distance where they can reach the flow safely. As you splash about, spare a thought for the stock that may be waiting patiently, and perhaps very thirstily, to get at the water too. This consideration also has a bearing on where you might choose to camp.

Fur Tor.

Routes

Quite a bit has been made already of the glories offered by Dartmoor to the meanderer. With a good map and compass, and a reasonable familiarity with high ground environments, the experienced walker can indulge any desire for wandering to the full, letting the passion of the moment forge a path from stream edge to lofty tor, from shady oak woodland to the bright sunlit ridge.

All this meandering doesn't suit everyone of course, and there's also plenty of enjoyment to be had on the moor in following a route, working from waypoint to waypoint, letting a written account guide you along a particularly good journey. So here are my route offerings; a few of my favourite paths, or more often than not, lack of paths, that head out along an extra special journey. Along the way, I'll try to highlight a few features from Dartmoor's rich library of natural history, archaeology and more recent accounts of human endeavour.

The routes in the following chapters are divided according to length: under 10km, 10–15km, 15–20km and those over 20km, which I class as potential two-day walks. I've also added a couple of multi-day treks. To avoid the problem of vehicle shuttles, almost all are circular routes, or something close, returning to the place from which you set out.

Wild Tor.

While the moor may offer little in the way of any real barriers to travel, most of these walks cross genuine Dartmoor wilderness along at least one stretch. They should all, therefore, probably be classed as reasonably demanding. Where the route is particularly challenging, often due to extended stretches of peat bog or wild unimproved grassland, I'll aim to make that clear.

As no walker travels at the same speed, times given for each route are approximations. They are based on my own experience, not counting meal stops or any deviations to explore.

The guides for each route have been prepared using the Ordnance Survey 1:25,000 OL28 sheet, and it is strongly recommended that one of these maps, or a Harvey's Dartmoor version, is carried by anyone giving any of these walks a go. The maps in the following pages provide an excellent general guide to the routes, but with the divergent scales involved cannot offer the detail provided by the OS cartographers. Where I mention a particular boundary wall, prehistoric cairn or abandoned mine building in one of the route descriptions, it would be extremely helpful, out on the moor, to be able to see it on the map being used.

Branscombes's Loaf.

Routes Under 10km

These might be the shorter walks in this collection, but that doesn't always mean they're that easy. The Branscombe's Loaf and Yes Tor routes, for example, both include quite a clamber. However, four of the following walks, the Wistman's Wood, Taw Marsh, Nun's Cross and Princetown Railway routes, cover ground that's been chosen deliberately for its relatively level and forgiving nature.

1 Branscombe's Loaf

Start / Finish	Sourton car park SX 535 903 / 50.6938, -4.0756
Distance	4.5km / 3 miles
Ascent	265m
Time	1 – 1.5 hours

Crossing Corn Ridge many centuries ago, and on meeting a seemingly friendly stranger, Bishop Branscombe was offered lunch. Fortunately, an observant companion spotted the generous traveller's cloven hooves, brushing the satanic snack aside before it was accepted. The cursed bread fell, petrified, to the ground.

Something tells me the origins of Branscombe's Loaf may have more to do with superheated geology, but whatever the truth, this isolated lump of stone remains one of my favourite Dartmoor features. The walk out to take a look is short but exhilarating.

After a steep climb from the village of Sourton, you'll probably feel you deserve a breather, and the rocky outcrop of Sourton Tors deserves a little exploration. Amateur geologists will soon spot that this is no ordinary Dartmoor exposure, and

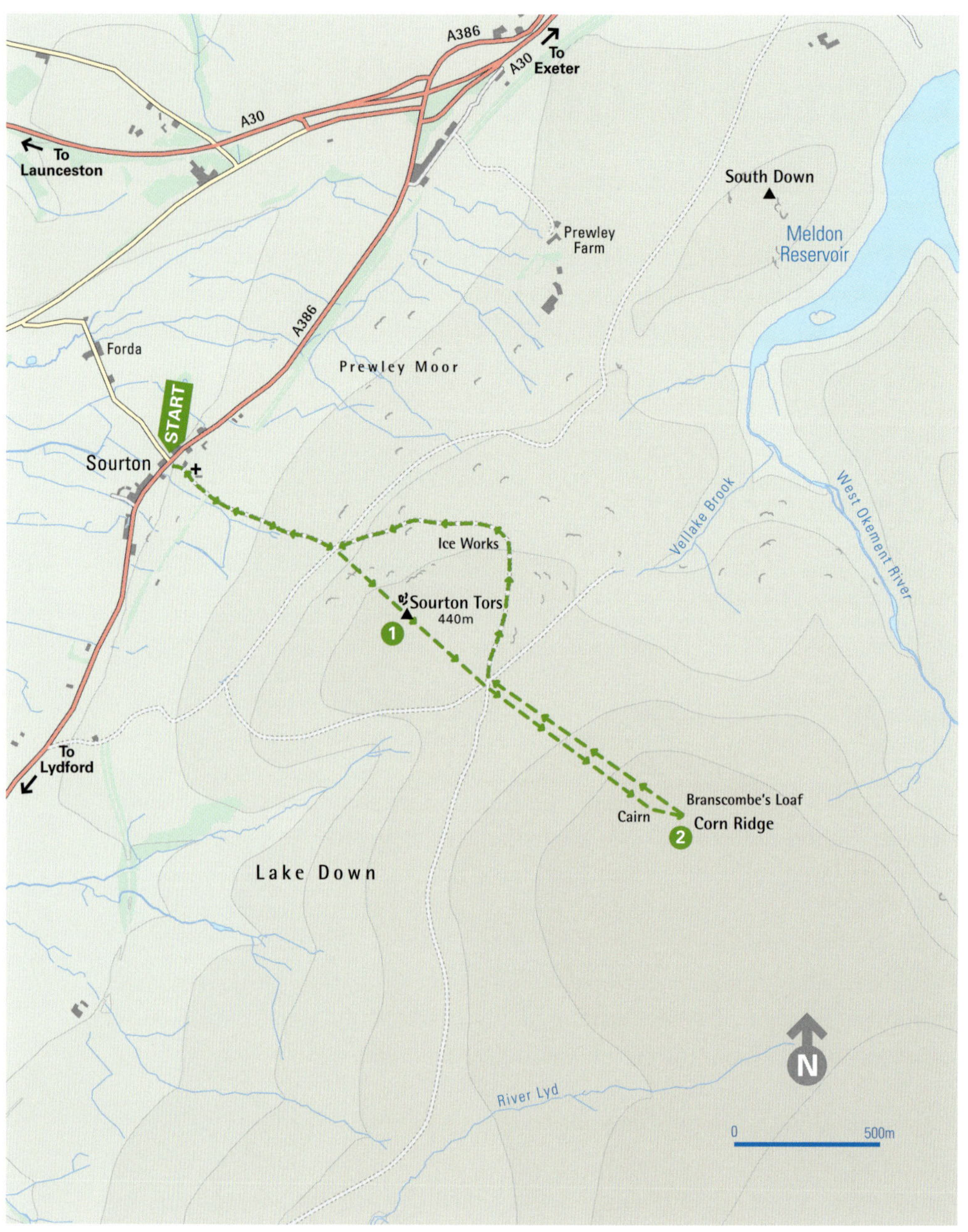

A386
To Exeter
A30
A30
To Launceston
South Down
Meldon Reservoir
Prewley Farm
A386
Forda
Prewley Moor
START
Sourton
Ice Works
Sourton Tors
440m
1
Vellake Brook
West Okement River
To Lydford
Branscombe's Loaf
Cairn
Corn Ridge
2
Lake Down
River Lyd
N
0
500m

Sourton represents one of only a handful of tors on the moor not formed from granite. I'd like to give a concise description of the geology responsible for this outcrop, but after trying to read the complex arguments presented in various academic papers, I'll make do with stating, I believe accurately, that the tor is the result of some form of odd superheated limestone.

The loaf itself is no less intriguing. Prehistoric man obviously agreed and encircled this very odd granite formation with a low bank. Before weathering filled it back up, there was probably once a ditch too, and the site represents a rare example of a Bronze Age monument sometimes referred to as a ring cairn. It's easy to imagine all sorts of dramatic ritual taking place on and around the outcrop.

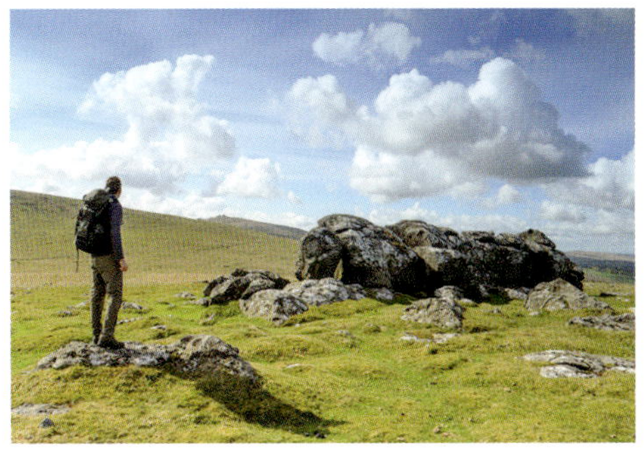

Sourton Tors, with Great Links Tor on the horizon.

Beyond the Loaf, with Sourton Tors back in view and the wooded splendour of western Devon spread out below, some rather extraordinary earthworks are now visible off to the right. These represent the remains of Sourton Ice Works, established in the late 1800s, when water from a spring was caught in channels, to freeze in winter. Collected and stored in a vast collection of peat-lined pits, this ice could then be carried away by cart to preserve fish landed in Plymouth.

You can follow the cart track away from this bizarre spot and back towards the church, trailed by the imagined creak and grind of ice-laden wagons.

START From the car park, head E alongside Sourton's church, then straight uphill to Sourton Tors.

1 Continue SE, looking for a reasonably clear trodden grass path that climbs uphill to find first a couple of low Bronze Age burial cairns, and then the outcrop of Branscombe's Loaf itself.

2 Return via the same route, but before reaching Sourton Tors, take a right turn, following an old cart track that leads to the remains of the abandoned ice works. A continuation of the track heads west, back to the car park.

Approaching Wistman's Wood in winter.

2 Wistman's Wood

Start / Finish	Two Bridges car park SX 609 750 / 50.5587, -3.99649
Distance	5km / 3 miles
Ascent	80m
Time	1.5 hours

Like Black-a-tor Copse, mentioned on page 205, Wistman's Wood represents a very rare survival of high-altitude oak woodland. Yet while Black-a-tor is a touch tricky to reach, with an approach along the steep slopes overlooking Meldon Reservoir, the track out to Wistman's from the tiny settlement of Two Bridges, is relatively level. It leads along the West Dart River valley pretty much to the woodland edge.

The wood itself is an extraordinary collection of wind-stunted and contorted oak trees, growing amongst a tight spread of sometimes massive, rounded granite boulders, both stones and trees swathed in lichen and green moss. It is claimed that over one hundred different forms of lichen have made their home in this shady upland copse. It's not to everyone's taste mind you, and in 1797, the Reverend Swete stated that, "It is hardly possible to conceive anything of the sort so grotesque as this wood appears."

Anyone experiencing the walk back in warm weather might be pleased to find that the car park sits only a stone's throw from the Two Bridges Inn, and a waterside beer garden.

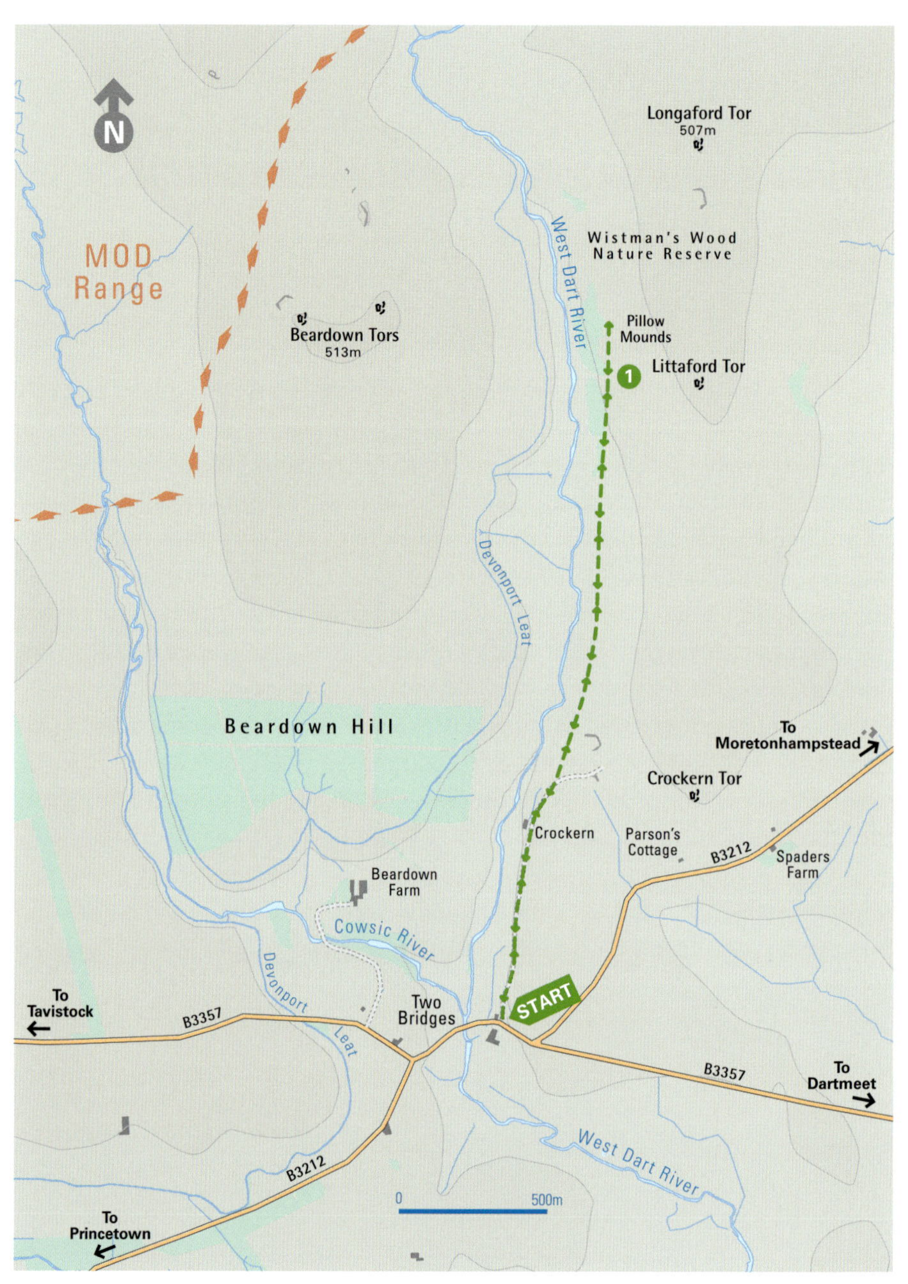

N
MOD Range
Longaford Tor
507m
Wistman's Wood Nature Reserve
Beardown Tors
513m
West Dart River
Pillow Mounds
Littaford Tor
1
Devonport Leat
Beardown Hill
To Moretonhampstead
Crockern Tor
Crockern
Parson's Cottage
B3212
Spaders Farm
Beardown Farm
Cowsic River
To Tavistock
Devonport Leat
B3357
Two Bridges
START
B3357
To Dartmeet
West Dart River
0
500m
B3212
To Princetown

Wistman's Wood in winter.

START ▶ Leave the car park using the gate in the north-west corner, following the track, then a clear footpath, which can be a little rugged in places, out to the wood. When you cross a wall, by way of a stile, you're almost there.

1 Return by the same route.

Heading south out of Taw Marsh.

3 Taw Marsh

Start / Finish   Belstone car park SX 621 938 / 50.7275, -3.9548

Distance   6km / 4 miles

Ascent   95m

Time   1.5 – 2 hours

Although some of the stream valleys on the high moor are relatively narrow, most are fairly open, even if the watercourses themselves tend to be restricted to a fairly tight slot. None, however, feel quite like the wide expanse containing the Taw, which possesses a great bowl of sometimes marshy ground just to the south of the village of Belstone.

Partly as a result of water extraction schemes, a good track heads out from the settlement; this makes for a very pleasant and fairly level walk, surrounded by the high ground of Cosdon Beacon, Metherel, Steeperton and the Belstone Ridge.

This is a 'there and back' walk, but once out in the amphitheatre of Taw Marsh it can be developed as the mood takes you. In low water conditions, the river can even be forded relatively easily at (SX 620 915), allowing an exploration of the east bank.

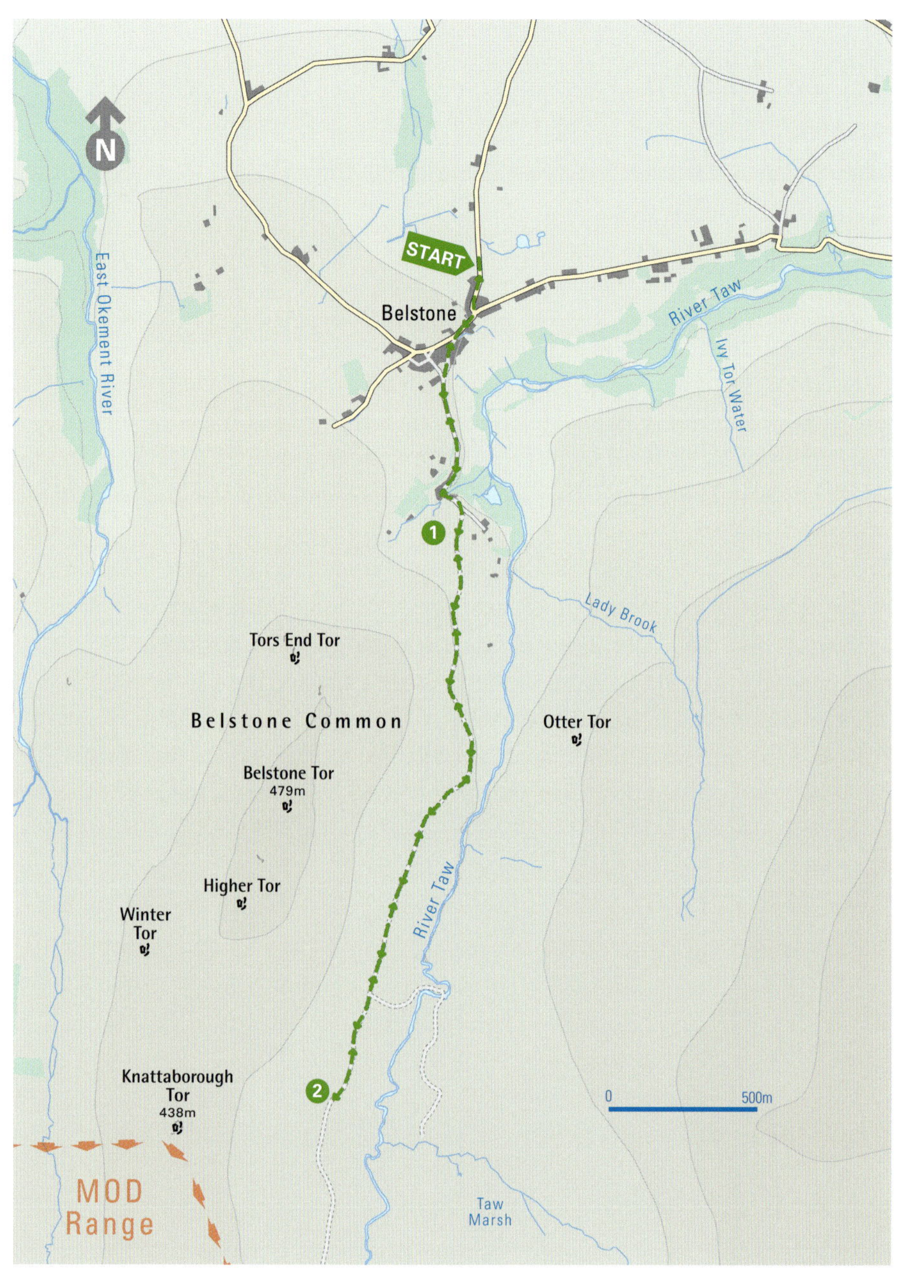

N
START
Belstone
East Okement River
River Taw
Ivy Tor Water
Lady Brook
1
Tors End Tor
Belstone Common
Otter Tor
Belstone Tor
479m
River Taw
Higher Tor
Winter
Tor
Knattaborough
Tor
438m
2
Taw
Marsh
MOD
Range
0
500m

Taw Marsh, with Steeperton Tor on the horizon.

🚶 **START** From Belstone car park walk through the village, taking the left fork at the village green. Follow the road uphill, and out through a gate.

1 A track, a little rough in places, heads out along the western side of the river.

2 Return the same way.

Nun's Cross.

4 Nun's Cross

Start / Finish	Princetown car park SX 589 735 / 50.5441, -3.9928
Distance	8km / 5 miles
Ascent	30m
Time	1.5 – 2 hours

Nun's Cross, or more correctly Siward's Cross, will crop up again (pages 167 and 201), representing, as it does, one of the ancient Dartmoor Forest boundary markers. While these later routes approach this medieval cross over some pretty rough ground, here is a much less demanding alternative.

Princetown is something of a city in Dartmoor terms, and very much a focus for population and services. The large village also offers ample parking, and the chance to walk out along relatively level ground to this elderly stone marker.

In the right light, when shadows highlight the letters, the word SIWARD can be made out on one upright flank of the cross. This was the Earl of Northumberland, who held the Manors of Mary Tavy and Willsworthy during the reign of Edward the Confessor. On the opposite face, the words BOC LOND refer to Buckland Abbey, which was granted an estate on the west side of the moor in 1278 by Amicia, Countess of Devon.

I rather doubt that either Amicia or Siward ever visited the spot.

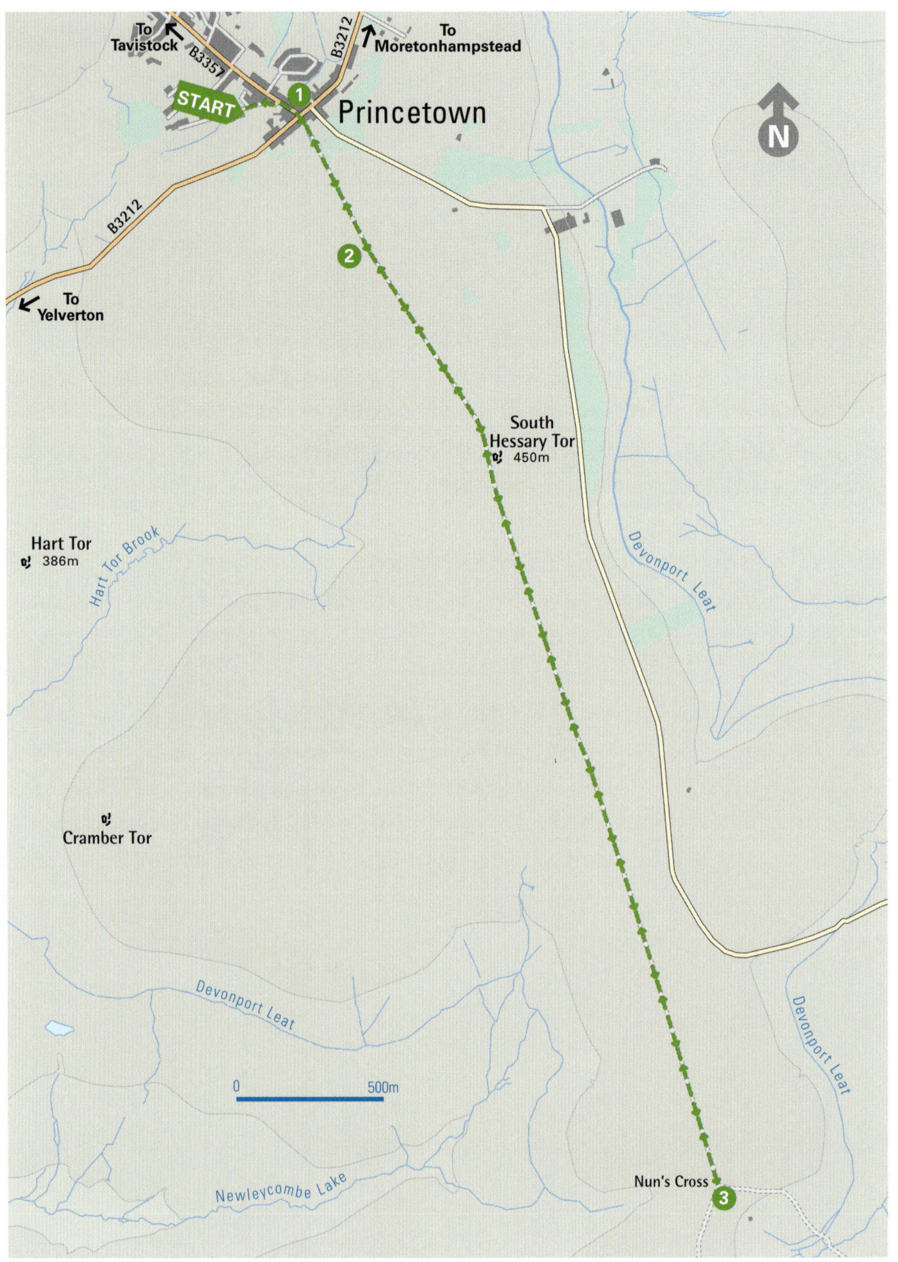

To Tavistock
To Moretonhampstead
B3357
B3212
B3212
START
Princetown
1
To Yelverton
2
South Hessary Tor
450m
N
Hart Tor
386m
Hart Tor Brook
Devonport Leat
Cramber Tor
Devonport Leat
Devonport Leat
0   500m
Newleycombe Lake
Nun's Cross
3

Heading back towards Princetown.

START Turn right at the car park entrance, then right again to follow Tavistock Road to the square.

1 Carry on across the crossroads, to follow the road opposite, which soon becomes a footpath.

2 After a slight rise, follow this relatively level track to the cross.

3 Return the same way.

Yellowmead stone circle.

5 Ditsworthy Warren

Start / Finish	The car park east of Nattor SX 578 673 / 50.4883, -4.0049
Distance	8km / 5 miles
Ascent	210m
Time	2 – 3 hours

As the cinema lights fade, a cheery swathe of Dartmoor springs into view on screen. A small village nestles beneath a craggy slope. Lifting fast, we soar high over the ridge, and the full sunlit panorama of this glorious corner of the moor is revealed. Steven Spielberg's film, *War Horse*, has begun.

Sadly, to obtain this view of Sheepstor, the reputed home of Albert Narracott and his thoroughbred horse Joey, you'll need to hire a helicopter too, but on this route I can offer a vista from the same direction, if not quite the same height.

To provide a suitably filmic finale, I wanted to finish this modest walk at the farm where Joey amazed the gathered critics (and me), by managing to plough the neighbouring stony hillside. This aim favours a route that begins at a car park beyond Nattor, before heading first in a north-west direction across rough ground towards Sheeps Tor; not the village though, but the impressive block of granite looming over it to the north-east.

Marshy conditions make the initial escape from the car park interesting. Heading for the projecting corner of enclosed land, it's best to keep close to the wall, before heading uphill to find the impressive Yellowmead quadruple stone circle. These are actually rings of stone that once revetted a burial mound, but they're still very definitely prehistoric.

Sheeps Tor is certainly worth a close look. Beloved of novice rock climbers, with numerous suitably simple routes (and a few tough ones), this fissured block of stone can also be climbed easily without a rope, from the right direction at least. The views from the top are pretty impressive. I was once buzzed here by a peregrine falcon. It passed so close overhead that the air was cut with a sound similar to a distant fighter jet.

After a satisfying clamber on the tor, and possibly another falcon sighting, you can drop down the bracken covered south slope to find a narrow road leading into the village itself. This holds an ornate well-head, a fine church and a good collection of traditional cottages.

To gain the view of that cinematic intro, you'll need to set your sights on the higher ground beyond, leaving the tarmac beyond the village to head out again, east onto open moorland. And it is here that you can turn to see that *War Horse* view of the village, just. A helicopter would improve things.

Setting out along the northern ridge of Ringmoor Down, the views in other directions more than make up for this slight anti-climax, particularly those from the top of Gutter Tor. Winding your way south-east amongst scattered granite, you'll find a track heading towards Narracott's farm.

In reality, this is Ditsworthy Warren House, once home to a family whose job it was to turn a few shillings breeding rabbits. The grassy remains of the pillow mounds, thrown up to provide cosy bunny homes, can be found all around, intermixed with more prehistoric remains.

Fans of the film might be a little disappointed by the buildings at the farm, which were given quite a makeover by the Hollywood architectural cosmeticians. Still, what remains is very pleasing.

A final stroll along Edward's Path, and through the wooded grounds to the Scout hut, leads – as imaginary credits roll – back to the car park.

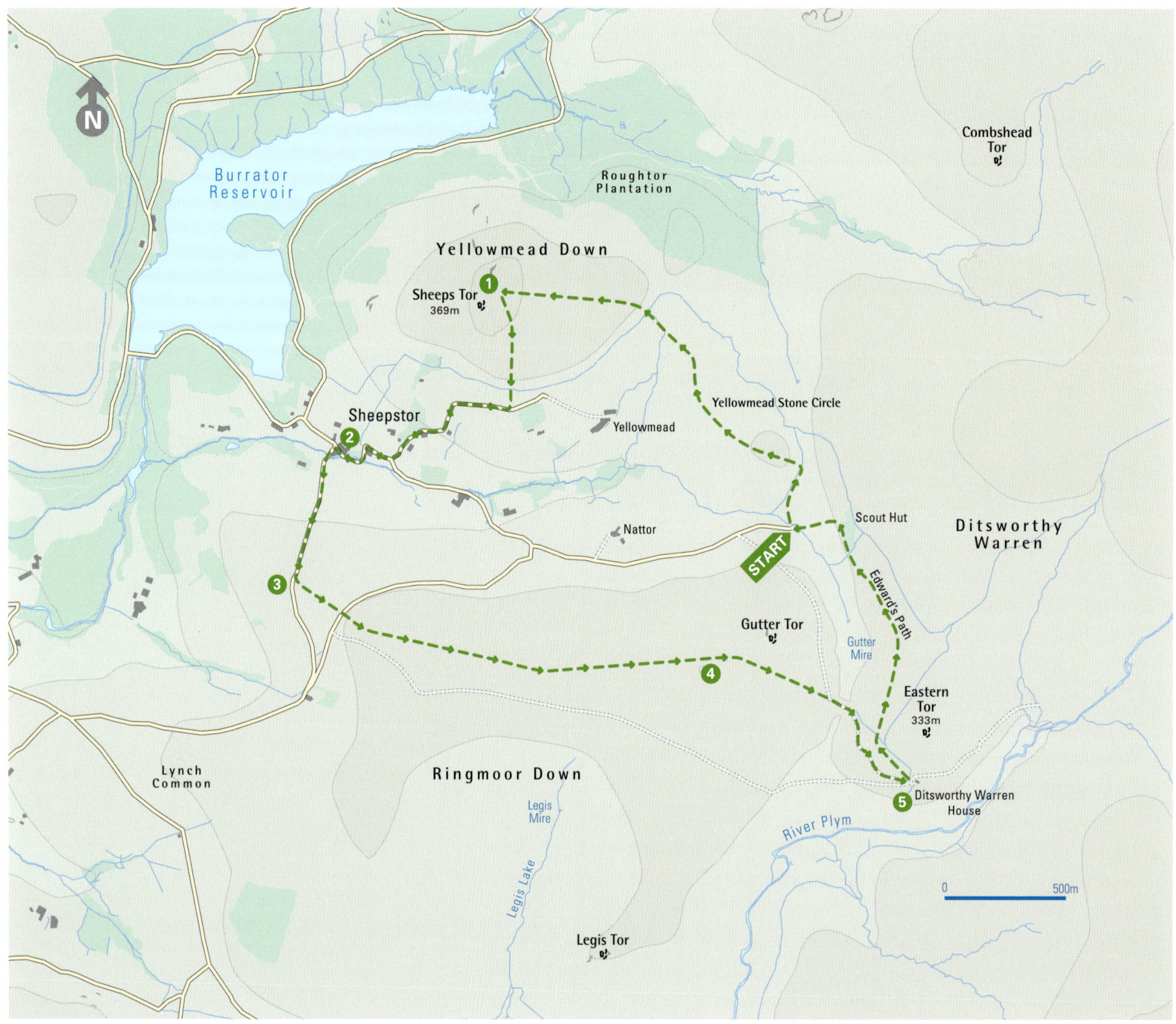

N
Burrator Reservoir
Yellowmead Down
Roughtor Plantation
Combshead Tor
Sheeps Tor
369m
1
Sheepstor
2
Yellowmead
Yellowmead Stone Circle
Scout Hut
Ditsworthy Warren
Nattor
3
START
Edward's Path
Gutter Tor
Gutter Mire
4
Eastern Tor
333m
Lynch Common
Ringmoor Down
Ditsworthy Warren House
5
Legis Mire
Legis Lake
River Plym
0   500m
Legis Tor

🚶 **START** From the car park, head NW alongside enclosed farmland to Sheeps Tor (tor), pausing to inspect Yellowmead stone circle.

1 Drop S from Sheeps Tor (tor) to follow a small road W towards Sheepstor (village), turning right at the T-junction.

2 Pass the church and turn left into Portland Lane.

3 Near the top of the hill, emerging onto unenclosed land, turn E along the down to Gutter Tor.

4 Leave Gutter Tor to the SE, to find a track leading to Ditsworthy Warren House.

5 Head N from Warren House to find Edward's Path, walking though the grounds to the Scout Hut, before turning W to return to the car park.

High Willhays.

6 Yes Tor and High Willhays

Start / Finish	Anthony Stile SX 587 927 / 50.7157, -4.0018
Distance	8km / 5 miles
Ascent	245m
Time	2 – 2.5 hours

Many motorists over the years will have looked up from their journey along the A30, to revel in the view of Yes Tor, perched high over the northern edge of the moor. It certainly looks imposing, and for many years, this rugged outcrop was considered the highest point on Dartmoor. I often meet people who will argue vehemently that it still is. A brief look at a map indicates otherwise, with the 619m elevation of Yes Tor, overtopped by High Willhays, sat 1km south, and a full 2m higher.

Despite holding the two highest points on the moor, and the rest of southern England for that matter, the ridge is very easy to climb. One popular route leads from the car park at Meldon Reservoir climbing the western side. My preference is for a circular walk that heads out from somewhere close to the Okehampton army camp.

Not only is this a slightly easier route, but taking in a final ascent that tackles the north-east slope, the tumble of fallen granite boulders provide just enough of a minor scramble (a technical term where an easy hill or mountain route requires the use of hands) to make this feel like a proper climb. The views from the top of Yes Tor are excellent, looking north over that green ocean of Devon pasture or south into the dark interior of the moor.

A short and near level wander along a broad ridge leads to the elongated granite wave of High Willhays, complete with a superfluous modern cairn. The walk back to the camp follows good tracks, the last stretch tarmacked. Perfect for slightly tired feet.

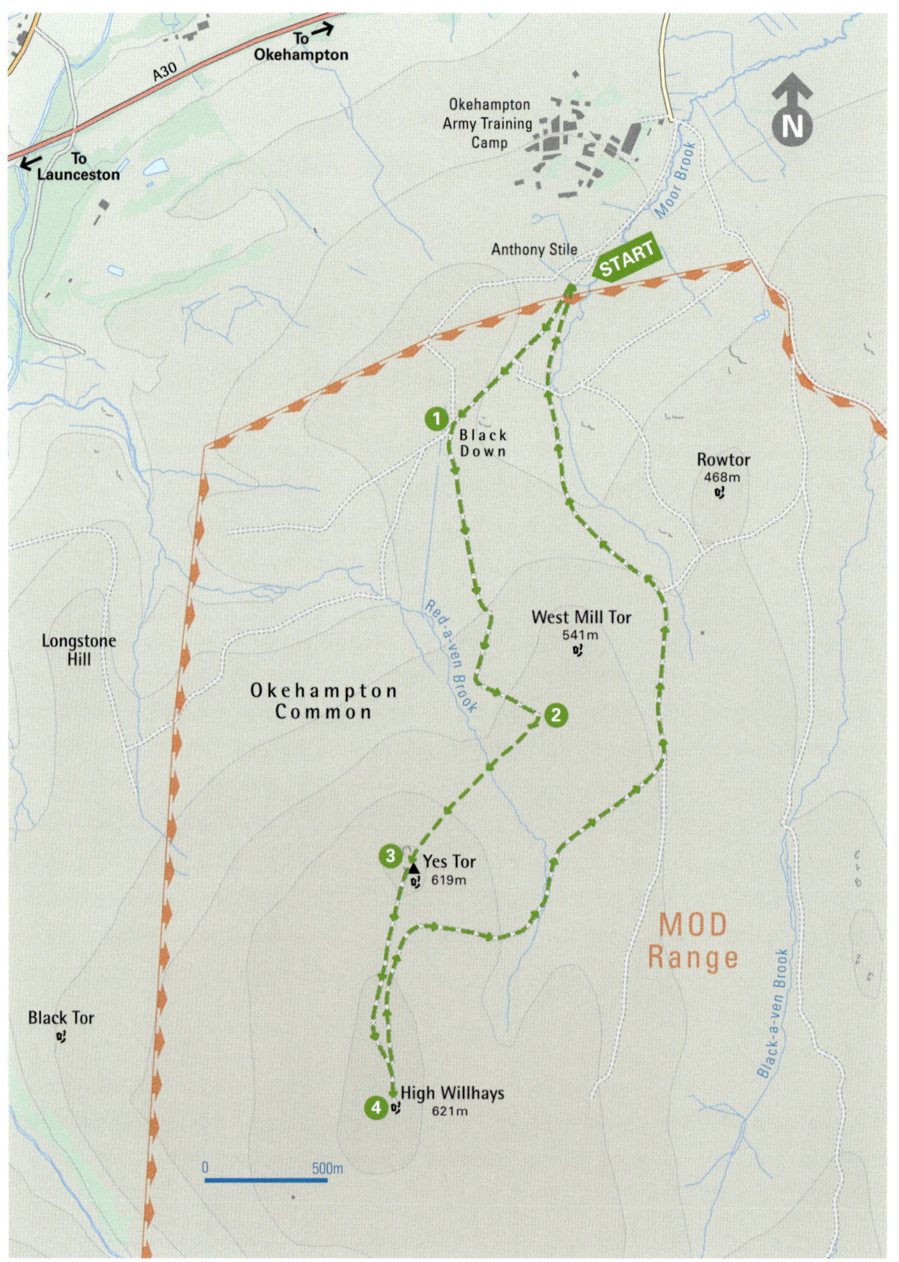

A30
To Okehampton
To Launceston
Okehampton Army Training Camp
Moor Brook
Anthony Stile
START
1
Black Down
Rowtor
468m
West Mill Tor
541m
Red-a-ven Brook
2
Longstone Hill
Okehampton Common
3 Yes Tor
619m
MOD Range
Black Tor
Black-a-ven Brook
4 High Willhays
621m
0 500m

START There are various parking options around the camp, but this route starts from Anthony Stile (SX 587 927), heading out along a stony track towards Black Down.

1 At a clear junction at the top of the rise, take the rough track to the left, climbing towards the valley between West Mill Tor and Yes Tor.

2 The turn off to the right isn't always obvious, but a well-trodden grass path heads south-west to a stream crossing, before you climb up through an increasingly boulder filled slope, to reach the top of Yes Tor. At times you may need to place a hand on a rock or two, but this is never true scrambling.

3 Head south along a clear track to High Willhays.

4 Return on the same route to find a junction with a track that heads east from close to Yes Tor, heading around the south side of West Mill Tor, onto a tarmac section, and back to Anthony Stile.

The old railway line.

7 Princetown Railway

Start / Finish   Princetown car park SX 589 735 / 50.5441, -3.9928
Distance   9km / 7.5 miles
Ascent   110m
Time   2 – 3 hours

Princetown, or Prince's Town as it was first known, was founded towards the end of the eighteenth century by Sir Thomas Trywhitt. His ambitious plan was to turn the barren centre of Dartmoor into productive farmland, the new town serving the burgeoning enterprise. While ultimately fruitless and involving the enforced loss of many acres of common land, the project did result in the building of the famous prison, and the opening of a string of quarries to provide stone.

Key to the success of Trywhitt's plans was a railway. This engineering marvel was forced up the inhospitable moorland slopes, with the dual aim of supplying the increasingly busy farmers and to extract granite for the many new building projects in Plymouth. The eventual failure of the schemes, while bad news for the railway, today provides a very fine, level route out along the old line and around Little King's Tor. This fairly long but trouble-free walk provides impressive views of the many dramatic quarry remains.

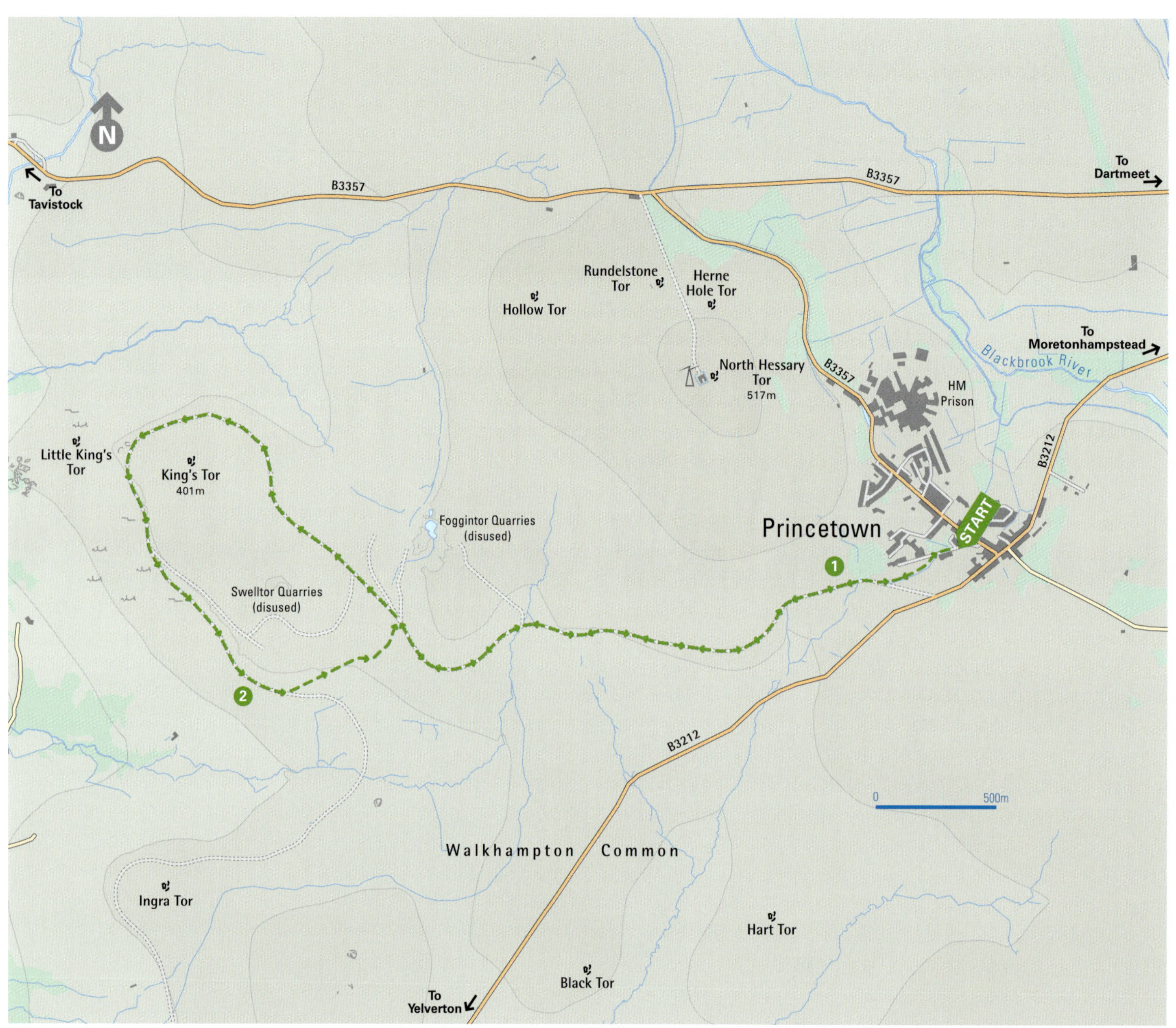

N
To Tavistock
B3357
B3357
To Dartmeet
Rundelstone Tor
Herne Hole Tor
Hollow Tor
To Moretonhampstead
Blackbrook River
B3357
North Hessary Tor
517m
HM Prison
B3212
Little King's Tor
King's Tor
401m
Foggintor Quarries (disused)
Princetown
START
1
Swelltor Quarries (disused)
2
B3212
0
500m
Walkhampton Common
Ingra Tor
Hart Tor
Black Tor
To Yelverton

START Turn left at the car park entrance, taking a left turn to leave the track before the cottages (signed 'Princetown Railway Cycle Route').

❶ Follow the old railway line route out around King's Tor.

❷ As the track turns to the right beyond the Swelltor Quarry remains, take a clear path to the left that climbs gently back to railway line, and the route back to Princetown.

Looking out from White Tor.

Routes 10–15km

8 White Tor

Start / Finish	Car park at SX 531 751 / 50.5575, -4.0756
Distance	10.5km / 6.5 miles
Ascent	250m
Time	3 hours

Taking in five Dartmoor tors, a standing stone, stone row and a stone circle, and crossing prehistoric enclosures, modern farmland, medieval tracks and historic tinworks, this walk has plenty going on. Yet White Tor still manages to stand out.

Reach the top on a good day and the views are quite extraordinary. Bodmin Moor sits off to the west, a wavy horizon beyond a broad sea of green farmland. Know where to look, and you can pick out Brown Willy, Cornwall's highest point. Spread over a full 180 degrees, Dartmoor fills the view in the other direction. Great Links Tor, Tavy Cleave, Fur and Great Mis Tors, each are easy to identify. Further examination reveals High Willhays and Hangingstone Hill, the most elevated ground on this moor.

With so much to look at, it may take quite a while before the ground closer at hand is considered. Gaze about though, and it's soon possible to make out the tumbled remains of stone walls or ramparts. There are two concentric rings in fact, enclosing an area of about 0.75h and a good handful of hut circles, shelters and cairns.

Sites like this aren't that uncommon, with many areas of high ground in Britain holding late Bronze Age or Iron Age hilltop enclosures. The thing is, this site may well be older, perhaps as much as a couple of thousand years older.

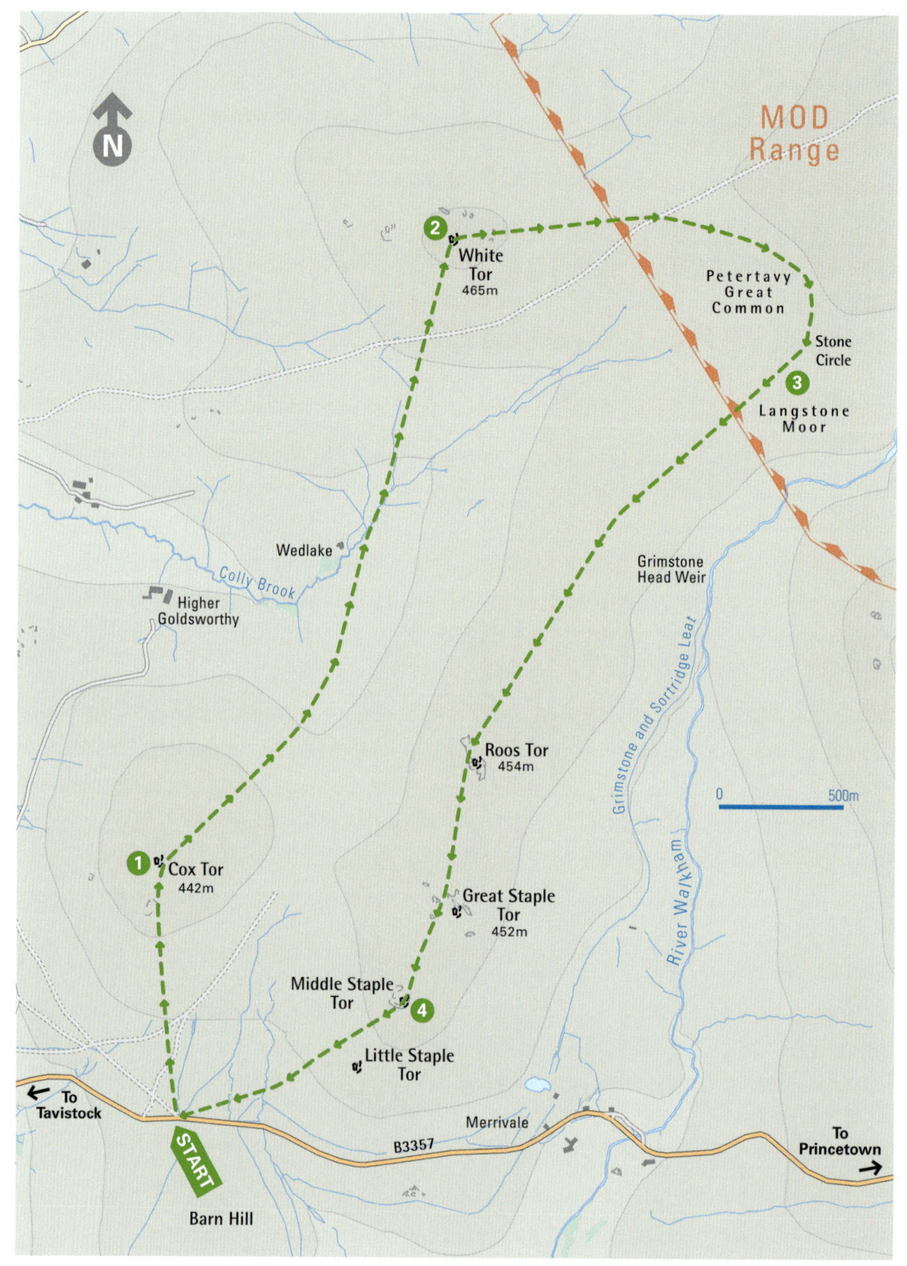

N
MOD
Range
White
Tor
465m
Petertavy
Great
Common
Stone
Circle
Langstone
Moor
Wedlake
Colly Brook
Grimstone
Head Weir
Higher
Goldsworthy
Grimstone and Sortridge Leat
Roos Tor
454m
River Walkham
0   500m
Cox Tor
442m
Great Staple
Tor
452m
Middle Staple
Tor
Little Staple
Tor
START
To
Tavistock
Merrivale
B3357
To
Princetown
Barn Hill

The hilltop was excavated, or at least parts were dug, in the late 1880s. No obvious evidence of Bronze or Iron Age activity was exposed. Instead, struck flints were found, the sort of flints you'd expect to find at a Neolithic settlement. Until further investigation takes place, the true age of the site remains a mystery.

Impressed? Well, there's more, and immediately to the north of this enigmatic site lies a settlement that probably is of Bronze Age date. This rambling collection of prehistoric remains includes another three enclosures, with 28 hut circles, and it's just one of another eleven Scheduled Monuments on this broad hill. These include a standing stone, stone row and stone circle that turn up next on this heritage packed walk.

The stone circle on Langstone Moor.

 **START** Cross the road and head straight uphill to Cox Tor.

1 Drop NE to find a gate to a footpath through the fields around Wedlake, before climbing to White Tor.

2 The standing stone is clearly visible, just north of east from White Tor, and once this is reached, the stone circle is also easy to spot at the crest of the ridge to the SE. Follow a reasonably clear path / quad bike track to skirt around the marshy ground and reach the circle.

3 Take a clear path SW to Roos Tor, then on to Great Staple Tor and then Middle Staple Tor.

4 Drop SW back to the car park on one of many paths.

Crossing the Higher White Tor wall.

9 Brown's House

Start / Finish	Two Bridges SX 609 750 / 50.5587, -3.99649
Distance	12.5km / 7.5 miles, partly within the Merrivale Range
Ascent	275m / 900ft
Time	4 – 5 hours

Dr Brown's wife was so beautiful that in order to keep her safe from the advances of numerous admirers, her troubled husband resorted to building them both a house in as remote a part of Dartmoor as he could find. Or so local legend would have us believe.

In truth, Benjamin Brown, 'Doctor of Physic', was inspired by no more than a wish to be a farmer. Some might argue that he was plagued by bad luck, although bad judgement might be closer to the mark.

Presumably filled with high hopes, Brown built his farmhouse in 1810, but alas, not before obtaining the all-important lease from the owners, the Duchy of Cornwall. This over-enthusiasm evidently irritated the Duchy, which responded by setting a rent he simply couldn't afford. Abandoned only two years later, the farm changed hands repeatedly, soon crumbling back into the folds of its isolated south-facing hill slope, not far from Great Mis Tor.

Despite Brown's intention to build an access road, none was ever laid. Any sortie to survey the evocative remains therefore requires some typical, if rather grand, Dartmoor trudging.

Setting out from a handy car park north of the road at Two Bridges, an enjoyable upland circuit begins by heading up and out along a broad tor-studded ridge. A

couple of fine granite walls protect the approach, pierced by convenient gateways. The last boundary before reaching Littaford Tors is straddled by a substantial stile.

From then on, as with all the best Dartmoor walks, one fine tor leads on to another, and Longaford Tor provides some spectacular views over the surrounding moor.

Following a slightly scrambly descent, Higher White Tor is up next. Flat-topped and fairly modest, it makes up for this by offering a fine sight of our destination, off to the north beyond Lower White Tor, and a rather boggy valley bottom.

In fact, once there you'll find little of Brown's short-lived farmhouse left – just some tumbled moss-covered walls and the outline of a yard or vegetable plot. Nonetheless, lunch eaten while sat on one of these walls gives time to contemplate

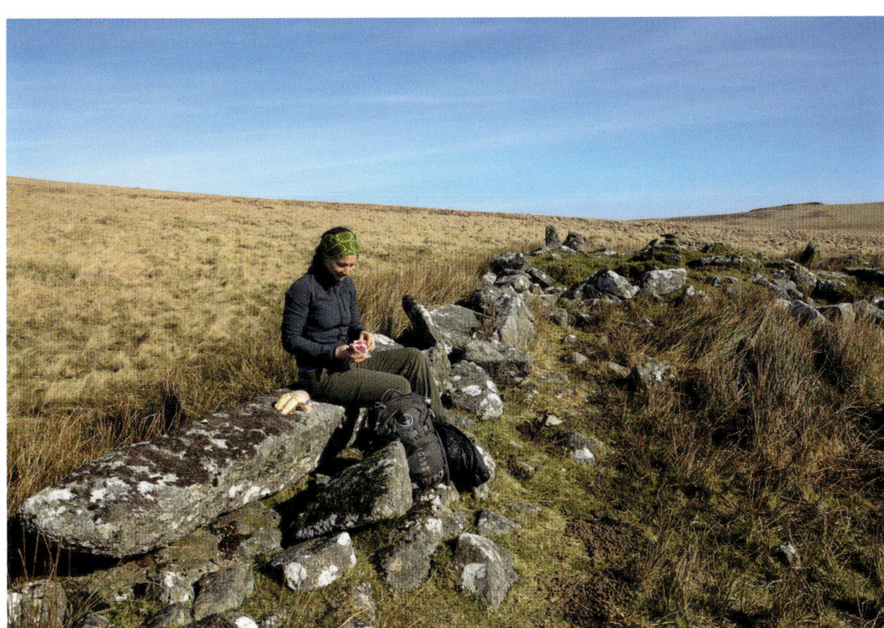

the commitment, and perhaps foolhardiness, of that two-hundred-year-old attempt to set up home at such an out of the way spot. It is wonderfully quiet though.

Rough Tor, beyond a crossing of the West Dart, is perhaps a bit of an anti-climax, not exactly living up to the rugged promise of its name. Beardown Tors, a couple of kilometres to the south compensates for this however, providing an excellent chance for a gentle exploratory clamber.

A drop downhill to the south-east leads to Devonport leat; a rather more successful project than poor Dr Brown's farm. Built in 1790, the leat provided water for the dockyard way off to the south. It still bubbles along sweetly, and on a warm day the easy path alongside the gentle flow, then through the shady wood above Beardown Farm, is very welcome. As is the final riverside route under trees to the car park.

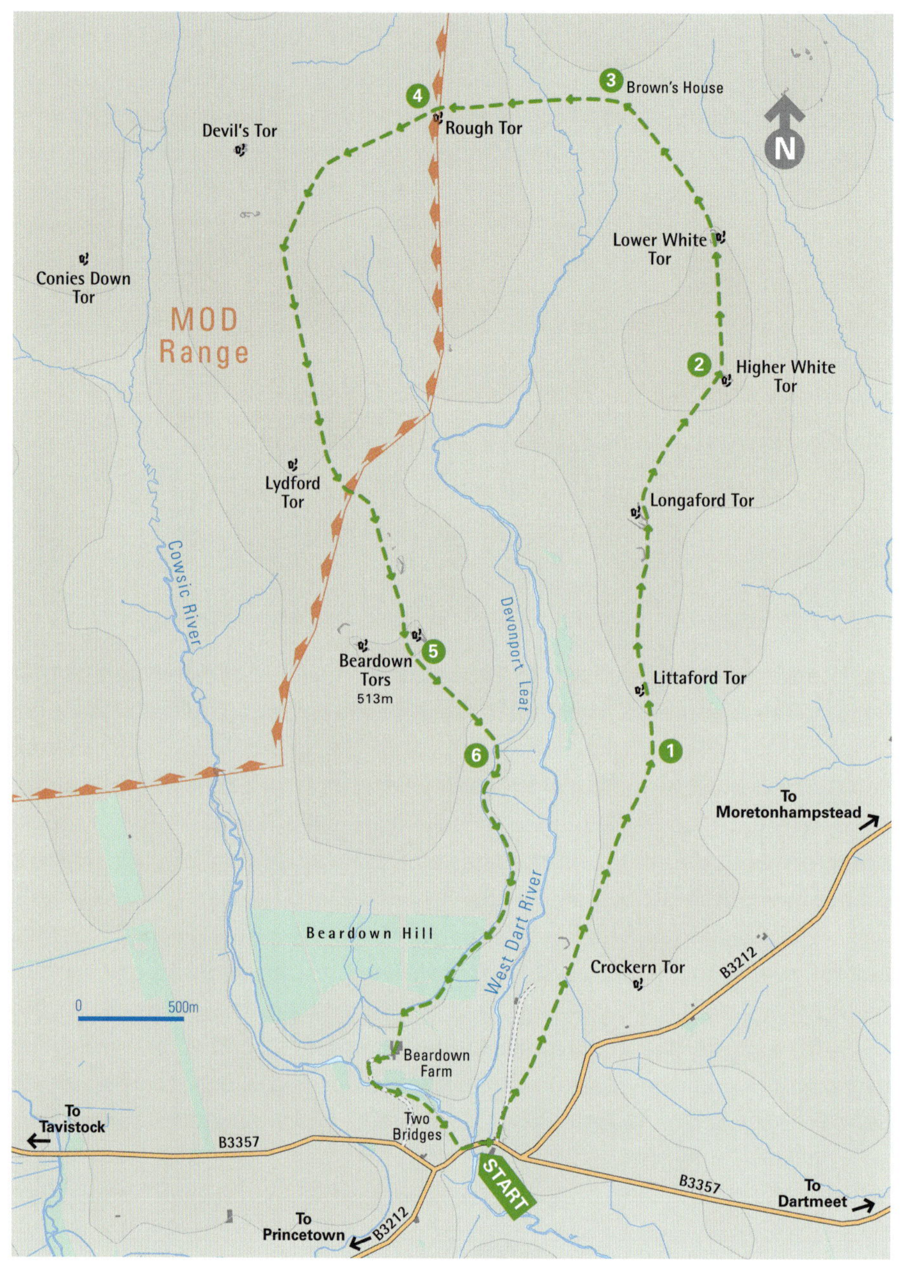

Devil's Tor
Rough Tor
Brown's House
N
Conies Down Tor
Lower White Tor
MOD Range
Higher White Tor
Lydford Tor
Longaford Tor
Cowsic River
Beardown Tors
513m
Littaford Tor
Devonport Leat
To Moretonhampstead
Crockern Tor
B3212
Beardown Hill
West Dart River
0   500m
Beardown Farm
To Tavistock
Two Bridges
B3357
START
B3357
To Dartmeet
To Princetown
B3212

🚶 **START** Leave the track to the N of the car park almost immediately, climbing to meet the ridge at Littaford Tors.

1 Continue N to Longaford Tor and then Higher White Tor.

2 Cross the wall to the N of Higher White Tor to pass Lower White Tor, crossing boggy ground to reach Brown's House.

3 Head W to cross the West Dart River, before climbing to Rough Tor.

4 Contour SW around the valley head before heading S to Beardown Tors.

5 Drop downhill to the SE, to find a small bridge over Devonport Leat.

6 Follow the leat-side path through coniferous woodland, then around Beardown Farm to the road.

Eastern White Tor.

10 Eastern White Tor and the Avon Valley

Start / Finish	Shipley Bridge car park SX 680 629 / 50.4510, -3.8601
Distance	12km / 7.5 miles
Ascent	285m
Time	4 hours

Head out onto the moor from Shipley Bridge, and other than the odd farmer, or perhaps a fellow walker on a distant ridge, you're unlikely to see another soul all day. Much of Dartmoor is now equally quiet, but as we've already seen, this relative human absence is only very recent. Many corners of the moor were once hotbeds of activity, and few have seen more industry than this. This river crossing must once have heaved with people.

Drive to Shipley Bridge today and you'll park in the middle of a derelict clay-drying pan. In the mid 19th century, liquid china clay was run off the moor to the site in open gulleys, but a poor quality product soon closed the business. It wasn't the first enterprise to go under here. Both a naphtha distillation plant and a peat charcoal factory had already been abandoned. As a result, industrial relics litter the area, disappearing slowly beneath birch woodland, blankets of moss and brackeny turf.

The peat was shipped to the valley along a tramway from Red Lake, and the route of this former railway provides a convenient start to the walk. With the bed of the tramway astern, and after walking through the various prehistoric remains on Brent Moor, the impressive bulk of Eastern White Barrow soon catches the eye on the horizon.

Some say it looks like a submarine, and the resemblance is definitely there. Originally built as a burial mound in the Bronze Age, the cairn long marked the south-east corner of the ancient Forest of Dartmoor. It features in the account of the Dartmoor Perambulation walk, starting on page 257. It's uncertain when the stone tower was added, with one story suggesting it was built in the 1930s by children from South Brent. An alternative account claims it was the handiwork of bored soldiers during WWII.

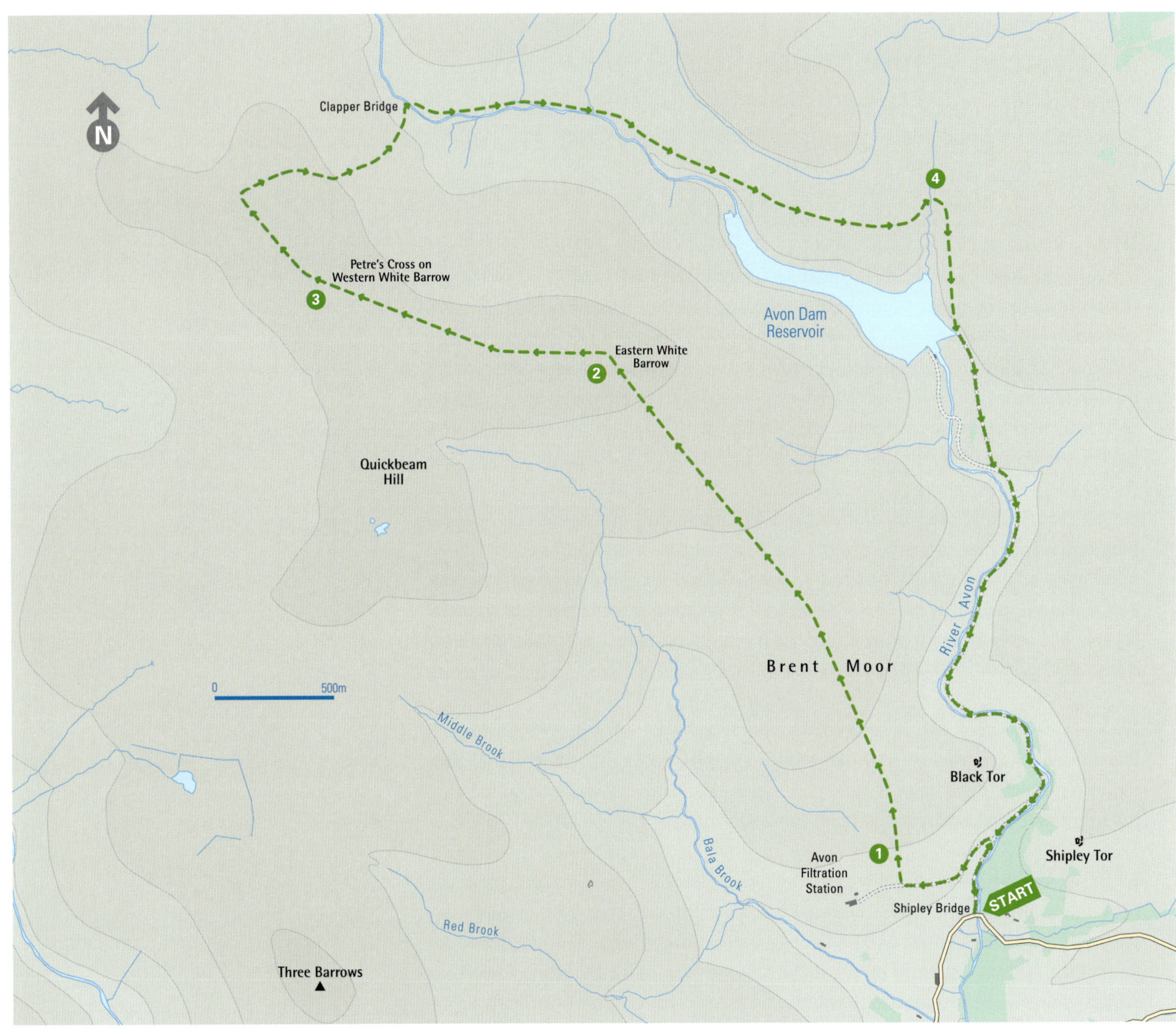

N
Clapper Bridge
4
Petre's Cross on
Western White Barrow
3
Avon Dam
Reservoir
Eastern White
Barrow
2
Quickbeam
Hill
Brent Moor
River Avon
0   500m
Middle Brook
Black Tor
Bala Brook
Avon
Filtration
Station
Shipley Tor
1
START
Shipley Bridge
Red Brook
Three Barrows

You might think that here, high atop a hill in the moor, you'd have left the scars of industry far behind, but almost as soon as you leave the cairn, heading for Western White Barrow, you have to wend your way through the pits and undulating spoil heaps left by tin miners. Heading north from the second barrow to find the Two Moors Way, onto that abandoned tramway again, and the vast conical spoil at the former Red Lake clay quarry dominates the view ahead. Mind you, all else in view is now open moorland, dotted with ponies. It might have been busy here once, but the only mass human activity here today involves other fellwalkers.

In the valley below, the last trace of the clay extraction industry gives way to those of past rabbit farming. Pillow mounds, former bunny homes associated with long closed Huntingdon Warren, dot the hillsides. These vie for space with prehistoric enclosures and hut circles as you head on to the Avon Reservoir, built in 1957.

Crossing the Avon.

START Head N along the private road from the Shipley Bridge car park, turning left at the first junction.

1 Just before the Avon Filtration Station, leave the road to the right and head up onto the broad ridge of Brent Moor. In good weather, you'll soon see Eastern White Barrow to the NW.

2 From the barrow, head just north of west along the ridge to Western White Barrow, which again, will be visible in good weather.

3 Head straight on from the barrow to find a clear path (the old tramway) that leads NW to the Two Moors Way. Turn right onto this clear path, dropping down to a clapper bridge that crosses the River Avon, before following the north side of the river to find a track that leads on to the Avon Reservoir.

4 Skirt around the edge of the reservoir, crossing Brockhill Stream before following a reasonably clear path to the end of the dam, where a track falls to the road leading back to the car park.

Drizzlecombe stone rows.

11 Evil Combe

Start / Finish	Nattor car park at SX 579 673 / 50.4883, -4.0049
Distance	10.5km / 6.5 miles
Ascent	240m
Time	3 – 4 hours

Great lumps have been torn from the ground. Deep scars criss-cross the moor, and abandoned buildings huddle, shattered amidst the desolation. Evil lies at the heart of this walk. And once there, at the edge of these impressive tin mining remains, Evil Combe turns out to be a pretty, if rather uneven, little spot, speckled with Galloway cattle.

Even on a moor renowned for its archaeology, the boggy folds in the ground tipping down towards the infant River Plym manage to stand out. Almost as soon as you leave the Scout hut near Sheeps Tor, walking out along Edward's Path, you come across the first lumpy remains.

Many of the artificial earth or stone heaps you come across on the moor were thrown up to cover a grave. The hummocks at Ditsworthy were built to house rabbits, live ones, and these elongated 'pillow' mounds lie scattered all around the old warren house at the end of the footpath. On this walk, Susannah and I didn't quite reach the farm itself (although you can on page 139), leaving the well-trodden route to weave our way through the old field walls and mounds above, heading instead for the low ridge holding Eastern Tor, and its view out to our main, ancient destination.

It's been suggested that as well as forming ceremonial procession routes, the stone rows on Dartmoor, built in the late Neolithic and early Bronze Age, also helped in navigation. It's true that many seem to line up naturally with a good walk, and the Drizzlecombe rows, one with a stone over 4m high, certainly matched our route out towards Higher Hartor Tor and beyond.

Newleycombe Lake
Down Tor
Combshead Tor
Narrator Brook
Nun's Cross
Nun's Cross Farm
4
Eylesbarrow
Eylesbarrow Tin Mine (disused)
Evil Combe
Great Gnat's Head
3
Higher Hartor Tor
Lower Hartor Tor
Calveslake Tor
START
Scout Hut
Ditsworthy Warren
Edward's Path
To Yelverton
Gutter Tor
Gutter Mire
1
River Plym
2
Eastern Tor 333m
N
0   500m

Once through an impressive collection of prehistoric settlements and burial mounds, and past the tor, it's those tin mining remains that take over. Apart from the impressive medieval cross that marks the turning point, the outer half of the walk is dominated by what's left of Eylesbarrow Mine, worked over a wide area in the first half of the 19th century. Deep holes pepper the hilltop, with great rifts cut down across the hillsides towards the river. Piles of spoil and those derelict buildings complete the scene of past industry.

And just to spoil the dramatic introduction, the name evil is said to derive from the Dartmoor mining name for a pick-axe.

Higher Hartor Tor.

START Take the track E from the car park to find a gate to the Scout hut, and a path leading out to Edward's Path.

1 After 400m or so, leave Edward's Path at the slight bend to head SE, climbing gently to pass through the northern edge of the Eastern Tor stone scatter, before continuing downhill to meet a clear track.

2 Follow the track north east to cross the stream, before heading uphill, past the stone rows, to Higher Hartor Tor.

3 From the tor, head north-east, passing close to the mining scars above Evil Combe, before finding a track, then a path, that crosses the hill, heading for Nun's Cross Farm (the path does grow a little faint, but by then, even in poor visibility, you should be able to see the farm).

4 After visiting Siward's, or Nun's, Cross, turn south to follow a clear path, then a track, back to the car park.

Looking down towards the crash site in the West Okement valley.

12 The Liberty walk

Start / Finish	Parking between the A386 and the Prewley Water Treatment Works
	SX 545 910 / 50.7006, -4.0622
Distance	10.5km / 6.5 miles
Ascent	328m
Time	4 – 5 hours

Aircraft 63926's radio operator transmitted his crew's last radio message at 22.15hrs, late on a December night in 1943. Their navigator estimated a return to base in about five minutes. They never arrived.

Setting out from RAF Dunkeswell in East Devon, the US Navy Liberator had been hunting a group of ten enemy destroyers in the Bay of Biscay. A couple of Dorniers had fired on them, but pilot William Parish reported only 'slight problems' as a result. Perhaps the altimeter was damaged. We'll never know. Whatever the reason, on their return, the bomber hit Dartmoor's Corn Ridge, not far from Kitty Tor, before falling into the West Okement valley. All ten aircrew lost their lives.

Not that much is left to mark the event, but there's enough to make this section of the walk deeply moving. Reaching the edge of the steep slope overlooking the river below, Black-a-tor-Copse lies spread along the bank beyond. When Susannah and I visited, it took us a while to spot the uppermost pile of debris; a small patch of tangled silver aluminium, heaped in a hollow on the hillside. We clambered down, picking our way amongst the granite boulders, the mood, despite the spring sun, suddenly sombre. Further exploration revealed more fuselage a little way down the slope, some melted by the resultant fire. In a small pit, the remains of one of the Liberty's four Pratt and Whitney engines slowly crumbles away into the peaty soil. Further debris cairns lie closer to the river.

At least 40 WWII air crash sites are recorded on the moor. At the time, this area of high ground was ringed by airfields. A Wellington bomber had come down close

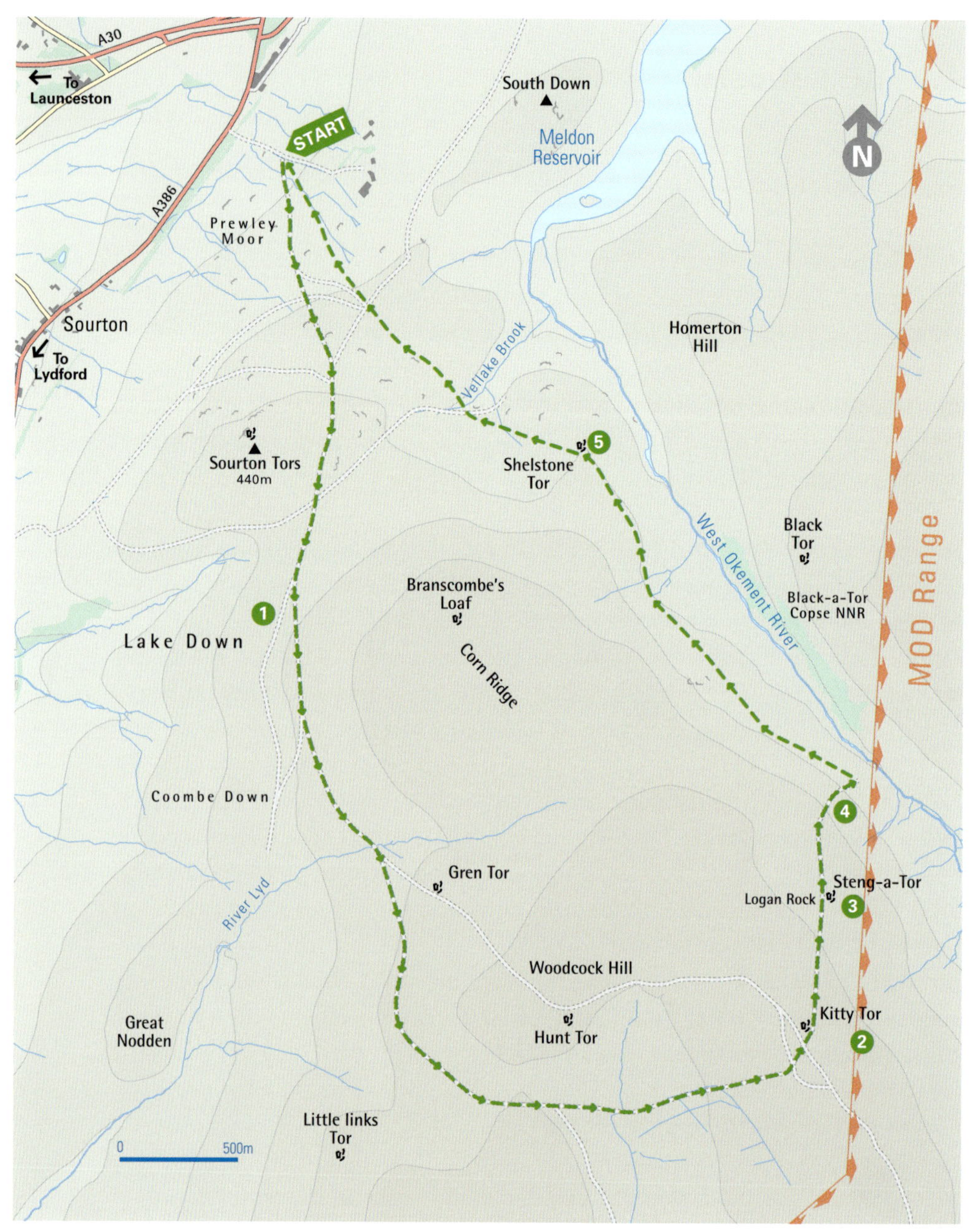
To Launceston
A30
A386
To Lydford
Sourton
Prewley Moor
START
South Down
Meldon Reservoir
Vellake Brook
Homerton Hill
Sourton Tors
440m
Shelstone Tor
5
Black Tor
West Okement River
MOD Range
Branscombe's Loaf
Black-a-Tor Copse NNR
Lake Down
Corn Ridge
Coombe Down
River Lyd
Gren Tor
Steng-a-Tor
3
Logan Rock
4
Woodcock Hill
Great Nodden
Kitty Tor
2
Hunt Tor
Little links Tor
0   500m
1
N

to Kitty Tor only the year before, with the loss of all life. December 1943 seems to have been a particularly bad month in this corner of Dartmoor, and on Christmas day, a USAF Flying Fortress struck the other side of Corn Ridge, not much further north. On this occasion there were at least some survivors, and three of the eight crew managed to stagger away to find help at the nearest farm.

Few of these crashes have left any visible remains. Amongst the scatter of Liberator 63926 fragments, spread wide along this side of the West Okement valley, there are two distinct cairns, no doubt gathered together over the years. Standing on the rugged, empty slope below Stenga Tor, surrounded by the astonishing beauty of this quiet spot, it's painfully easy to picture the crumpled sheets of riveted metal, even lengths of hydraulic hose, as a complete aircraft. Little was said before we continued our journey to Shelstone Tor, then on towards the dog walkers of Prewley Moor and the growing rumble of the A30.

A Pratt and Whitney engine.

START From Prewley Moor, follow a fairly clear path S, climbing to find an old track that runs away from Sourton Tors.

1 Leave the track where a path forks to the left, rising gently to find another good track (if you find yourself on a track heading downhill you've missed the turn and can rectify the problem by turning left to head upwards). The correct track, once found, is an old railway line bed that swings round to the E, before climbing through wet ground to Kitty Tor.

2 In good weather, Stenga Tor (Steng-a-Tor on the map) is visible to the N of the Army huts. If it isn't visible, a faint path runs on through the grass.

3 Continue on, beyond the tor to meet the top edge of the valley side. From here, you should be able to make out the small patch of debris below (SX 568 885). Other remains lie in heaps farther downhill, where you will also find the engine.

4 Follow the valley NW at about the same level, climbing at the end to find Shelstone Tor.

5 Drop NW towards the corner of the enclosed land, before following the wall, and continuing in the same direction beyond the next corner to find the parking area.

The south edge of Whitchurch Common.

13 Walkham Valley

Start / Finish   Car park at SX 539 749 / 50.5566, -4.0626

Distance   10.5km / 6.5 miles

Ascent   300m

Time   4 hours

While much of Dartmoor's high ground sits within access land, the upper extent of the Walkham Valley, close to the western edge, is still out of bounds. A circular walk over here will require a couple of roadside tramps to negotiate the barrier.

Before reaching the enclosed section, Whitchurch Common bristles with granite exuberance. Humble Feather Tor leads on to Pew Tor, where a wonderful spread of folded rock lies ripe for investigation. Fairly close to three popular car parks, and with fine views over the edge of the moor, this can be a busy spot.

Close scrutiny of the granite fragments spread about these tors will reveal frequent examples of ad hoc quarrying. Numerous surface 'moorstones' still bear the scars, having been split, ready to be carted away.

You'll need no close scrutiny to spot quarrying evidence on the other side of the valley, where quite astonishing efforts have been employed to remove vast tonnages of stone. A fair stretch of this walk takes place along the bed of an abandoned railway, built in large part to carry this stone off the moor and away to build large chunks of Plymouth.

Of course these 19th-century quarrymen were not the first to exploit the local geology. Not far to the north, and spread out across a rare, flat piece of ground that seems almost purpose built for the job, is a remarkable collection of prehistoric standing stones, stone circles and stone rows. Nobody knows quite what our ancestors got up to here, but I'm fairly sure it was a lot quieter then.

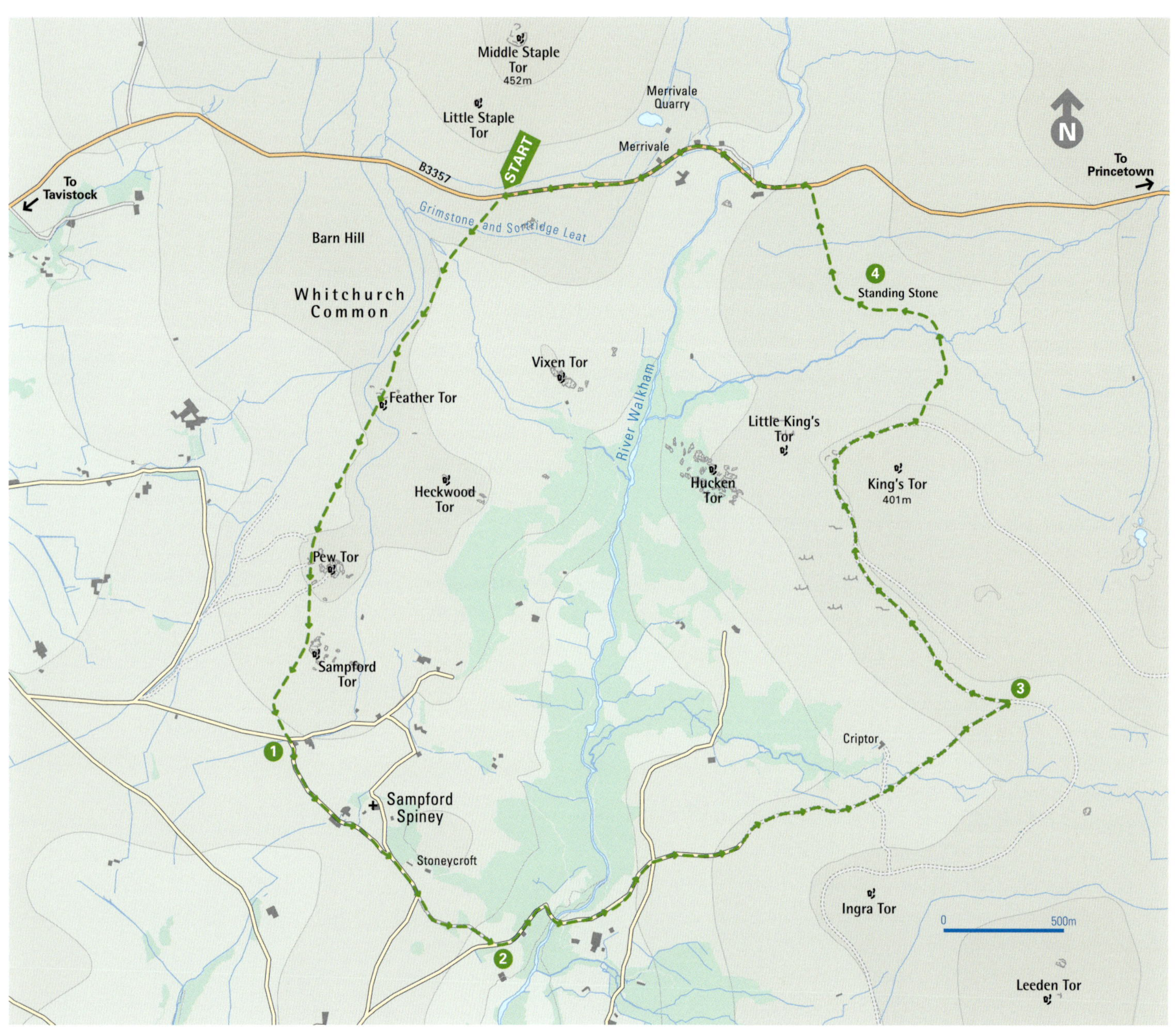

Middle Staple Tor
452m
Little Staple Tor
Merrivale Quarry
Merrivale
START
B3357
To Princetown
To Tavistock
Grimstone and Sortridge Leat
Barn Hill
Whitchurch Common
4
Standing Stone
Vixen Tor
River Walkham
Feather Tor
Little King's Tor
Heckwood Tor
Hucken Tor
King's Tor
401m
Pew Tor
Sampford Tor
1
Criptor
3
Sampford Spiney
Stoneycroft
Ingra Tor
2
Leeden Tor
0   500m

Still, the almost constant flow of traffic on the nearby B3357 must help keep the Dartmoor Inn in business, and here a short restorative break can be enjoyed before taking to the verge again. It's not far now to the car park.

START Cross the road to head SE, climbing gently on the other side of the valley to Feather Tor, before continuing to Prew Tor, then along a clear path to the end of the common, keeping to the right of a small enclosure.

1 Cross the road, taking the narrow road through Sampford Spiney to Stoneycroft, where you continue downhill along a good track.

2 Turn left on meeting the road again, crossing the River Walkham and heading straight up, and back out onto the moor. Turn left to follow a track towards Criptor, where a sign will direct you along a footpath heading towards the abandoned railway.

3 Turn left to join the old rail line, leaving it to the left at the corner below King's Tor. Skirt the enclosed land (ignore the inviting stile over the field boundary wall) and find a way over the stream, bearing NW on the other bank to find the standing stone.

4 Continue north, to pass through the double stone rows, turning left onto the B3357. Care needs to be taken. There is a path, of sorts, along the left hand verge, and you can cross beyond Merrivale Quarry to walk back to the car park along the edge of the moor.

Heading away from Prew Tor.

Gidleigh Common.

14 Gidleigh Bounds

Start / Finish   the tiny Scorhill car park SX 662 878 / 50.6738, -3.8963

Distance   13km / 8 miles

Ascent   250m

Time   4 hours

Look closely at your OS OL28 sheet, and you'll see a fair stretch of this walk follows a dotted line, or a route close to it. Despite being wholly within the bounds of the Dartmoor National Park, this spread of rough common lies outside the much more ancient Forest of Dartmoor. Instead, it forms the western edge of the parish of Gidleigh, and that dotted line marks the boundary.

For most of us, the exact extent of the parish we live in is probably a mystery. That certainly wasn't the case in the past. Go back only a hundred years or so, and your allegiance might be to your country and county, but foremost it was likely to have been to the parish.

Details of your birth, marriage and death would have been kept in the parish records. A parish constable monitored your behaviour, and the local Lord of the Manor expected your deference. Whatever your occupation, a tenth of your income or crop would go to the parish priest. At times in the past you wouldn't even have been able to seek work elsewhere without his written consent. If you fell on hard times, it would be the parish and it's workhouse that kept you from the gutter... just. And the bounds of the parish were known to all.

To ensure this fact, most parishes had a tradition of walking, or 'beating', these bounds. This ritual often meant literally beating each boundary marker in turn with sticks. What was inevitably a long walk often involved a whole host of other, sometimes odd, practices. Many Dartmoor parishes would beat not just the stones or cairns on the route, but the youngsters dragged along too, presumably on the grounds that knocking the memory of their location into them would ensure it stuck. Some rituals went further still, upending the children over each boundary marker, even dropping them onto the stone headfirst.

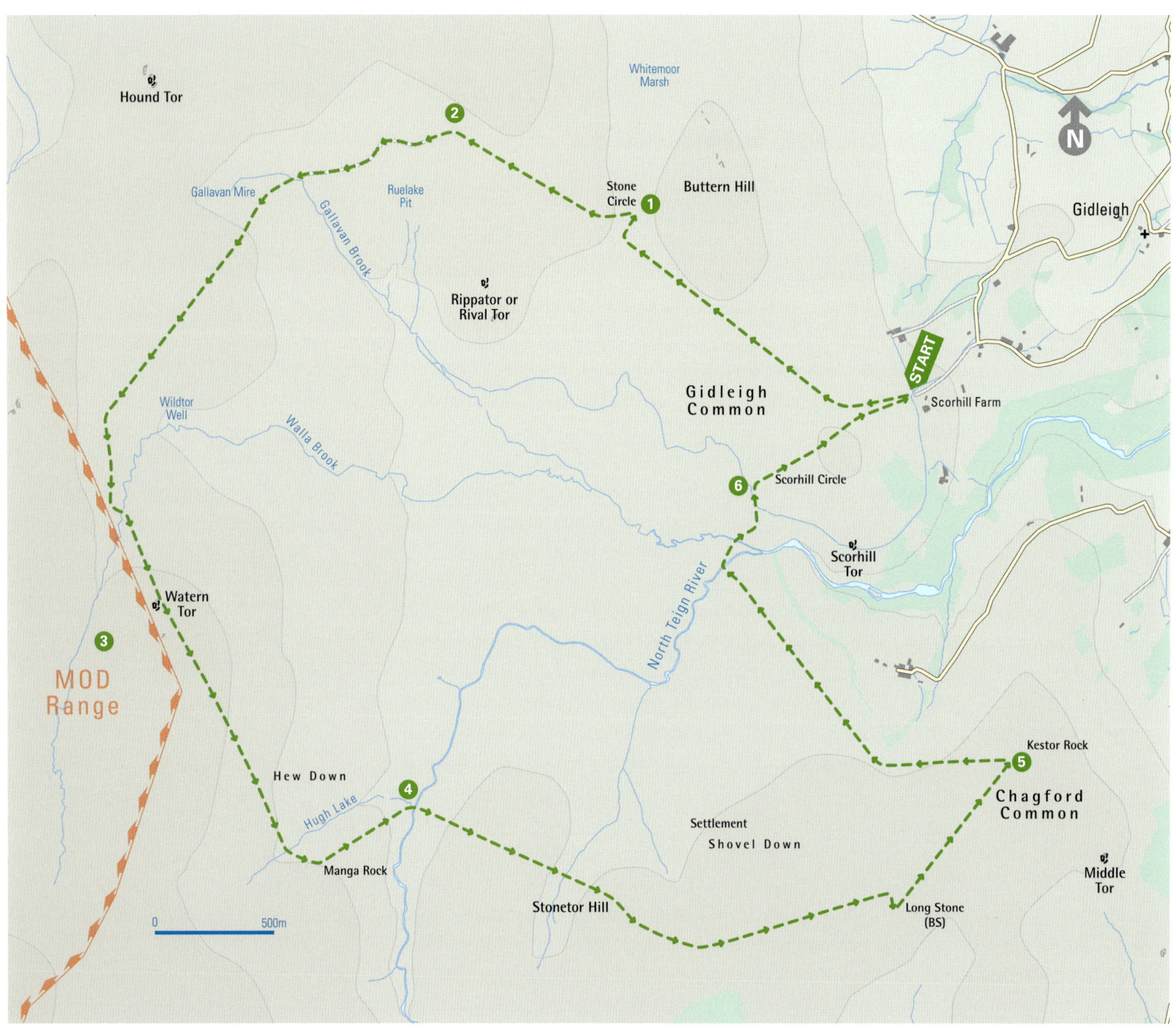

Hound Tor
Whitemoor Marsh
Gallavan Mire
Gallavan Brook
Ruelake Pit
Stone Circle
1
Buttern Hill
Gidleigh
2
N
Rippator or Rival Tor
Wildtor Well
Walla Brook
Gidleigh Common
START
Scorhill Farm
6
Scorhill Circle
Scorhill Tor
Watern Tor
3
MOD Range
North Teign River
Kestor Rock
5
Chagford Common
Hew Down
4
Hugh Lake
Settlement
Shovel Down
Middle Tor
Manga Rock
Stonetor Hill
Long Stone (BS)
0   500m

Today the bounds of Gidleigh are still beaten every seven years, before a traditional pint is drunk below Wild Tor. A 'race' is then held across part of the common.

One of the old parish boundary markers is Manga Rock, where GP, for Gidleigh Parish, is carved into one face. There was an enquiry in 1842, when the parish went to court, claiming that the owners of Teighnhead Farm had moved the marker. The parish won.

Long Stone on Shovel Down marks the meeting of Gidleigh with two other parishes, and traditionally there was a competition during the beating to see who could climb, or fight, their way to the top, first. Perhaps it's best though not to recreate this particular ritual when you meet this impressive megalith yourself.

Thurlstone.

START Head W from the car park, turning NW on gaining the open moor, to follow a clear path.

1 Turn right beyond Buttern Hill, to find the remains of the stone circle, before following a faint path W and back to the earlier track.

2 The junction with the next track is not clear, but you should see it heading W towards Gallaven Mire. This tinners' track fades to a wide path that eventually meets a clear route, heading towards the Walla Brook, which you cross to climb to Watern Tor.

3 Head SSE from Watern Tor to find a stile, then on beyond to cross Hugh Lake and find Manga Rock at SX 6361 8579.

4 Cross the North Teign at the rails, before climbing alongside the wall, leaving it to follow a wide path to Chagford Common, Long Stone (SX 6602 8567) and Kestor Rock.

5 Head west to the corner of the woodland, then along a clear path to recross the Teign by way of clapper bridges, before heading on to the Scorhill stone circle.

6 Take the clear path uphill and over to the car park.

Heading towards Arms Tor.

  Arms, Great Mis, Kitty, Stenga, Shelstone and Sourton Tors

15 Arms, Great Mis, Kitty, Stenga, Shelstone and Sourton Tors

Start / Finish	Nodden Gate car park SX 530 863, limited spaces, or, for the cost of a drink, the Fox and Hounds car park SX 525 867 / 50.6620, -4.0877
Distance	13km / 8 miles
Ascent	430m
Time	4 – 5 hours

Set foot on Dartmoor, whether on your first visit, or after many years of satisfying familiarity, and if you have a destination, it's likely to be a tor. Perched atop almost every bluff, rise or prominence, and ranging from mighty metamorphic monsters to humble heaps, these natural stone sculptures catch the eye and hold an impressive draw. This walk is a modest celebration of that variety.

Just to the east of Nodden Gate, the granite-strewn approach to our first objective makes a fine start to this tour of tors. Much of Arms Tor seems to have slipped quite a way down the hill. Even a direct approach will involve plenty of weaving.

The line to Great Links Tor is much cleaner and pretty straight, with an isolated outlier providing a fitting prelude to the main event. The main tor seems almost reluctant to display, and it's not until you bump right up against the imposing mass of once molten rock, that its Great prefix suddenly makes sense. This is a very impressive lump of granite.

Which Kitty Tor isn't. However, while this thin stone scatter may lack tor exuberance, it certainly makes up for this in views, with Great Links to the rear, and Yes Tor and High Willhays, Dartmoor's highest point, looming ahead. Just below, at the edge of the same broad ridge, lies Stenga Tor (marked as Steng-a-tor or Logan Rocks on OS maps). This is a fascinating outcrop, although be warned, the immediate vicinity can often be surprisingly soggy.

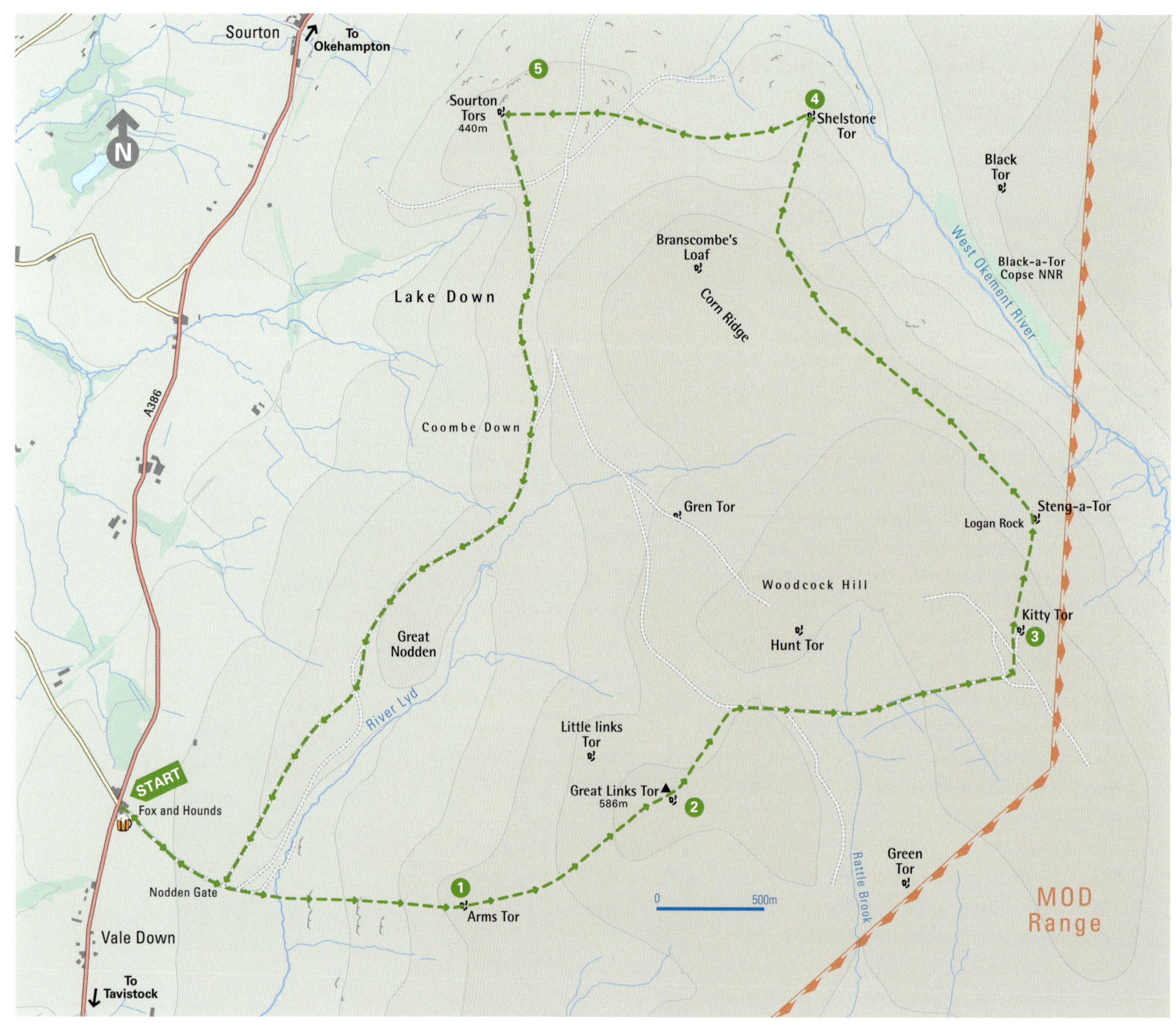

Sourton
To Okehampton
N
5
Sourton Tors 440m
4
Shelstone Tor
Black Tor
Branscombe's Loaf
West Okement River
Black-a-Tor Copse NNR
Lake Down
Corn Ridge
A386
Coombe Down
Gren Tor
Steng-a-Tor
Logan Rock
Woodcock Hill
Kitty Tor
3
Great Nodden
Hunt Tor
River Lyd
Little links Tor
START
Fox and Hounds
Great Links Tor 586m
2
Rattle Brook
Green Tor
Nodden Gate
1
Arms Tor
0   500m
Vale Down
MOD Range
To Tavistock

For a tor lying so close to the moor's edge, I suspect secretive Shelstone is relatively seldom trod. It deserves a visit though, and a wander along the top edge of the steep valley will bring you to less vertical ground and an easy descent. This low, multi-faceted stone pile of Shelstone calls out to be clambered over. Every inspection seeming to reveal yet another impressive eccentricity.

Finally, in our mini six-tor challenge, with superb views over the farmland below, Sourton Tors always manage to feel slightly set apart. It's not just the location; this extensive rocky exuberance, the result of heat altered limestone, represents one of the very few tors on the moor that isn't formed from granite.

Great Links Tor.

START From the Fox and Hounds, head SE along a good track to Nodden Gate. Beyond the gate, head east to cross the Lyd, before following a reasonably clear path to tackle Arms Tor head on.

1 From Arms Tor, head NE on a faint path to climb to Great Links Tor.

2 Head NE (towards Hunt Tor), finding a raised track that heads E, trying, but failing, to provide a dry route to Kitty Tor.

3 From Kitty, a clear grass path leads on an almost northerly bearing to Stenga Tor, before continuing along the top edge of the valley, until Shelstone Tor appears on the valley side below.

4 Sourton Tors is visible on high ground from Shelstone Tor, but not on the route in between. A clear path between the two, then a track, leads most of the way though.

5 Follow a clear path downhill, just east of south from Sourton Tors, joining a track on the far side of a slight dip. Follow this track, which eventually meets an even better one, leading past Great Nodden, and back to Nodden Gate.

Light scrambling in Tavy Cleave.

16 Tavy Cleave and Fur Tor (and variant)

Start / Finish   Lanehead car park SX 537 823 / 50.6224, -4.0691
Distance   13km / 8 miles
Ascent   385m
Time   4 – 5 hours, possibly more

Slowly our efforts to struggle through the Cleave began to fail. The route was just too demanding. As our pace slackened still further, our progress now almost at a standstill, I realised time was slipping away. Something dramatic needed to be done. Resigned to the inevitable, I put away my camera. The day was saved.

All walks have a PPM rating – that's Photos Per Mile. These exist in pretty much inverse proportion to the time taken to complete the route, and are most easily assessed once you return home and download the camera. Some outings, particularly those undertaken in rain or mist, can have a score as low as 0.5 – 1. Others will be much higher. Few routes, at least few on Dartmoor, have a PPM as elevated as Tavy Cleave. It took us ages to wend our way through.

To be fair, the route itself has much to do with this too, the traditional elements immediately underfoot that is. Set out along the level path flanking Mine Leat, and some may worry that this walk might be a little too manicured. No need to fret. The Cleave's upper sections will quickly remove any concerns. You may only take a step or two up there before the next photogenic opportunity appears, but the requirement to use your hands will soon have you putting that camera away. This twisting gash in the side of the moor is not only dramatic, but also pleasingly rugged in places.

True, once over Sandy Ford, and on the way out across the wide boggy stretch leading to Fur Tor, the PPM might drop. However, as you climb to the granite outcrop, with the great expanse of central Dartmoor opening up all around, the rating begins to rise again with every step.

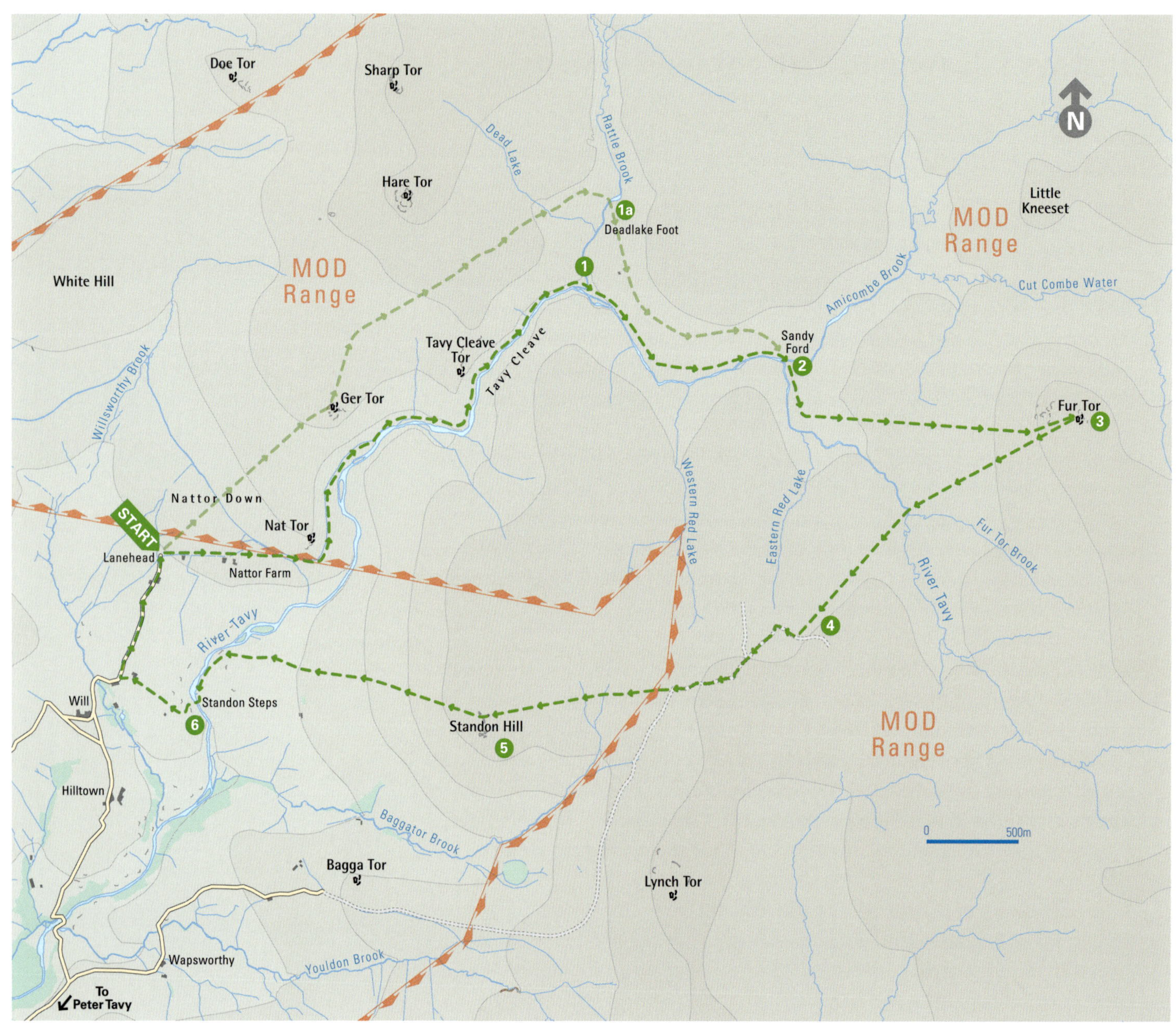

   Tavy Cleave and Fur Tor (and variant)

As for the accuracy of the route's time estimate, given above... well that all depends on the capacity of your camera's data card.

START Take the track E from the car park, swinging uphill beyond Nattor Farm to follow Mine Leat, which leads to a rough path running tight alongside the river, up through Tavy Cleave.

1 Cross Rattle Brook (tricky in high water conditions), picking your way along the steep, stony, eastern bank to the Tavy, before breaking out onto more open ground leading to Sandy Ford.

2 Once over the ford, head S a little along the Tavy to find a less boggy route to Fur Tor, then make for the summit (a direct route from the ford may look appealing. It isn't).

3 From Fur Tor, drop back into the boggy valley, making for the point where the Firing Range boundary (marked by white and red posts) crosses the Tavy. From here, head SW up over the ridge to find an old trackway. This isn't easy to locate, and you may have to make for a short mast at the eastern end (where the track is still not obvious).

4 Either on the track (which becomes a little more pronounced as it wends its way W) or on a bearing, set out for Standon Hill (and the visible army shelter).

5 From Standon, drop downhill, just north of west, crossing ancient field boundaries to find a gate at the end of a walled funnel. Take the (often flooded) track, or skirt it to either side, before following the river round to Standon Steps footbridge.

6 Take the track uphill from the bridge, turning right at the road to find the car park.

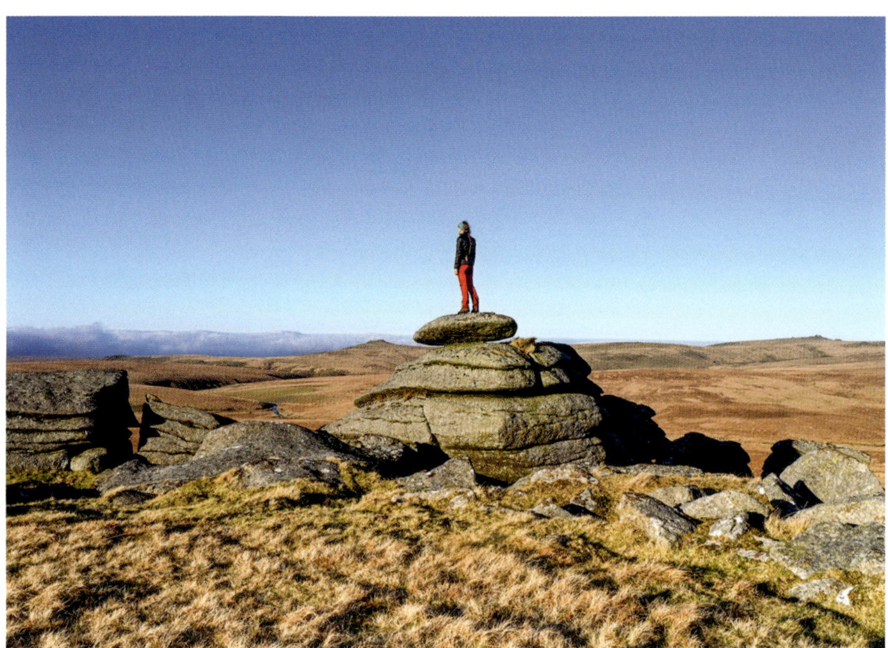

Alternative route

For those who don't much like the idea of the sometimes quite demanding scrabble through the Cleave, or simply fancy a change, the initial part of the route can be given a completely different feel. This route also takes you through the finest prehistoric village on the moor, in my books anyway, with numerous remarkably well-preserved hut circles.

START Take a clear and sometimes broad path NE from the car park, heading for Ger Tors, before making for a low saddle between Hare Tor and Tavy Cleave Tor, the rocky outcrops overlooking the Cleave. A well-trodden path leads on to a crossing of the stream at Deadlake Foot.

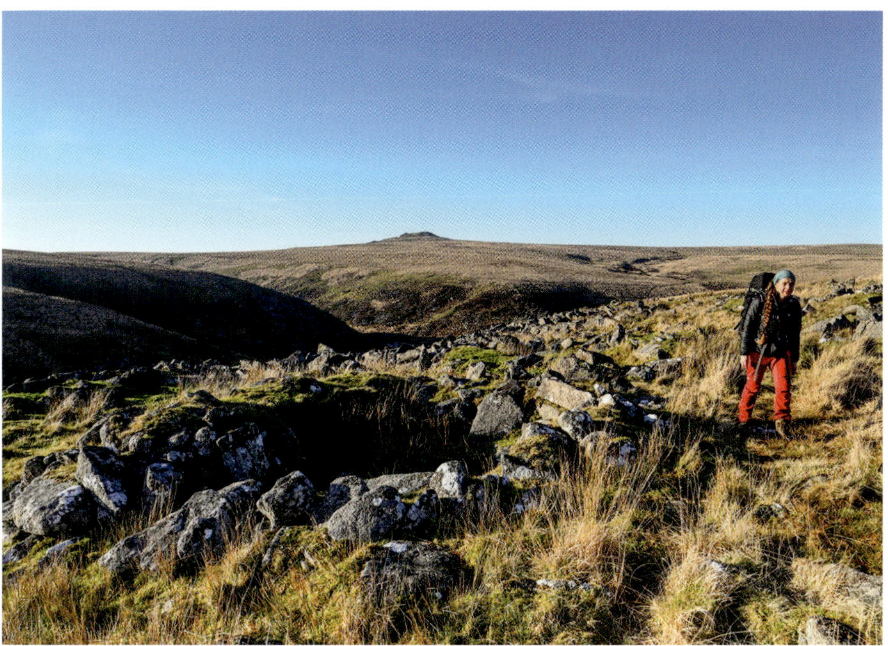

One of the hut circles in the prehistoric village on the alternative route.

1a Climb up the far slope, contouring around to the SE, heading for the area marked 'hut circles' on the OS 1:25,000 sheet, before continuing along the slope to Sandy Ford, and waypoint **2** in the main route above.

2a Return by either route.

Just beyond the former rail line, east of Great Links Tor.

17 Corn Ridge

Start / Finish	Sourton SX 535 903 / 50.6938, -4.0756
Distance	10.5km / 6.5 miles
Ascent	390m
Time	4 – 5 hours

We've met the odd granite upswell of Branscombe's Loaf already, following a 2km saunter up onto the moor from the village of Sourton (page 123). This is a fine little walk, but if you fancy something a little longer, the Loaf can be left to near the end of a good circular tramp.

As you turn south off the A30, Sourton Tors form the first bumpy bit, high on the moorland edge. Parked near the church, with the sun rising behind this scattered collection of geology, the climb looks somewhat tougher than the map suggests. In the end, the rock-strewn slope provides just the right warm up for the walk ahead. The view south towards your next goal is inspiring, and Great Links Tor only falls briefly from view as you approach along a sturdy track.

From a distance, Dartmoor tors often look larger than they really are, and while from the ridge Great Links Tor seemed quite sizable, you might expect the same shrinkage. With a final stroll up a grass slope, you'll probably be pleased then to find this gate-like formation continues to look satisfyingly solid, standing as a fitting sentinel on the moorland edge.

It also provides the first glimpse of the metamorphic understatement that is Kitty Tor. This put upon (quite literally) little outcrop isn't the most inspiring spot on Dartmoor. However, while the modest collection of low granite mounds and military detritus isn't much to look at, the views are excellent, taking in the curved ridge holding High Willhays up and away to the north-east.

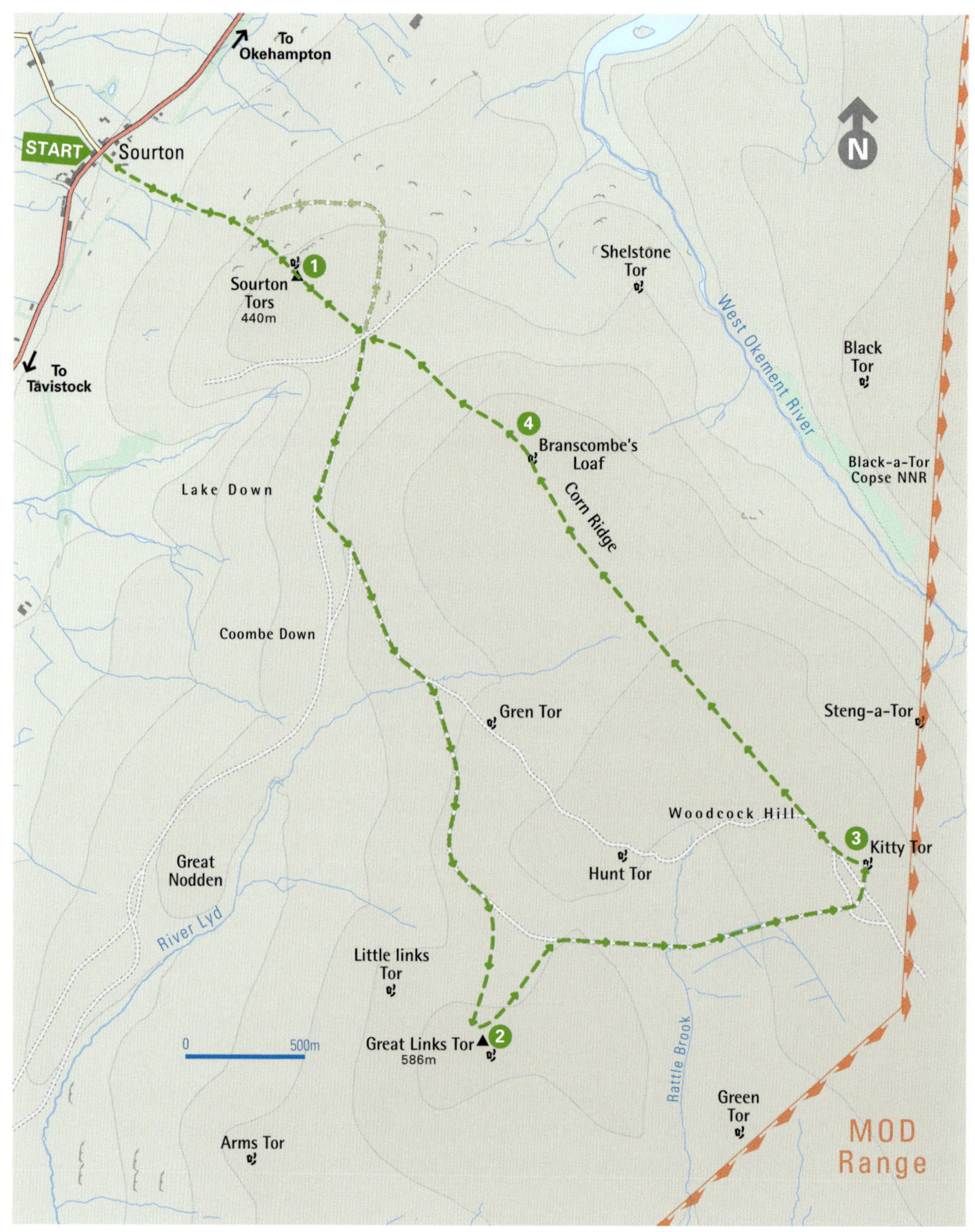

To Okehampton
START
Sourton
To Tavistock
Sourton Tors 440m
1
Shelstone Tor
West Okement River
Black Tor
4
Branscombe's Loaf
Black-a-Tor Copse NNR
Corn Ridge
Lake Down
Coombe Down
Gren Tor
Steng-a-Tor
Woodcock Hill
3
Kitty Tor
Great Nodden
Hunt Tor
River Lyd
Little links Tor
Rattle Brook
Great Links Tor 586m
2
Green Tor
Arms Tor
MOD Range
0   500m
N

Revelling in the sense of space, set out on a bearing to tramp across Corn Ridge. Lots of sky and a remarkable feeling of isolation more than make up for the squidgy and ephemeral apology for a path.

After wandering around and perhaps over the Loaf, possibly trying to picture the Bronze Age activities within the ditch and bank that encircles the outcrop, the view out from the cairns at the top of the slope that drops to Sourton Down rarely disappoints. Quite a bit of Cornwall is visible along the horizon in good weather.

 **START** Head E alongside Sourton's church, and uphill to Sourton Tors.

1 Continue SE from the tors, dropping slightly to a union of tracks, where you take the route heading south. Leave this track where a path veers off to the left, climbing gently to another good track, which continues uphill towards Great Links Tor. Leave this track after it turns SE and head up onto the tor.

2 Drop NE to regain the track before the valley bottom, walking through a demolished building and up to Kitty Tor.

3 Walk on a bearing across Corn Ridge towards the invisible Branscombe's Loaf.

4 Continue NW towards Sourton Tors, returning the way you arrived (alternatively, visit the abandoned ice factory, described on page 123).

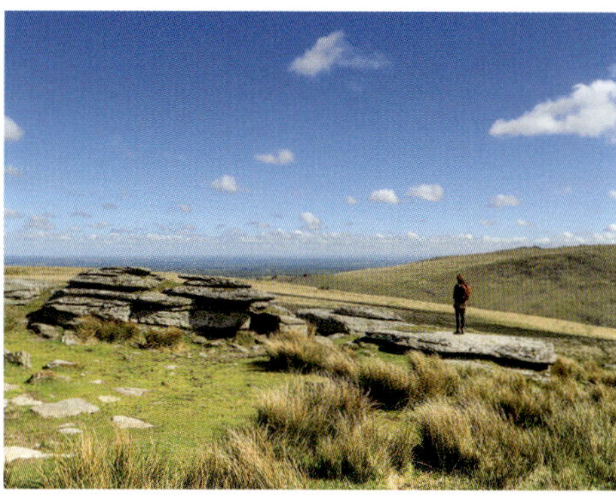

Looking out from Kitty Tor.

Approaching Hen Tor.

18 Lee Moor

Start / Finish	Car Park at SX 561 644 / 50.4617, -4.0288
Distance	14km / 8.5 miles
Ascent	310m
Time	4 – 5 hours

Setting out from this corner of the moor it's a little hard to ignore the 3,000-hectare elephant in the Dartmoor room. Clay extraction started at the edge of Lee Moor in the 1830s as individual farmers began to open small pits. By 1883, there were five large clay works in the area, and the English China Clay Company, or ECC, was formed in 1919 after a merger of several companies. Production in the 1980s was about half a million tons per annum. This quickly produced quite a big hole.

Initially, it's a scar that's pretty hard to overlook. Oddly though, as you head up-hill, weaving between thick patches of reed, you do start to forget. Perhaps this is because there's so much else to look at. The Trowlesworthy tors are certainly impressive, the untouched elements still standing proud amidst a swathe of in-triguing granite quarrying debris.

Head on, and archaeological remains arrive thick and fast; 19th-century rabbit farming (warren) features, medieval houses, and a swathe of early Bronze Age and Neolithic domestic and ritual monuments. The slopes here heave with enclosures, hut circles, and standing stones. Looking out from Hen Tor, the Plym Valley bristles with walls and you cross a couple as you head for Shavercombe Brook.

The waterfall in this tight valley sits below one of the few genuine fall hazards on the moor. It's quite a drop from the mini cleave edge, and not a spot you'd want to stumble upon in the dark. Deep in this little cleft the surrounding moor disappears, and this would be a wonderfully cool spot on a summer afternoon.

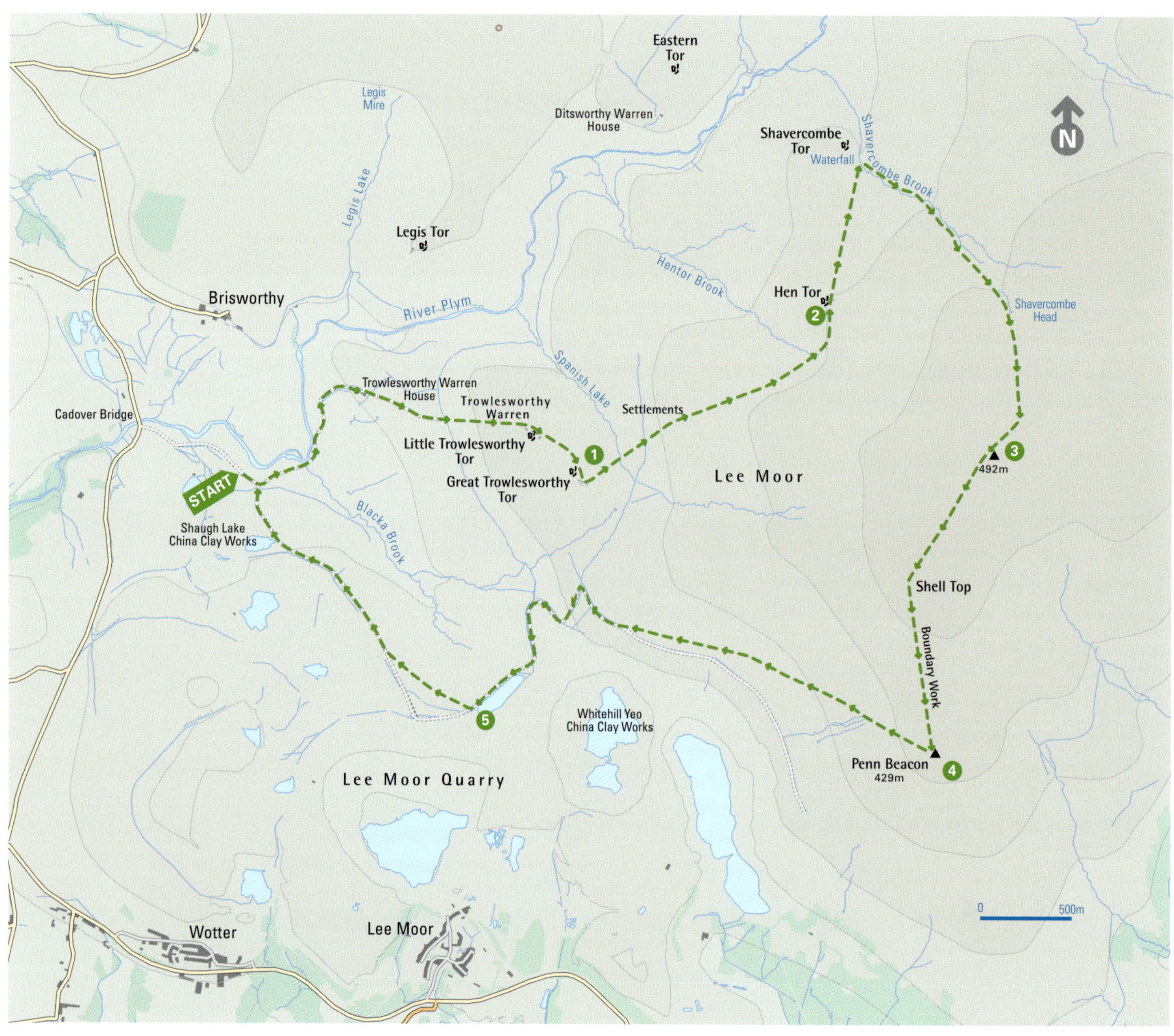

Eastern Tor
Legis Mire
Ditsworthy Warren House
Shavercombe Tor
Waterfall
Shavercombe Brook
Legis Lake
Legis Tor
Hentor Brook
Shavercombe Head
Brisworthy
Hen Tor
2
River Plym
Spanish Lake
Settlements
Cadover Bridge
Trowlesworthy Warren House
Trowlesworthy Warren
1
Lee Moor
3
492m
Little Trowlesworthy Tor
Great Trowlesworthy Tor
START
Shaugh Lake China Clay Works
Blacka Brook
Shell Top
5
Whitehill Yeo China Clay Works
Boundary Work
Penn Beacon
429m
4
Lee Moor Quarry
0   500m
Wotter
Lee Moor
N

Climbing out, we followed the stream uphill in thickening cloud, and could see little more than a couple of hundred metres until we met Penn Beacon. Here, as we sat eating a snack, the mist lifted suddenly, and the full extent of the clay pit spread out before us. Yes, quite a big hole.

START Turn left out of the car park, heading along the track to Trowlesworthy Warren Farm, where you skirt around to the north of the stead, before continuing, up to Little and then Great Trowlesworthy Tors.

1 Turn north to cross Spanish Lake and climb the opposite slope. From the top, in clear weather, Hen Tor should be visible beyond some rough and sometimes damp ground.

2 Head N, perhaps on a bearing, to find the waterfall in a deep cleft, then follow the stream uphill along the south bank. A quad bike track will eventually swing round to head for the trig point.

3 Veer slightly left to follow a clear path to Shell Top, before following the low remains of a boundary bank out to Penn Beacon.

4 Drop NW to eventually meet an old quarry road which bends around a deep excavation.

5 After crossing the leat, you can cut the corner to get back to the road, heading on towards the river and the car park.

Looking out over the clay works from Penn Beacon.

Mount Misery.

Routes 15–20km

19 Cross country

Start / Finish   Combestone Tor car park SX 670 718 / 50.5307, -3.8779

Distance   16km / 10 miles

Ascent   290m

Time   5 hours

It's likely there was once a full string of medieval crosses set out across Dartmoor, marking a safe route between Buckfast and Buckland Abbeys. Most stood between the modern reservoirs of Venford and Burrator and at least fifteen still survive. The route is usually called the Monk's Path.

Following the slightly meandering line from one stone marker to the other makes for a great walk, and even today it can be undertaken pretty successfully without a map, at least in good weather. Reach a cross, head on in the same direction, and you're likely to spot the next before too long.

Mind you, it's hard to make a circular walk of the whole collection. The only reasonable option, unless you've placed a shuttle vehicle at the end of the journey, is to head right back along the same path. Not the best outcome, and for most a touch too far for an enjoyable day out anyway. Taking in just eight of the old markers, however, this walk allows for something of an elongated horseshoe. Not the full cross clutch, but still a fine cross-linked saunter over the uplands.

Stood at Horn's Cross, it's easy to imagine a group of monks stopping to check a well-thumbed scrap of vellum, peering at a hand-written route guide. They would have forded O Brook next, before climbing in search of Horse Ford Cross. It's then a case of crossing crosses from the list; Skaur Ford, then two more on Ter Hill.

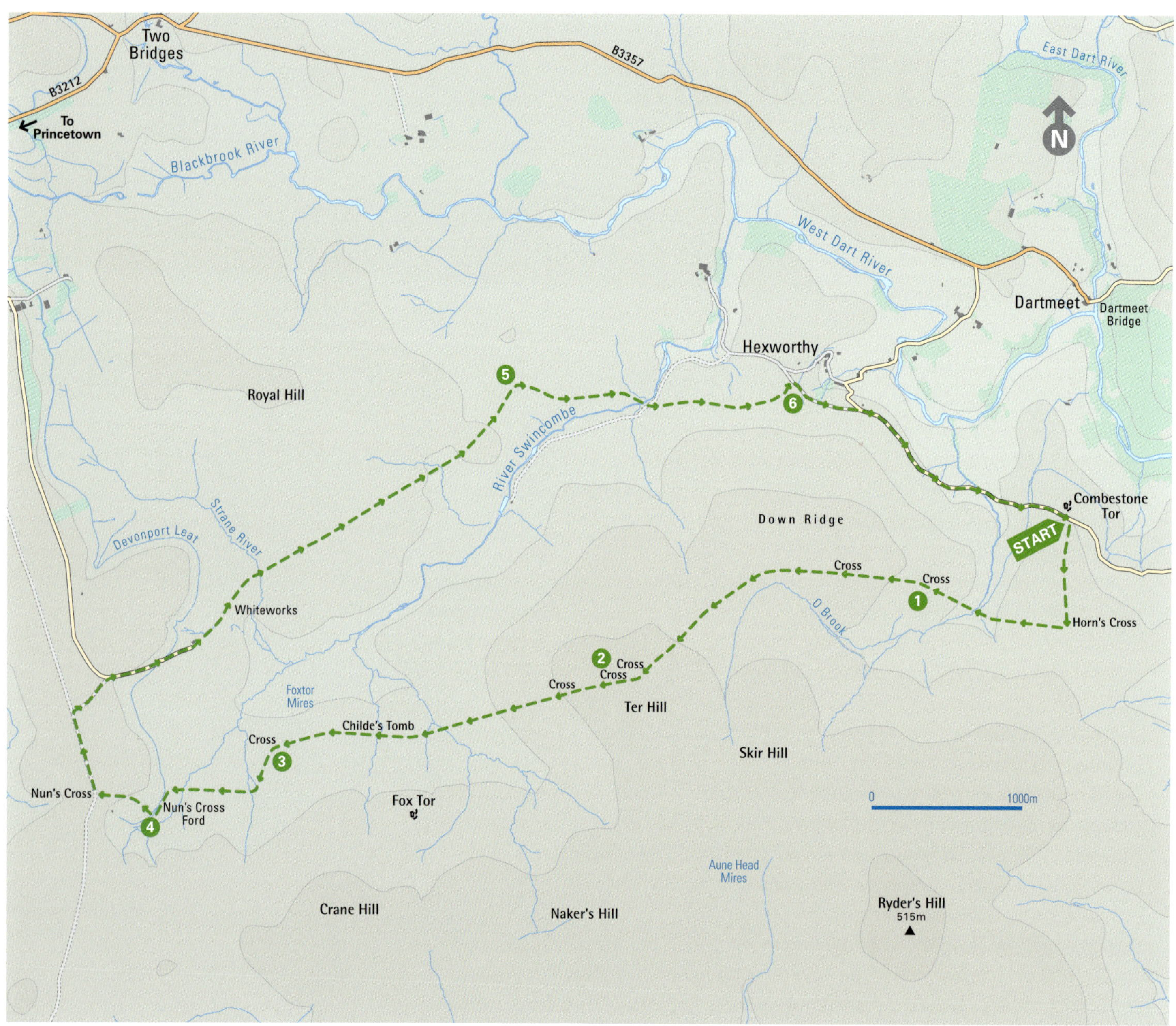

Two Bridges
B3357
East Dart River
B3212
To Princetown
Blackbrook River
West Dart River
Dartmeet
Dartmeet Bridge
Hexworthy
Royal Hill
5
6
River Swincombe
Combestone Tor
Down Ridge
START
Strane River
Devonport Leat
Cross
Cross
1
O Brook
Whiteworks
Horn's Cross
Foxtor Mires
2
Cross
Cross
Cross
Ter Hill
Childe's Tomb
Cross
3
Skir Hill
Nun's Cross
Nun's Cross Ford
4
Fox Tor
Aune Head Mires
Crane Hill
Naker's Hill
Ryder's Hill
515m
0
1000m
N

The wonderfully named Mount Misery Cross stands at the corner of an old field, commanding magnificent views over the notorious Foxtor Mires. From here it's pretty easy to make out the stone structure of Childe's Tomb, sat in the expanse below. Amongst some lumpy ground, diminutive Goldsmith's Cross is less obvious, even when you're close, and it's a slight relief to cross Devonport Leat and find Siward's, or Nun's, Cross so easily.

Half way round then, and the last of the crosses, but not an end to the interest. The extensive remains of a long abandoned tin mine around Whiteworks are still to come, and close by the river, you'll find the evocative and impressive ruins of Swincombe. This abandoned settlement still had residents as recently as the 1960s.

Approaching Childe's Tomb.

START Follow a path uphill to Horn's Cross (SX 6699 7104; all crosses are shown on the OS map) before dropping west to cross O Brook to climb to Horse Ford Cross (6600 7136).

1 Continue in the same direction to find Skaur Ford Cross (65475 7143; in poor visibility take a bearing), then skirt the stream before heading SW, along an increasingly obvious path, for the high ground of Ter Hill (642 707) and its two crosses.

2 Continue west from the westerly cross to Mount Misery Cross (6366 7059), then walk on sight, or a bearing, to Childe's Tomb Cross (6258 7030).

3 Skirt a derelict boundary across rough ground to Goldsmith's Cross (6165 7016), continuing along this boundary to follow a distinct wall west to Devonport Leat, turning SW to cross a footbridge.

4 Follow a distinct path NW to Nun's Cross (604 699), turning right along a clear track, before turning right again at the next track junction to find the road through Whiteworks, and out to a clear path skirting the southern edge of Royal Hill.

5 Turn right at a boundary wall, dropping to cross the River Swincombe, before climbing out beyond to take a path to the road.

6 Turn right at the road, then right again at the junction to follow the tarmac back to the car park.

Taking a break by the West Okement.

20 Black-a-tor Copse

Start / Finish   Meldon Reservoir car park SX 562 917 / 50.7079, -4.0386

Distance   17km / 10.5 miles

Ascent   454m

Time   4 – 5 hours

Many years ago, thumbing through a booklet, I found Black-a-tor Copse described as 'one of the best examples of a high-altitude oak woodland in Britain'. High-altitude oak woodland? Who could resist that?

To be fair, we knew this narrow stand of English oaks quite well already, at least from above. One of my favourite stony lumps on the moor is the outcrop after which the copse is named, and we'd often looked down from Black Tor, either on the cushiony summer canopy, or the close-packed bare branches of colder months. It was about time we shunned the ridge for a change and paid a visit.

Once there, after clambering over the moss and lichen covered boulders, working our way through the wood between the wonderful collection of contorted trunks, the West Okement River valley stretched out alluringly ahead. Instead of heading as usual for high ground, why not keep at the same level and follow that instead?

Admittedly, a decision like this is a lot easier if you live locally. Fellwalkers do like to walk fells after all, and the draw of higher ground is ever present. But comforted by having been up there a few dozen times before, we decided to make a looping return to the van, keeping as low as possible.

And our walk along the valleys turned out to be quite an eye-opener. Even if we'd not yet visited the high ground of the Yes Tor and High Willhays ridge, or the two Mill Tors, I'm sure this low route would have been fascinating. For us, as is so often the case when experiencing a new and unexpected perspective on an old friend, the day was fascinating.

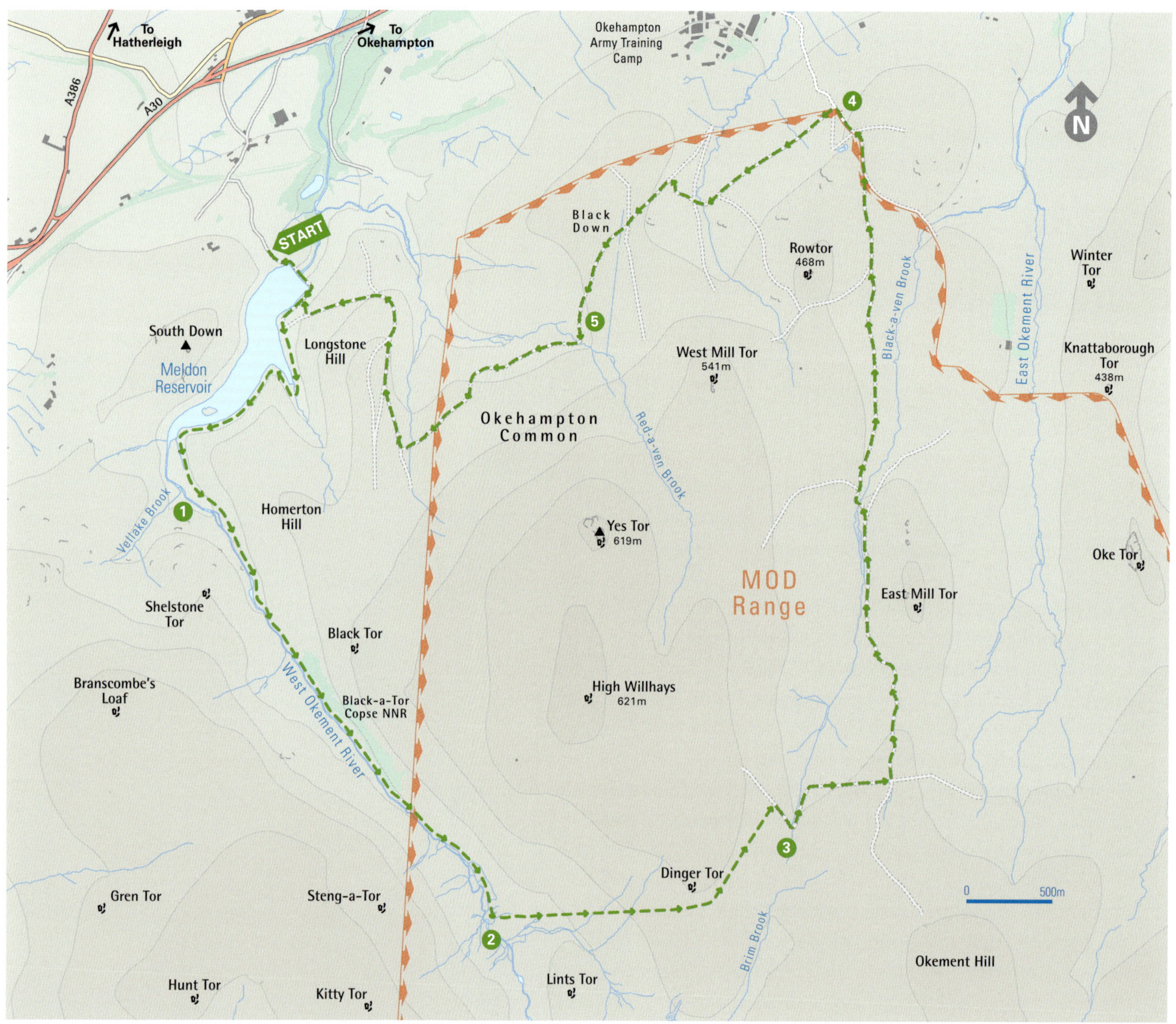

To Hatherleigh
To Okehampton
A386
A30
Okehampton Army Training Camp
START
N
Black Down
Rowtor 468m
Winter Tor
South Down
Meldon Reservoir
Longstone Hill
West Mill Tor 541m
Knattaborough Tor 438m
East Okement River
Black-a-ven Brook
1
5
Okehampton Common
Red-a-ven Brook
Homerton Hill
Yes Tor 619m
MOD Range
Oke Tor
Shelstone Tor
Vellake Brook
East Mill Tor
Black Tor
West Okement River
Branscombe's Loaf
High Willhays 621m
Black-a-Tor Copse NNR
3
Gren Tor
Steng-a-Tor
Dinger Tor
Brim Brook
0   500m
2
Okement Hill
Hunt Tor
Kitty Tor
Lints Tor

Meeting the old army track, just beyond our low altitude avoidance of Dinger Tor, our eyes no longer fixed on the next step, we had the chance to lift our gaze. With heads held high, we took in all that stunning ground, lifting high on every side.

While discussing Black-a-tor Copse it would be a shame not to mention the swimming. The West Okement River, which flows alongside, is hardly big, but as it tumbles from one slew of rounded granite stones to another, it does possess some lovely pools, many shaded by outstretched oak limbs. Quite a few of these are large enough for a dip, and on a hot day mid walk, or if camped here on a sultry summer evening, they are hard to resist.

START Turn left at the car park to cross the dam, following the far side of the reservoir SW to its end.

1 Before reaching the bridge, turn SE, at first on a good track, to follow the valley through Black-a-Tor copse and on towards Lints Tor.

2 As you meet the boggy ground close to the hillock holding Lints Tor, turn east, climbing to contour around the south and east side of Dinger Tor before finding a firm track to the NE of the tor.

3 Turn right onto the track, turning left again at a crossroad on the ridge to follow another track south.

4 As you drop downhill beyond Rowtor, and a couple of hundred metres beyond an old quarry depression, follow a clear path that strikes out to the left, crossing a stream and a tarmac road before meeting a firm track, where you turn left.

5 Follow the track (avoiding any forks to the right), to cross Red-a-ven Brook and Okehampton common, before contouring around Longstone Hill and back to the car park.

Black-a-tor Copse.

Ryder's Hill, with the Red Lake spoil heap in the distance.

21 Red Lake clay works

Start / Finish	Car park at SX 698 700 / 50.5150, -3.8383
Distance	17.5km / 11 miles
Ascent	450m
Time	5 – 6 hours

Set deep at the centre on the southern side of the moor, in the middle of a wide featureless plain, sits a perfect miniature mountain. It's a bit of a surprise, and looks as if some reclusive model maker has been hard at work on their obsession with Mount Fuji. It's hard to resist the urge to take a closer look.

Any walk out to the spoil heap at the abandoned Red Lake china clay works is quite a trek. This route is one of the shortest, but there is a penalty to pay. As a Dartmoor Rescue friend put it recently, this walk is "a bit of a slog." While this route might appear on the map to chart a safe course midway between the Fishlake and Ryder's Mires, it's still a remarkably wet experience.

Water seems almost part of the geology in these parts, and blanket peat holds moisture close to the surface, even on the highest ground. Arrive at Ryder's Hill, with mini-Fuji directly ahead, and your feet are probably damp already. As you head out along a farmer's quad bike track, water pools ominously around every step. You then reach the sprawling mire-zone alongside the infant River Avon.

As if enjoying your discomfort, and just as you think you've reached your goal, this route saves the very worst section for the last 50 to 100 metres. My suspicion is that those clay miners threw up this mound of spoil simply to provide themselves with somewhere dry on which to stand.

The China Clay Corporation Ltd was founded in 1910, only a few years after the discovery of usable clay deposits around Red Lake Brook. Somewhere in excess of

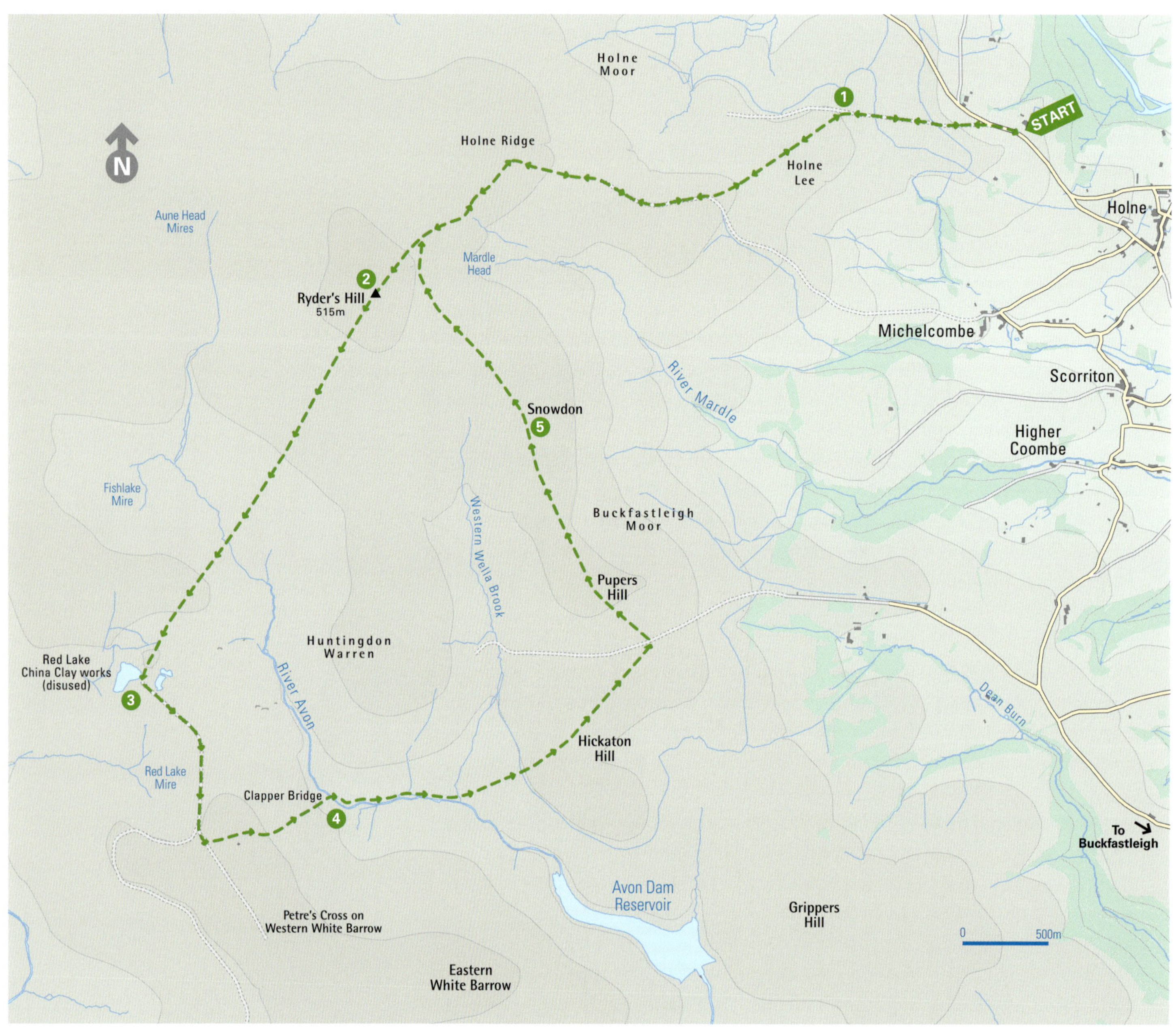

N
START
1
Holne Moor
Holne Ridge
Holne Lee
Holne
Aune Head Mires
Mardle Head
Ryder's Hill
515m
2
Michelcombe
River Mardle
Scorriton
Higher Coombe
Fishlake Mire
Snowdon
5
Buckfastleigh Moor
Western Wella Brook
Red Lake China Clay works (disused)
3
Huntingdon Warren
Pupers Hill
River Avon
Red Lake Mire
Hickaton Hill
Dean Burn
Clapper Bridge
4
To Buckfastleigh
Petre's Cross on Western White Barrow
Avon Dam Reservoir
Grippers Hill
Eastern White Barrow
0   500m

two-million tons of the stuff was thought to lie below the soggy surface, justifying the cost not only of a new pit, but a railway to serve it (and the drainage to make that rail link usable). In the end, excavation continued only until 1932, when diminishing returns forced an abandonment. Today we're left with the bed to that railway line (and a very useful dry route into the central moor), three lakes and that alluring landmark, just waiting for another pair of soggy feet.

START Turn left onto the road, then left again soon after to follow a good track uphill.

1 Soon after a boundary stone (on the right), turn left onto a clear path/quad track that leads up onto Holne Lee. On meeting another quad bike track, turn left to head up onto Ryder's Hill (take the right fork after the dip).

2 In clear weather, the track out to Red Lake is obvious. Otherwise, take a bearing and follow the quad bike route. The river crossing can be a little tricky in wet weather.

3 Take the abandoned railway away from the demolished buildings, then turn along a path on the left just before the second bend, that leads downhill to a clapper bridge over the Avon.

4 Follow a clear path to the stile and medieval cross SE of Huntingdon Warren, before taking a clear path over Hickaton Hill, tuning left at the path junction to climb to Pupers Hill and on to Snowdon.

5 Avoid the clear route to Ryder's Hill, instead taking a quad bike track that contours below the summit to the east, before meeting the earlier route above Mardle Head.

Approaching the Red Lake spoil heap.

Belstone Ridge.

 Hangingstone Hill and Cosdon Beacon

22 Hangingstone Hill and Cosdon Beacon

Start / Finish	Belstone car park SX 621 938 / 50.7275, -3.9548
Distance	18km / 11 miles
Ascent	510m
Time	5 – 6 hours

When a visitor suggests they'd like to be taken on a good walk, most of us will turn to a favourite. No matter how many times it's tramped, this is the route that never seems to pale.

Actually, most of us will probably have a collection of these 'turn-to' walks, ranging in length and severity to suit the experience and suspected stamina of the enthusiastic guest. Well, this is the one I choose if a request is made for a proper hill walk, an appeal from a cousin or niece with a pair of well-used three-season boots clasped eagerly in one hand.

By chance, the starting point sits at the closest point on the moorland edge to our home. This, though, certainly isn't the only reason for its high ranking in the Gent walking route league.

From the moment the village of Belstone is left behind, the walk climbs purposefully, soon placing host and guest on a classic Dartmoor tor. On a good day, the views across the lowlands of mid and north Devon are unlikely to disappoint even the most discerning visitor.

A clear, cropped-grass path then leads along what I consider the most interesting ridge on the moor. Not the highest, that's true. This honour goes to the whaleback lump off to the west, High Willhays at the centre, Yes Tor a touch lower at the northern end.

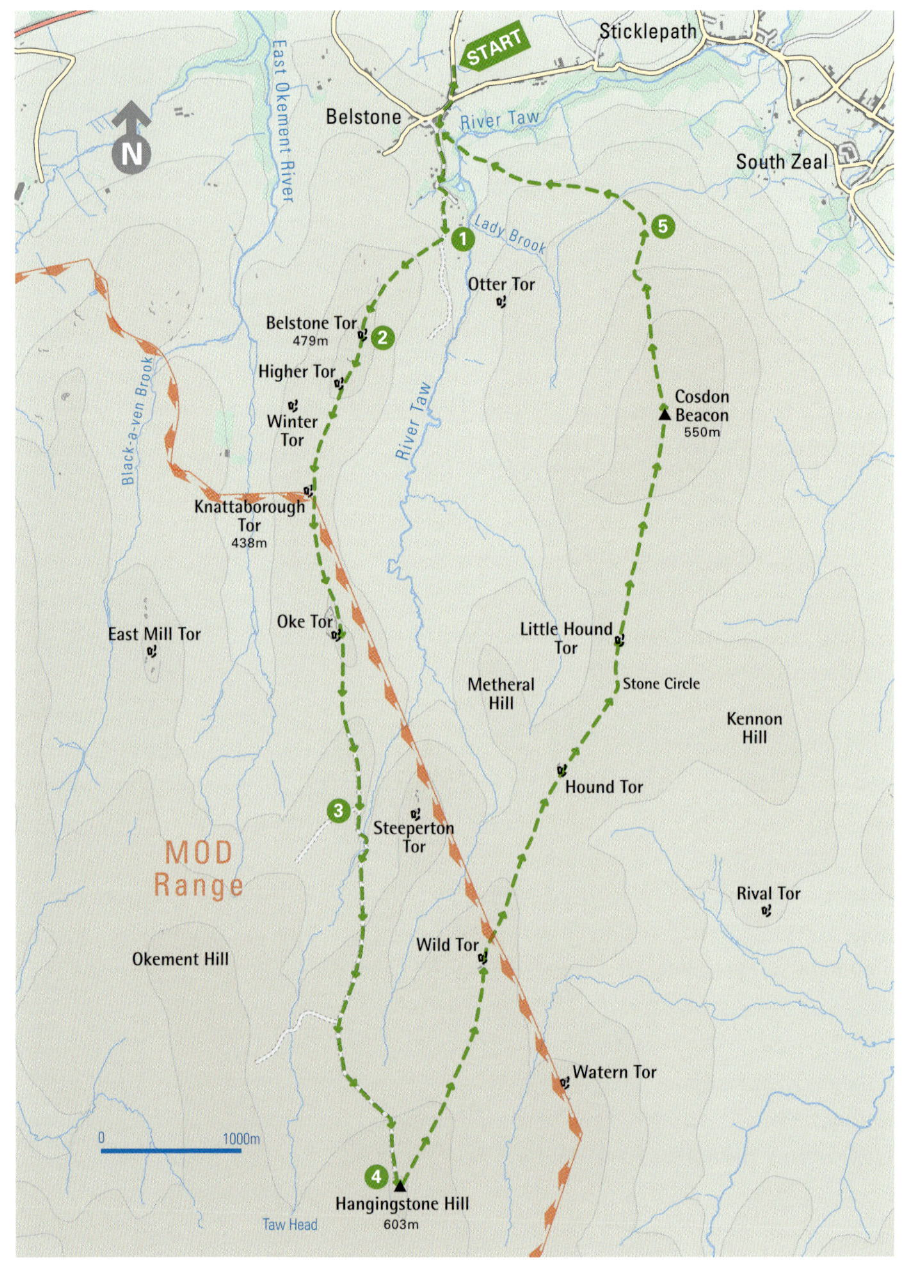

START
Sticklepath
Belstone
River Taw
South Zeal
East Okement River
Lady Brook
1
Otter Tor
5
Belstone Tor
479m
2
Higher Tor
Winter Tor
Cosdon Beacon
550m
Black-a-ven Brook
River Taw
Knattaborough Tor
438m
East Mill Tor
Oke Tor
Little Hound Tor
Stone Circle
Metheral Hill
Kennon Hill
MOD Range
3
Steeperton Tor
Hound Tor
Rival Tor
Okement Hill
Wild Tor
0   1000m
Watern Tor
4
Hangingstone Hill
603m
Taw Head
N

Back on our chosen ridge, pretty tor follows pretty tor as you head for a stream crossing, sunk deep in a cleft to the side of Steeperton. This granite exuberance is perhaps fortunate. It has to be admitted that the outward destination, the turning point of the walk, doesn't exactly offer the most dramatic of summits. What it lacks in geological aesthetics, it more than makes up for in character and views. Hangingstone Hill is bleak and bare, but remote and high. It always feels like the heart of the moor to me.

Impressive metamorphic lumpiness is soon back on the menu again, and Wild Tor manages to live up to its name, with what are now stunning views of Belstone Ridge and the early part of the walk.

After the rather retiring qualities of the two Hound Tors, and a chance to visit a Bronze Age stone circle, it's up over 'Cawsand' (as it is known to the locals), or Cosdon Hill as it is named on the OS sheets, and a final chance to gaze back across a fine Dartmoor walk. It's an overused term, but this one really is a classic.

Watching a retreating hailstorm from Cawsand, or Cosdon Beacon as it's named on OS mapping.

START From Belstone car park walk through village, taking the left fork at the village green. Follow the road uphill, through a gate, and out onto the open moor.

1 After about 200m, bear right off the track (there is a faint but dependable path) and climb the broad hill, working through scattered stones on the left (east) side of the first, unnamed, tor.

2 Clamber through Belstone Tor (there is a path, of a sort), crossing Irishman's Wall to to pass Higher Tor to the left, before following a now clear path along the broad ridge, meeting a rough track that drops to a rough stepping-stone crossing of the Taw.

3 Follow the track to Hangingstone Hill.

4 Almost turn back on yourself to follow a rough, sometimes soggy, path past Wild Tor, over Hound Tor, Little Hound Tor and Cosdon Hill.

5 At the far side of Cosdon follow the path west to contour around the end of the hill, before dropping to a bridge to recross the Taw and climb back to Belstone.

Passing quarry waste from King's Tor, to look out over west Devon and Bodmin Moor.

23 King's Tor, Sharpitor and South Hessary Tor

Start / Finish	Princetown car park SX 589 735 / 50.5443 -3.9921
Distance	18km / 11 miles
Ascent	316m
Time	5 – 6 hours

Dartmoor might look wild and untouched today, an island of grey-green emptiness left thoughtfully unsullied amidst a sea of lowland bustle, but for a long time this certainly wasn't the plan. In fact, for many years there was every intention of making this heathery upland dome look just like the surrounding farmland below – fenced in and subjugated, made to pay its way. Culminating in the late eighteenth and nineteenth centuries, huge effort was expended in order to turn this aim into reality, and a closer look at the moor soon reveals the impact.

One of the most remarkable acts of exploitative determination saw a railway line carved in huge sweeping arcs up the south-west side of the moor to Princetown. The builders had two key aims, to supply a collection of intrepid farmers with the equipment needed to tame the incalcitrant wilderness, but most importantly, to assist in the removal of as much granite as possible. In the end, thankfully, these exploits failed, leaving us with some of the biggest man-made holes on the moor – and an excellent surface for easy walking.

Cut through the high bits, raised over the low, the level bed of the old railway, offers a very smooth route into the wild. It's a rare and ideal opportunity for anyone wishing to experience a little Dartmoor rough stuff, from a forgiving surface. Along the way, with none of the hillwalkers' usual need to keep an eye out for safe footing, there's also the chance to look up and enjoy some outstanding views lying out beyond those broad sweeping curves.

To Tavistock
To Moretonhampstead
Rundelstone Tor
Herne Hole Tor
Hollow Tor
B3212
North Hessary Tor
HM Prison
Blackbrook River
River Walkham
Little King's Tor
King's Tor
401m
Foggintor Quarries
(disused)
Princetown
START
Swelltor Quarries
(disused)
South Hessary Tor
450m
Devonport Leat
Walkhampton Common
Ingra Tor
B3212
Leeden Tor
Black Tor
Hart Tor
386m
Hart Tor Brook
1
2
Cramber Tor
5
Devonport Leat
Older Bridge
Sharpitor
Leather Tor
Leather Tor Bridge
Newleycombe Lake
Peak Hill
4
Lowery Tor
3
Down Tor
0   500m
To Yelverton

It doesn't last though. This is Dartmoor after all. And as the middle section of this walk leaves the railway, it soon grows lumpy. As you meet Sharpitor there's even the pleasing opportunity for a bit of a scramble.

A short extension of this bumpy bit soon leads down an extremely brief section of road. And then it's time to meet another example of mans' moorland taming activities. This time it's tin miners that are responsible, and possibly the church; the tracks they built to cross this rough corner of the moor wend their way to Princetown over ground that's almost as even as that old railway.

START Turn left at the car park entrance, taking a left turn to leave the track before the cottages (signed 'Princetown Railway Cycle Route') to follow the old railway line around King's Tor.

1 As you leave an enclosed area to the south of Ingra Tor, turn left to follow a clear path uphill to the road.

2 Cross the road, and either climb Sharpitor or detour around to either side, before heading downhill to the right of Leather Tor, following a rutted path along the fence line to the road below.

3 Almost as soon as you meet the road, leave it to the left to follow a signed footpath along the lower edge of a leat, turning right onto a track where the leat is crossed by a bridge. Follow the track downhill to Leather Tor Bridge over the River Meavy.

4 Bear left beyond the bridge, then take the right fork. On reaching a T junction at the edge of the wood, turn left (east) to follow the new track uphill.

5 At a crossroads in the track above Older Bridge, turn left, which takes you to the track heading N to Princetown.

Up onto Sharpitor.

Following the Staldon Row.

24 Erme Valley

Start / Finish	Car park at SX 643 594 / 50.4200, -3.91106
Distance	19km / 12 miles
Ascent	350m
Time	6 – 7 hours

At some rain-drenched point on this walk I joked that providing a route guide would require only three words: follow the stones.

Admittedly, this seemingly insubstantial advice doesn't really work at the start, and you have to work your way up the Erme valley for quite a distance before reaching the Dancers stone circle. From here on though, you really can simply wander alongside an incredible row of upright granite lumps.

Even today, following millennia of pilfering and disturbance, the Staldon row is reputed to contain as many as 1,000 stones. Often placed no more than a metre or two apart, the constituent elements of the monument head out across the slopes, flanking the river, before crossing it to extend as far as Green Hill. In all that's a distance of 3.3km. Some claim it's the longest stone row in the world. It's certainly the longest on Dartmoor by quite a margin, and a very useful navigation aid.

We didn't follow the Staldon stones as they met the rain-swollen flow of the River Erme near Red Lake, choosing instead to head further upstream to cross at Dry Lake Ford (still a boots off and near knee-deep wade). We then met the stone row again on the slopes near Red Lake (a stream, as you may recall, rather than a body of water) before climbing in search of Western White Tor.

From here, as the ridge led away into the early winter gloom, it was back to stone stalking again. Now placed much further apart, and set up a lot later than their prehistoric cousins on the other side of the valley, these stones mark the line of

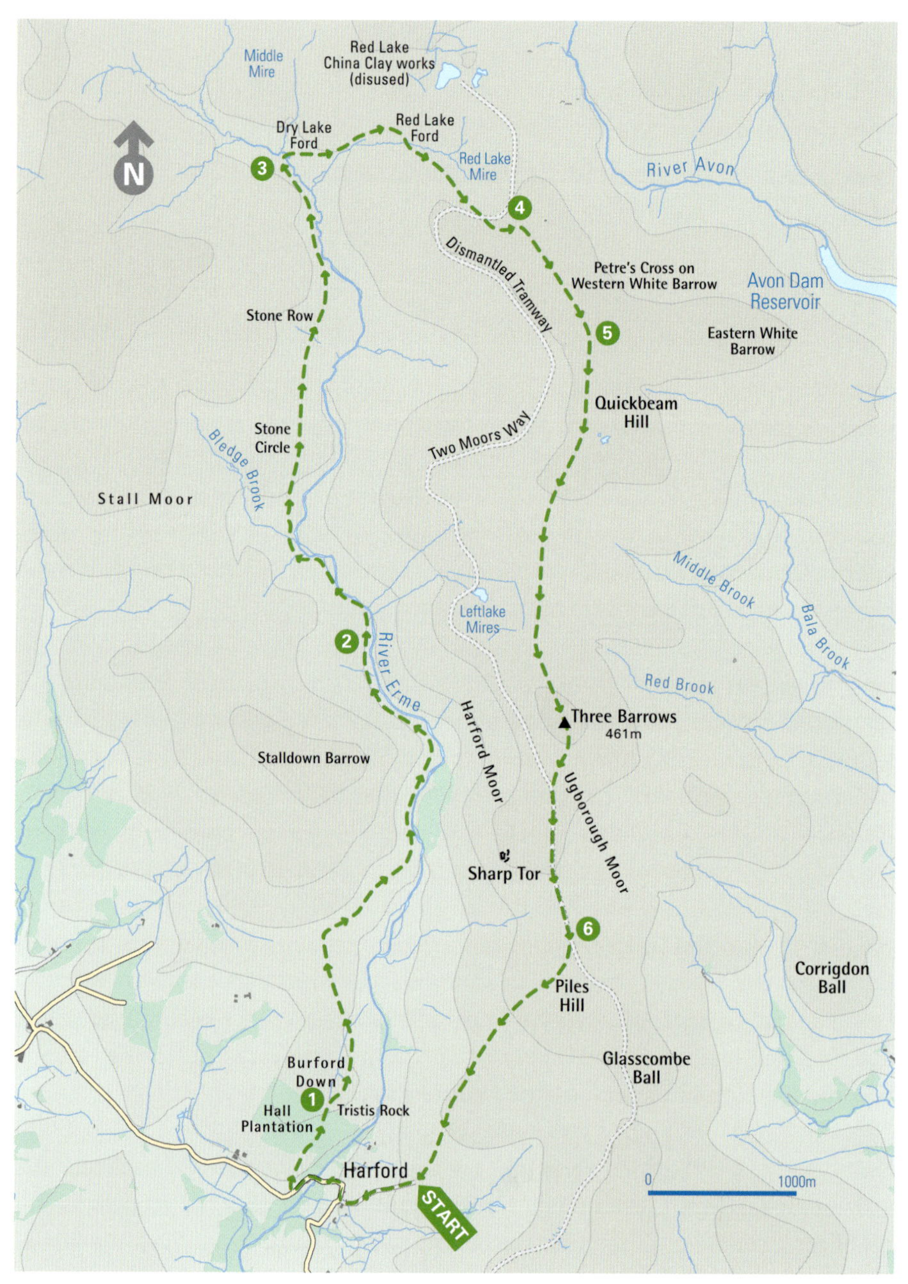

N
Middle Mire
Red Lake China Clay works (disused)
Dry Lake Ford
Red Lake Ford
Red Lake Mire
River Avon
3
4
Dismantled Tramway
Petre's Cross on Western White Barrow
Avon Dam Reservoir
Stone Row
5
Eastern White Barrow
Stone Circle
Quickbeam Hill
Bledge Brook
Two Moors Way
Stall Moor
2
River Erme
Leftlake Mires
Middle Brook
Bala Brook
Red Brook
Stalldown Barrow
Harford Moor
Three Barrows
461m
Ugborough Moor
Sharp Tor
6
Corrigdon Ball
Piles Hill
Glasscombe Ball
Burford Down
1
Tristis Rock
Hall Plantation
Harford
START
0   1000m

a parish boundary. They still worked well as route markers though, and as each granite 'post' faded into the low cloud to the rear, another would appear almost magically up ahead.

🏃 START ▶ Head back down the road from the car park, turning right at the church to cross the river, taking the second gate (a five-barred type) on the right to head out past Hall Plantation.

❶ Pass Tristis Rock, and make for the top field ahead, where a gate leads to the open moor. You then climb gently to turn right, onto a good track which takes you to a reservoir.

❷ Continue upstream, skirting the edge of the floodplain, leaving the valley floor after crossing Bledge Brook, then climb gently to find the Dancers stone circle and follow the stone row.

❸ In dry summer weather you could follow the stone row to cross the Erme, but in higher water conditions, continue up the valley to cross at Dry Lake Ford, before turning to cross Red Lake (a stream), following a clear path to the bed of the old railway line, turning left.

❹ After about 2–300m, at a granite Two Moors Way marker, take a path to the right, being careful not to follow the TMW itself (which will soon head downhill; this crossroad is not shown accurately on OS mapping). Instead, climb to pass Western White Tor and continue along the broad ridge.

❺ Meeting a fork, take the path on the right, following the stone markers to the large stone cairns atop Ugborough Moor, continuing beyond as it veers right to again meet the abandoned railway line, where you turn left.

❻ The right turn before Piles Hill is not marked, but once found, a clear path leads back to the car park.

Passing Western White Tor.

Dartmoor ponies on Hamel Down.

Routes Over 20km (potential two-day walks)

25 Soussons, Corndon and Hamel Downs

Start / Finish	Bennett's Cross car park SX 680 816 / 50.6190, -3.8678
Distance	21km / 13 miles
Ascent	555m
Time	6 – 7 hours

Asked at the end of this walk which bit I'd enjoyed most, I struggled a little for an answer. There had been a very cute foal, struggling to its hooves on brand new legs on the north slope of Corndon Down. Foals are always hard to beat. Then there was the woodland trail, winding alongside the West Webburn river. Even in its bare winter state, this slightly muddy stretch of hazel, holly and oak flanked path was pretty spectacular. The stream rushed nearby between rounded granite stones, before swirling into some surprisingly deep pools, the sunlight reflected gold off the sand at the bottom.

A plethora of archaeological remains vied for attention along almost the entire route. Right from the start, on leaving the medieval cross at the car park, a great expanse of ground had been altered completely by long-abandoned tin mining. A team of mechanical diggers building a modern 4WD training course couldn't have done a more thorough and impressive job.

After this upheaval there then followed huge Bronze Age cairns, a deserted medieval village, a collapsed stone beacon and hut circles, the whole route criss-crossed by the low banks of some truly vast prehistoric field systems. This walk also runs right through the centre of Grimspound, possibly the best-preserved and most impressive pre-Roman settlement on the moor.

In spite of all this, including the simple exhilaration of striding across wide open spaces, it was the colours that provided the star turn of the walk for me.

Corndon Down.

Lit by a low sun, the slopes above Widecombe, seen to the east from Hamel Down, were simply breathtaking. In broad, distinct and very bright bands, these leapt from emerald green across the grass fields near the valley bottom, to the burnt orange of dead bracken on the slopes above. Then, over a bold horizon dotted by the stone eruptions of Honeybag, Chinkwell and Hound Tors, the blue of the sky stepped in, deepening in hue as it soared up and overhead. Even the ponies in the foreground were forgotten for a while.

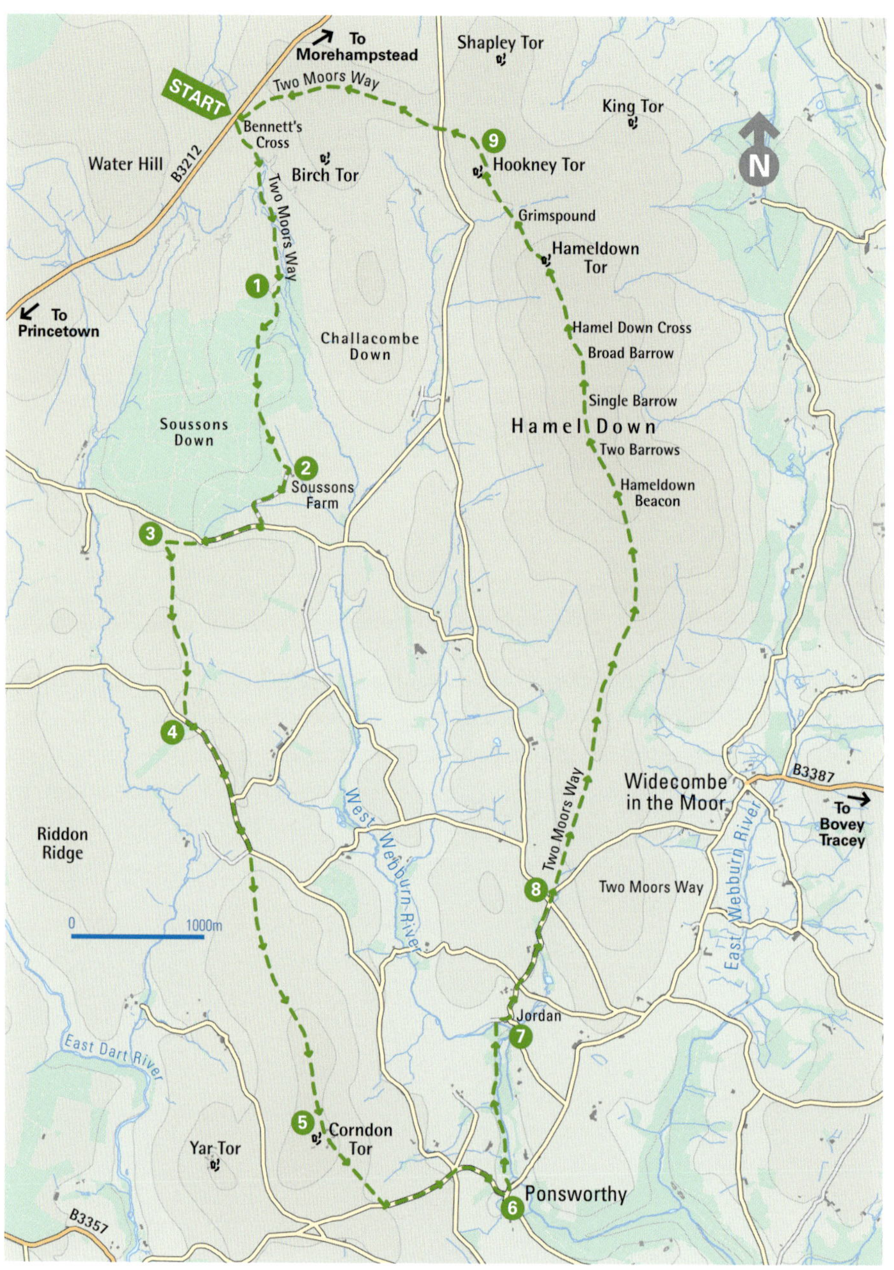

To Morehampstead
Shapley Tor
START
Two Moors Way
King Tor
Bennett's Cross
Water Hill
B3212
Birch Tor
9
Hookney Tor
Two Moors Way
Grimspound
Hameldown Tor
1
To Princetown
Challacombe Down
Hamel Down Cross
Broad Barrow
Single Barrow
Soussons Down
Hamel Down
Two Barrows
2
Soussons Farm
Hameldown Beacon
3
4
Riddon Ridge
West Webburn River
Widecombe in the Moor
B3387
To Bovey Tracey
Two Moors Way
East Dart River
8
Two Moors Way
East Webburn River
0   1000m
Jordan
7
5
Corndon Tor
Yar Tor
6
Ponsworthy
B3357

START From the car park near Bennett's Cross, follow a winding path, downhill through a tin-mined landscape.

1 Soon after entering the wood, take a right turn, signed to Soussons Farm.

2 At Soussons Farm, take the track opposite the gate, signed 'Road Near Grendon', and follow this to the road, where you turn right.

3 After some 500m, take a track on the left, soon turning left again (signed 'Bridlepath'), to walk across the fields. Don't be tempted to follow the new farm track through the wood.

4 Turn left on meeting the road, heading up over Corndon Down, keeping to high ground and finding a path leading to the cairns.

5 Drop downhill SE from Corndon Tor to walk alongside the road, joining it at the junction to reach Ponsworthy.

6 Just before the stream, and immediately beyond a cottage, turn left (signed JORDAN), and then follow the Two Moors Way alongside the stream.

7 At Jordan, take the road uphill (perhaps diverging slightly to visit the abandoned medieval village of Hutholes – signed).

8 At the crossroads, take to the moor, following the Two Moors Way over Hamel Down, deviating at Hameldown Tor to follow the path through Grimspound and up to Hookney Tor.

9 Beyond the tor, on crossing a low bank, turn left onto a path that continues, beyond a road crossing, back to the car park.

One of the longhouses at Hound Tor deserted medieval village.

26 Hound Tor and Haytor

Start / Finish Car park NE of Bennet's Cross SX 682 819 / 50.6218, -3.8647
Distance 23km / 14 miles
Ascent 688m
Time 7 – 8 hours

Set out to explore the east side of Dartmoor and one granite lump in particular tends to catch the eye. If, as is suggested, Hound Tor really does resemble a pack of hunting dogs, lounging on a rise near Swallerton Gate, then Haytor must be their owner. Stood with his horse on the next rise, proud and rather overweight, he gazes out over his moorland edge domain. Haytor is anything but shy and retiring, and as a result, for many visitors to Devon, Haytor is Dartmoor.

True, after a short climb from the car park, a quick wander around will be pretty much their fill of the open moor. A cream tea at Widecombe awaits. Next day, during a drive in search of the prison, there might be a brief halt to photograph a roadside pony, and there will probably be a moment for a selfie on the clapper bridge at Postbridge, but that's often about it. Heading for home, that impressive granite lump will still provide the dominant moorland memory.

Yet despite its fame, for many regular Dartmoor walkers, Haytor, even if conspicuous, represents little more than a peripheral feature; often seen, rarely visited. To reach this tor, tucked right out on the rather busy eastern edge, you have to leave the main moor, threading a way between one unenclosed upland block and another. It is worth the trouble though. This meander amongst the tors of the Widecombe fringe, rarely beyond sight of that famous outcrop, offers a good look at a very different moorland setting. The route can be walked easily enough on a long summer day, but there are many spots where it would be very tempting to tarry a while and pitch a tent.

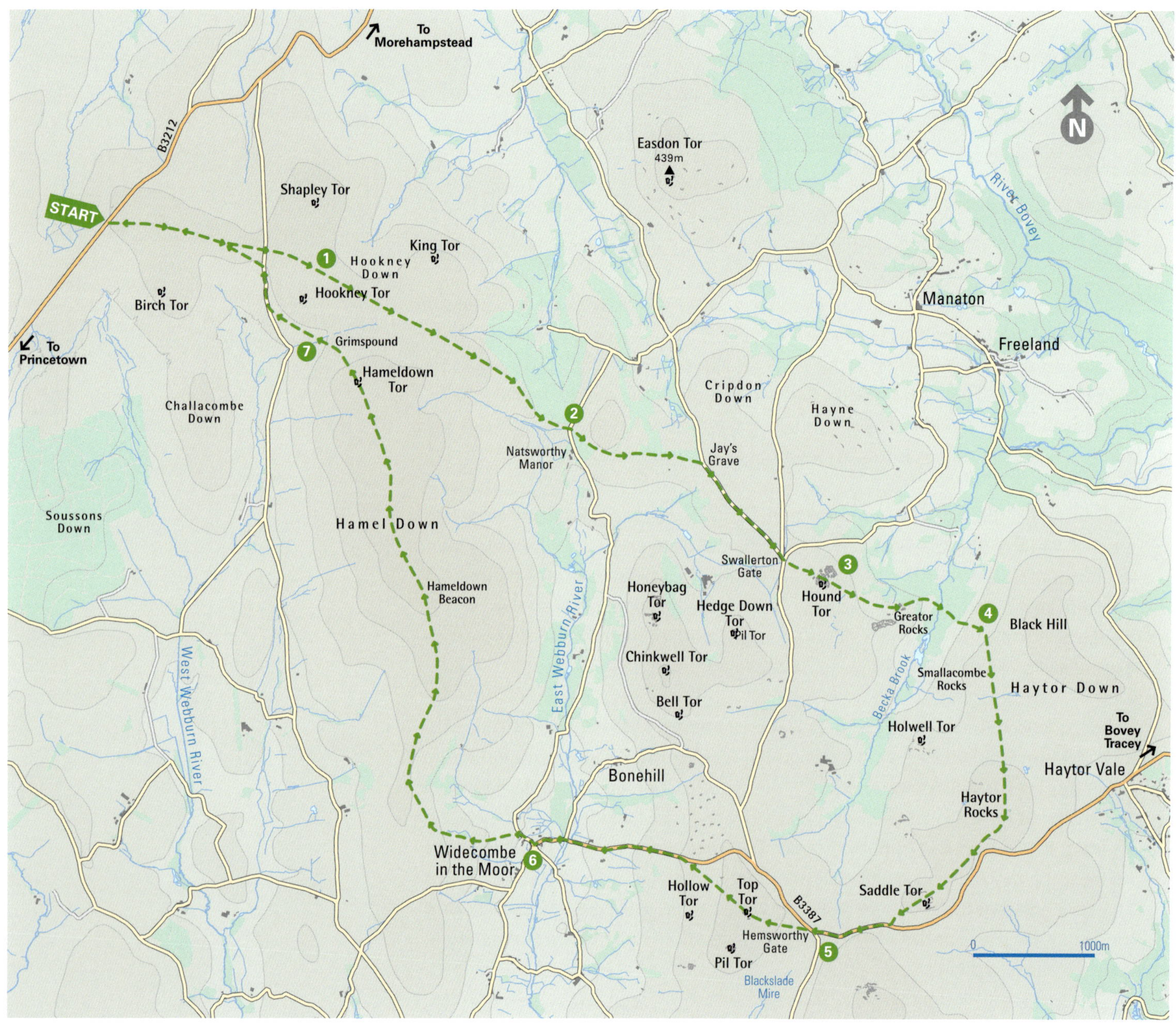

To Morehampstead
To Princetown
To Bovey Tracey
START
N
B3212
Easdon Tor
439m
Shapley Tor
King Tor
Hookney Down
Hookney Tor
Birch Tor
Manaton
Freeland
Grimspound
Hameldown Tor
Cripdon Down
Hayne Down
Challacombe Down
Natsworthy Manor
Jay's Grave
Soussons Down
Hamel Down
Swallerton Gate
Honeybag Tor
Hedge Down Tor
Hound Tor
Greator Rocks
Black Hill
Hameldown Beacon
Pil Tor
Chinkwell Tor
Smallacombe Rocks
Haytor Down
West Webburn River
East Webburn River
Becka Brook
Holwell Tor
Bell Tor
Bonehill
Haytor Rocks
Haytor Vale
Widecombe in the Moor
Hollow Tor
Top Tor
Saddle Tor
B3387
Hemsworthy Gate
Pil Tor
Blackslade Mire
River Bovey
0   1000m

While a map may suggest Dartmoor is a pretty uniform upland lump, the area is actually quite varied. The southern moor, tipped towards the sun, with its distant views of the channel, is quite unlike the high expanses to the north, and neither part feels much like the crinkly western flank facing the Atlantic, windswept and wet. Tucked away on this eastern side is a softer land, noticeably warmer, distinctly drier. Sheltered from the prevailing wind, the vegetation is more verdant. It stands taller and more full. This fringe might lack the sense of isolation of the central high moor, the almost endless sweep of bogs or the highest tors, but it more than makes up for this with a comforting blend of cosiness and occasional haughty drama.

Haytor.

START Follow the Two Moors Way east, away from the car park, crossing the road to climb the hill.

1 At the wall junction continue straight on, following the path along the south side of the wall, before dropping downhill to the gate close to Natsworthy Manor.

2 Turn left at the road, then immediately right to follow the signed footpath to Jay's Grave, turning right here to join the road, before leaving it at Swallerton Gate to climb through Hound Tor.

3 Drop SE to the deserted medieval village, continuing along a clear path that descends to cross Becka Brook.

4 Emerging from woodland, take the path straight uphill, eventually crossing the granite tramway. From Haytor, follow the path SW to Saddle Tor and beyond, along the road edge to Hemsworthy Gate.

5 Climb a path to Top Tor, before dropping NW to follow the road to Widecombe.

6 Beyond the village green take the right fork, very soon leaving the road to the left at a sign to Grimspound, before climbing to follow a path up and along Hamel Down.

7 Take the path running NE away from Grimspound to meet the road, leaving it again, opposite the wall dropping from Hookney Down, to rejoin the Two Moors Way.

The new find at Sittaford.

27 Stone Circles

Start / Finish	Postbridge car park SX 647 788 / 50.5939, -3.9121
Distance	26.5km / 16.5 miles
Ascent	570m
Time	10 – 12 hours

Built in the late Neolithic and early Bronze Age, so roughly 3,500 to 5,000 years ago, stone circles crop up all over Britain. Nobody really knows why they were built, although considering the effort involved they were obviously important. As if these monuments aren't intriguing enough individually, Dartmoor offers a whole new level of stone circle mystery. Depending on who's counting, there are about sixteen up there. But that's not the impressive bit.

It turns out that a great arc of circles was built across the north-east side of the moor, each set about 1km apart. Until recently, it was thought that the remains of this vast semicircle included the stone circles of White Moor, Buttern Hill, Scorhill, Shovel Down and Fernworthy. There are then two more, stood side by side, known as The Grey Wethers.

Suspecting this might not be the whole picture, one amateur archaeologist, Alan Endacott, decided to take a look at the next hill on. After many visits, and following a heather fire, circle number seven was announced in 2014. Remarkably, this Sittaford setting was found not far from a busy footpath, with all the stones toppled to lie flat amongst the low vegetation

This walk sets out first to visit that recent addition. It then strikes out north to find the White Moor circle, before heading back in an anti-clockwise route, following the arc formed by the remaining six.

Looking again at the map, I can't be the first to notice at least one other suspicious looking gap in the arc, so you never know what you might find out there. Who knows, there might once have even been a circle of circles, stretched out to encompass the whole of the northern half of the moor. Now that really would be something to think about.

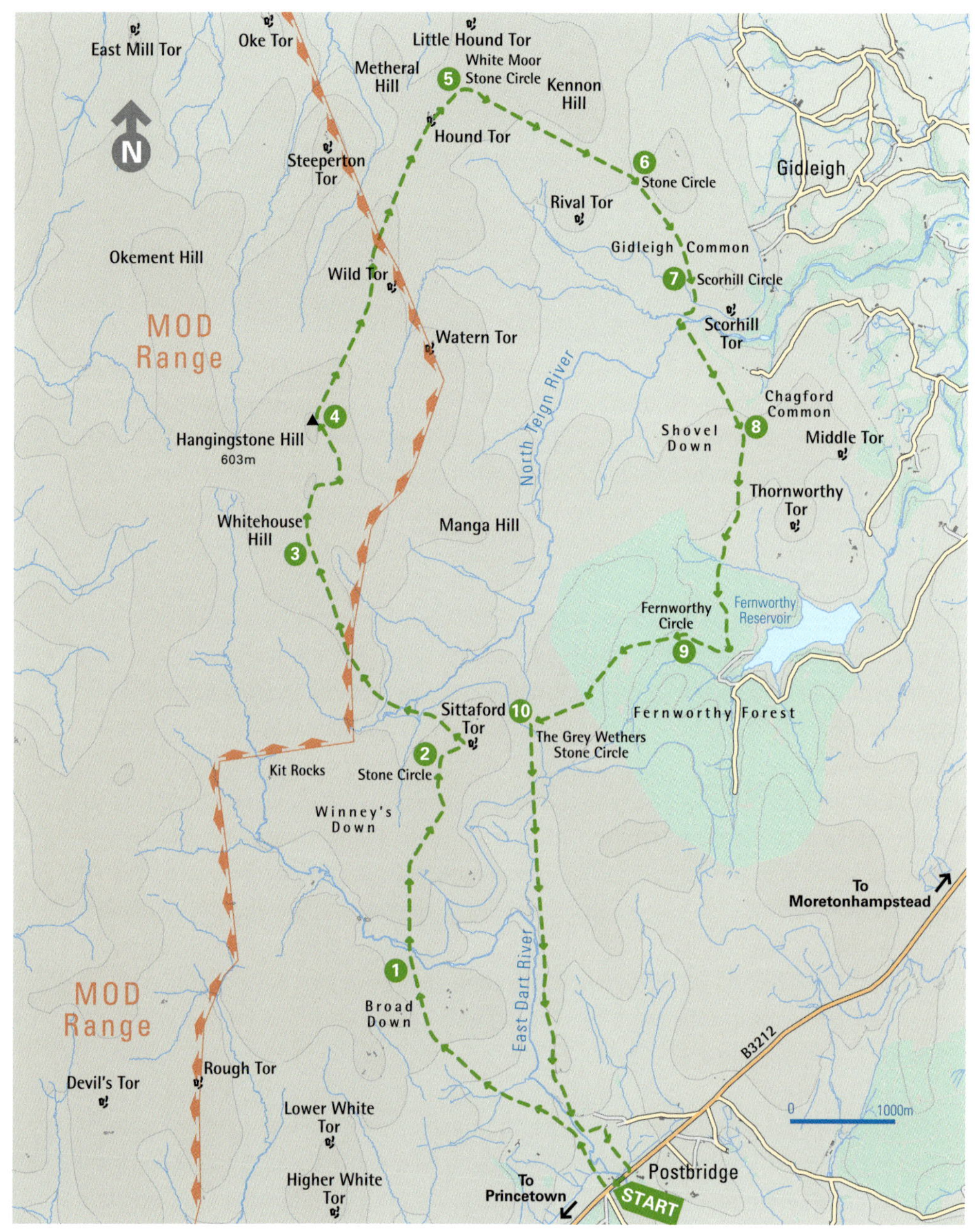

N
East Mill Tor
Oke Tor
Little Hound Tor
White Moor Stone Circle
Metheral Hill
Kennon Hill
5
Hound Tor
6
Stone Circle
Gidleigh
Steeperton Tor
Rival Tor
Gidleigh Common
Okement Hill
7
Scorhill Circle
Wild Tor
Scorhill Tor
MOD Range
Watern Tor
North Teign River
Chagford Common
8
Shovel Down
Middle Tor
4
Hangingstone Hill
603m
Thornworthy Tor
Whitehouse Hill
Manga Hill
3
Fernworthy Circle
Fernworthy Reservoir
9
Sittaford Tor
10
Fernworthy Forest
Kit Rocks
Stone Circle
The Grey Wethers Stone Circle
2
Winney's Down
To Moretonhampstead
1
Broad Down
East Dart River
MOD Range
B3212
Devil's Tor
Rough Tor
Lower White Tor
0   1000m
Higher White Tor
To Princetown
Postbridge
START

The Scorhill circle.

START ▶ Take the footpath to the west of the Postbridge car park, following the track before climbing over Broad Down.

1 Cross the East Dart at the waterfall (unless river conditions prohibit, then head upstream, possibly as far as Kit Rocks), climbing rough ground above Winney's Down Brook to search just SW of Sittaford Tor (SX 6302 8281: the circle lies close to a leaning upright stone).

2 From Sittaford Tor follow a wall NW to cross the infant River Teign, then climb Whitehorse Hill.

3 Head north to Hangingstone Hill, keeping well to the right of the boggy ground.

4 Follow a rough path NNE past Wild Tor, and over the Hound Tors to the White Moor circle.

5 Head SE on a bearing along the southern side of Kennon Hill, to find the Buttern Hill circle at SX 6494 8847.

6 Cross Gidleigh Common to the SSE, to find the Scorhill circle at SX 6546 8738.

7 Use the clapper bridges to the south, then follow a path SSE through the Shovel Down standing stone rows. You'll have to deviate from the path to find the elusive three remaining stones of the circle at SX 6582 8619.

8 Head south to follow a wall to a gate, into Fernworthy Forest. Turn left at the first track junction, then right as the track drops towards the reservoir. Fernworthy circle sits in a clearing.

9 Continue west along the track, taking the first turn on the left. Keep right at the first fork, then right again at the second, to follow a very eroded path uphill out of the woods.

10 From the gate follow the wall towards Sittaford Tor (but not meeting it). The Grey Wethers will be visible, just to the left. Follow the path through the stones and along the valley, turning right at the road to find the car park.

High Willhays and Yes Tor.

28 Modest Mountains

Start / Finish   Belstone car park SX 622 938 / 50.7293, -3.9486

Distance   29km / 18 miles

Ascent   460m

Time   10 – 12 hours

In 2000, as part of their Right to Roam legislation, the Department of the Environment Food and Rural Affairs (DEFRA) decided to classify all land above 600m as mountainous. Overnight, our upland regions suddenly bristled with 'Defras'. While I'm not actually suggesting the adoption of this new classification, I think our collection of Munros, Hewitts and Marilyns will do, a quick glance across an OS Explorer Map 28 shows four, maybe five such peaks. And while they may not deserve a new definition, a route that pulls them together makes a fine if slightly demanding walk.

Setting out from the generous car park at the edge of Belstone, this walk meets the high moor along one of my favourite Dartmoor ridges (which features in a shorter walk on page 213). While the route encounters a string of fine tors, it is the slightly less bristly mound to the south that forms our initial goal.

Apart from being one of those dodgy 'Defras', at a height of 603m, Hangingstone Hill offers fine views across the moor in all directions. This is at least some compensation for the fact that the flat summit, complete with army lookout post, is hardly pretty. What you can see well from the stone blockhouse, off to the north-west, is the whale-back ridge holding Yes Tor and High Willhays. But before we head that way, in search of Dartmoor's crowning glory, and if we want to bag those remaining 600m 'peaks,' we need to head on south.

While few would rate Hangingstone Hill for its aesthetic qualities, it does feel very remote, and a sense of genuine wilderness is soon enhanced as you set out to visit the Peat Pass, 200m beyond and 1m below Hangingstone. The often-bare peat route is very rough, and often very wet and soggy. While technically only a satellite top, Peat Pass does still lift, just, above the 600m DEFRA line.

A passing visit to Whitehorse Hill, then a crossing of the infant East Dart close to the marked tinner's hut, sets you up for a steady plod over rough ground to Cut Hill. The rather bleak top does possess lovely views of Fur Tor.

Almost anyone who knows anything about Dartmoor will have heard of Yes Tor, and many still believe that, at 619m, it represents the highest point in the National Park. This is not surprising, as any view of the north side of the moor seems to confirm this suspicion. In fact, it was not until Captain William Mudge and Isaac Dalby of the Ordnance Survey extended their Devon survey to cover the north side of the moor, that the true situation was revealed on the first map of the area, printed on 11th October 1809. Even so, it seems most people still choose to continue ignoring this inconvenient fact.

Oddly, a close squint at the Explorer Map suggests that the Ordnance Survey still seem keen to support the myth, with Yes Tor marked in their largest peak-depicting font. I guess this is due to the trig point cemented to the top of the tor. Yet, only 1km or so to the south lies the apparently less dramatic outcrop of High Willhays.

Its name may be shown on the map with less ink, and its height is given in even fainter red print, but that height does read 621m. Now, by some mountain classification this makes Yes Tor a mere subsidiary peak. Step forward High Willhays, or Mount Willhays as it is known affectionately in the family.

Of course, those who know where we live could well argue that all this promotion is merely a ploy to try to raise the value of our family home. We do like to claim it has mountain views after all. But by the 2,000-foot rule, High Willhays and Yes Tor have every right to be considered alongside their more illustrious mountain cousins, by just over 37 feet and a little under 31 feet, respectively, if you're counting. What's more, this makes them not only the sole mountains in southern England, but also, by default, the highest. This ridge is certainly the most elevated point south of the Brecon Beacons, and in England the highest point below the Peak District other than the Black Mountains on the Welsh border.

After the plod back from Cut Hill, a track can be followed, along a somewhat circuitous route, over Okement Hill and on to within a short distance of your destination. Here the track can be left for the final push (gentle climb) to the cairn at the top of our mountain. Oxygen isn't required.

It has to be admitted that the High Willhays top is hardly breathtaking, especially as the impressive rock outcrop of Yes Tor, that well known pretender to the throne, sits within clear view to the north, and really is rather impressive. It still manages to look higher too. The tor also commands even better views out across North Devon to Exmoor, and west towards the moors above Bodmin. But High Willhays is higher, just. High enough that on a clear day you can even see the mountains of the Brecon Beacons, some 80 or 90 miles away to the north.

The name High Willhays might derive simply from the two words High and Well, although I'm not convinced. Nor does a suggested connection with the Celtic word *Gwylfa*, or watching place, look particularly promising, particularly as the ever present Yes Tor does this job so much better. At various times through history, High Willhays has been recorded as High Willies and even High Willows, demonstrating just how tenuous place name study can be. One name that does crop up to describe the ridge holding both the mini mountain and Yes Tor is the Roof of Devon. That sounds about right. Out with the ridge ladder.

Walking into the mire from Hangingstone Hill.

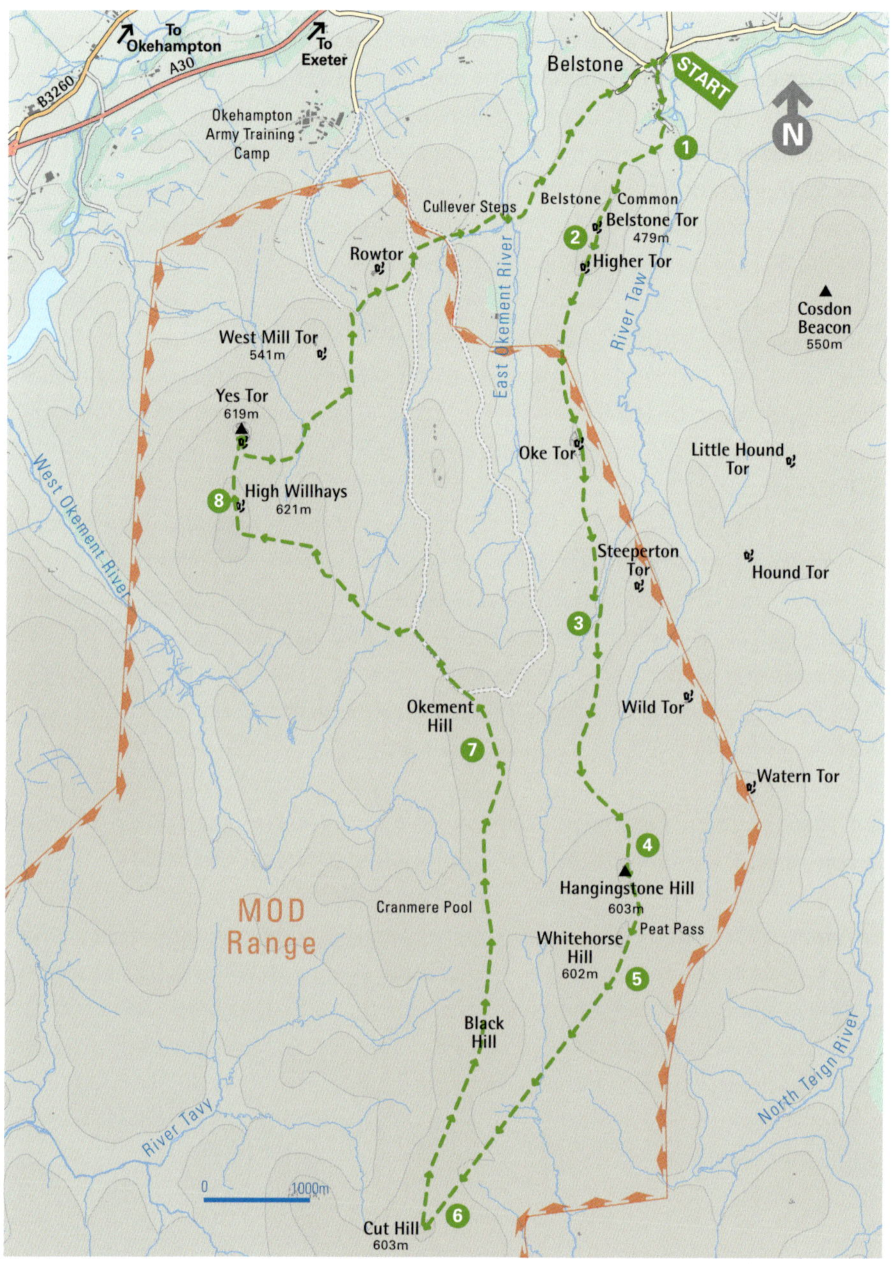

To Okehampton A30
To Exeter
B3260
Belstone
START
N
1
Okehampton Army Training Camp
Cullever Steps
Belstone Common
Belstone Tor 479m
2
Higher Tor
Rowtor
West Mill Tor 541m
East Okement River
River Taw
Cosdon Beacon 550m
Yes Tor 619m
Oke Tor
Little Hound Tor
8
High Willhays 621m
West Okement River
Steeperton Tor
3
Okement Hill
Wild Tor
Hound Tor
7
Watern Tor
4
Hangingstone Hill 603m
Cranmere Pool
Peat Pass
MOD Range
Whitehorse Hill 602m
5
Black Hill
North Teign River
River Tavy
0   1000m
Cut Hill 603m
6

START From Belstone car park walk through the village, taking the left fork at the village green. Follow the road uphill, through a gate, and out onto the open moor.

1 After about 200m, bear right off the track (there's a faint path) to climb the broad hill, working through scattered stones on the left (east) side of the first tor (this isn't named on OS maps).

2 Clamber through Belstone Tor (there is a path, of a sort), crossing Irishman's Wall to pass Higher Tor to the left before following a now clear path along the broad ridge, meeting a rough track that passes Oke Tor and then drops to a stepping-stone crossing of the Taw.

3 Follow the track to Hangingstone Hill.

4 Head southish across a soggy and very rough peat ridge to Whitehorse Hill. I'm still not sure of the best route, but skirting around to the east is a good idea.

5 Head SW on a bearing, to the tinner's hut marked on the OS map. After crossing the Dart, work your way slowly uphill to climb Cut Hill.

6 On a clear day, Black Hill is obvious just east of north. Otherwise, walk on a bearing again to cross this high ground before skirting, as best you can, the marshy ground around Cranmere Pool, making for the track at Okement Hill.

7 A reasonably good track can now be followed on a meandering route, towards the High Willhays ridge. Leave the track at around SX 587 891, to climb to the summit cairn.

8 A pretty clear track/path heads north to find Yes Tor, and another arm of this track heads east, then north, to skirt West Mill Tor and Rowtor, before crossing the East Okement River at Cullever Steps and leading back to Belstone.

Nine Stones circle, with High Willhays on the horizon.

Multi-Day Routes

29 Central Dartmoor

Start / Finish   Belstone car park SX 622 938 (50.7275, -3.9548)

Distance   54km / 34 miles

Ascent   715m

Time   3 days

I've mentioned my enthusiasm for meandering, so the origins of this walk should come as no surprise. One fine summer morning, after pouring over a map, spotting a favourite route here, a particularly enjoyable path there, we decided to just set out. Our carefully considered expedition aim? To head south.

Actually, our sortie was a little more developed. We would head south across Dartmoor until it grew dark, put up a tent, wake in the morning refreshed and keen to head on, walk south a bit more, turn east for a while, or maybe west, before striking north, perhaps popping up a tent once again if we hadn't reached our waiting van before dusk. We let family know we would be on the moor... for a while. Our route turned out to be a corker, and is presented here for those who fancy a few days out on the moor, but would prefer a route to follow.

Right from the start we were just making it up. Ah the freedom. Nowhere particular to be at any projected moment. No schedule, no waypoints, in fact no real destination. Just up onto the high bit, wander thataway for a while and see where we'd end up. Bill Tillman, mountain and ocean explorer, once suggested 'Any worthwhile expedition can be organised on the back of an envelope.' We decided to dispense with the effort. I think he would have approved.

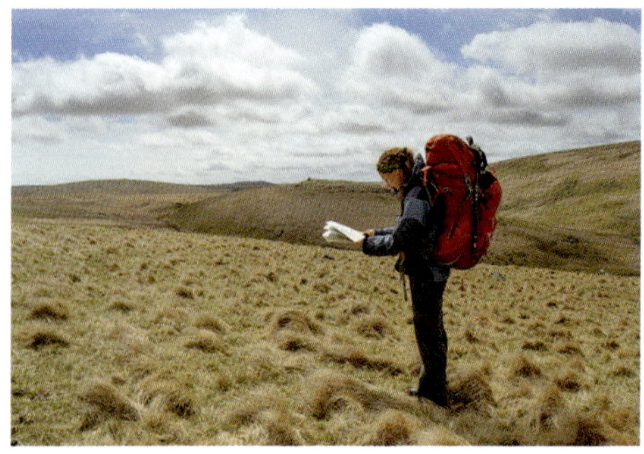

Looking north from the High Willhays ridge, with Lints Tor on the skyline.

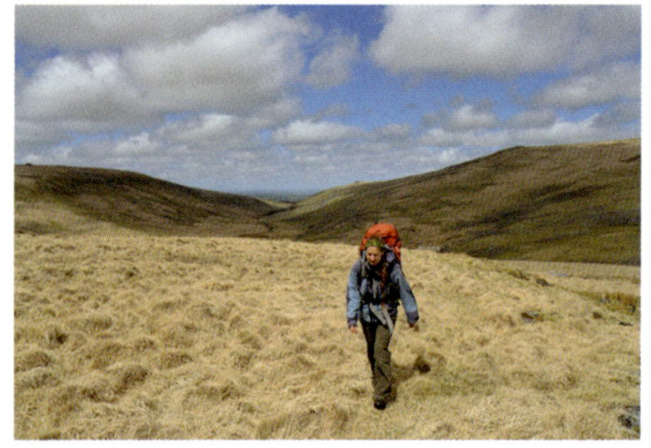

Heading up to Lints Tor.

To be fair, we had picked a starting point, the village of Belstone, set not far from our home on the northern edge of the moor. Reaching the last gate before open ground, still weighing up various appealing ridge options, the rarely walked (by us at least) path that sets out south-west past the Nine Stones circle suddenly looked the most alluring... but after that?

We ended up at High Willhays because of tarmac. Admittedly, this flat surface lay over only a short section, along the left-hand fork in a track. The route heading off uphill to the right was stony, vaguely uneven, and therefore far more adventurous. Up we went.

I'm not sure that the Lebanese-born poet Gibran Khalil Gibran had quite our situation in mind when he wrote 'and when you have reached the mountain top, then you shall begin to climb', but standing by the Willhays cairn, the highest spot in southern England and a popular family destination, this did seem a fitting physical and metaphorical stance from which to view afresh the empty upland prospect before us. Now we could start to explore, to find out how this unstructured encounter with the moor, one without design or expectation, might influence our perhaps rather settled response to its already proven charms.

Familiarity not only requires this sort of approach every now and then, but also helps in its application. At almost any point along the route we could picture much of the land ahead, or at least the general detail. It was easy, then, to assess the alternatives from a range of well-known, and sometimes less well-known options. As for decisions... well, we continued to leave those until they needed to be made; perhaps when we reached that rock outcrop over there, or the next bend in the stream. Aimless, perhaps literally, but then that was the point, to meet an old friend from a different perspective.

Not that someone with less in-depth knowledge of the moor might not benefit from the same approach. Perhaps to set out in this rather laid-back way with no Dartmoor experience would be pushing it. As already suggested, this reasonably sizeable chunk of shattered granite and bog really is quite wild after all. But for the accomplished walker, particularly one with at least a handful of Dartmoor

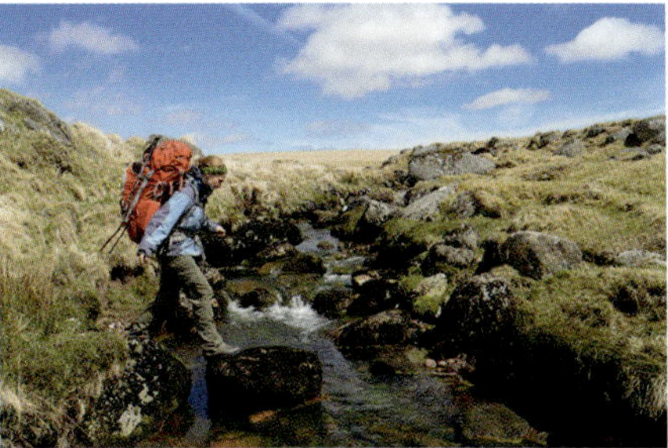

trips under their moulded hip-belt, this is a fine way to get to know that lofty bit between Exeter and Plymouth. Map, compass, bulging rucksack... and go.

So which way now?

We stood squinting into some very pleasing sunshine, surveying the familiar scene. Kitty Tor? Last visited late the previous summer. Hangingstone Hill? Late last week. The horizon was dotted with granite eruptions; all very pretty, but all rather well-known too.

As we cogitated, we sauntered. And as the broad ridge fell gently, so did we, until our gaze settled on... Lints Tor.

Looking out from the end of the High Willhays ridge, we'd often been intrigued by this small tor, set proud in the middle distance on its motte-impersonating hill like a tiny Norman castle. Somehow though, it never quite fell in line with any of our walks. Now, we realised, was our chance to take a closer look.

Sat low on its grassy mound alongside the West Okement River, this little tor proved to be a gem. Modest in size and elevation perhaps, overlooked on almost all sides by higher ground, it still managed to maintain a commanding air over its moorland domain. After a little feeble bouldering we moved on, our route already empty, wild and pathless.

It was also pretty people-less too. After speaking to a black Labrador and its owner at Lints, we didn't meet another soul until the B3357 the next day. Two walkers did

Left: morning light on the River Walkham.

Right: crossing the Walkham, before heading up towards Great Mis Tor.

appear briefly on the skyline a mile or so on, but seemed to share our preference for solitude, dropping quickly out of sight again.

Through the simple process of avoiding familiar ground, with a corresponding veer towards anything unusual or interesting, we nearly reached the top of Great Kneeset, crossing a pony-strewn flank to the west, and failing to summit by a few metres. In slow succession, we then failed to crest Fur Tor, Lynch Tor and Cocks Hill as well.

What we found instead were wonderful tracts of open moorland, unvisited (at least by us) slopes and rarely trodden (by anyone) stream valleys and low ridges. After a very pleasant night, camped alongside the infant River Walkham on the north side of Greena Ball, we cheerfully failed to reach the top of Great Mis Tor too.

Admittedly, heading south in the morning, we couldn't help sliding pretty close to North Hessary Tor, but then this granite outcrop, set below a vast telecommunications spike, is one we'd not visited before. It was now pretty clear that we were soon to meet Princetown too, but after that?

Even as we left the square, maintaining a now entrenched and very liberating air of indecision we still hadn't made up our minds. At the very last minute, and for no better reason than the track ran straight on ahead, we continued in a southerly direction to add South Hessary Tor to our list of new stony acquaintances. Sticking with the track, and overtaken by a succession of mountain bikers, we made for Nun's Cross.

We'd been here before, in fact only a few weeks earlier, following a more definite route, and an old one at that. That walk was about as different from our present one as is possible on the moor. While our current meander had all the permanence of a shifting summer breeze, that route was set in stone – literally.

Nun's Cross.

Nobody really knows much about the origins of what is most commonly called the Monk's Path. Legends abound of course, but then you need only the smallest standing stone on this open expanse of tumbled granite and waving grass to attract a story involving the Devil's pencil sharpenings, a headless ghostly rabbit or some rather unlikely hag-induced disaster. What is fairly certain is that a collection of granite crosses, stretching roughly east-west across the southern half of the moor, represents markers on the line of a now redundant path. This runs between the largely rebuilt Buckfastleigh Abbey, and the now closed (blame Henry VIII) abbey to the west, at Buckland. Nun's Cross, stood before us, even has the words BOC LOND carved into one face.

Horn's Cross.

Not all the surviving route-markers stand on the open moor. At least one (Hawson's Cross) overlooks a road junction between Buckfast and high ground, while to the west, Crossgate and Yennadon Crosses can still be seen on the road verge, approaching the B3212. Our walk had taken in the eleven still standing, in the intervening 13km of upland, between Venford and Burrator Reservoirs.

The western Ter Hill Cross, looking out along the line of the walk.

Looking west from Mount Misery Cross.

The Monk's Path

For those tempted to give this ancient path a go, the route extends between car parks at Venford (SX 686 713) and Burrator (SX 568 693) Reservoirs. Unfortunately, a circular route is impractical, and two cars and the old shuttle process will probably be needed. On the plus side, the whole route lies outside the military firing areas.

Walked from east to west, the monumental list, in order of appearance, includes:
Horn's Cross (669 711), tall on its replacement shaft
Horse Ford Cross (660 713), rather short on the remains of its original one
Skaur Ford Cross (655 715), followed by
two crosses on Ter Hill (642 707 and 641 706)
another lone monolith then braves its station on Mount Misery (637 706).

Continuing west you'll meet:
the slightly bizarre Childe's Tomb Cross (626 703), largely reconstructed, and complete with an unlikely suggested origin
Goldsmith's Cross (617 702), found and subsequently re-erected by a naval officer on leave from his ship, before arriving at
Nun's Cross, stood before us on our present walk (604 699).
Newleycombe Cross (591 703), and then
Crazywell Cross (584 704) forms the tail of the route, the last two are set a little to the south, and north, respectively of the track dropping downhill towards Burrator Reservoir.

An abridged version of the route is offered on page 201.

Those medieval road-sign teams certainly knew their job, and while a map and compass are always a good idea, I suspect it would be quite possible to walk this route relying only on these markers, on a clear day at least.

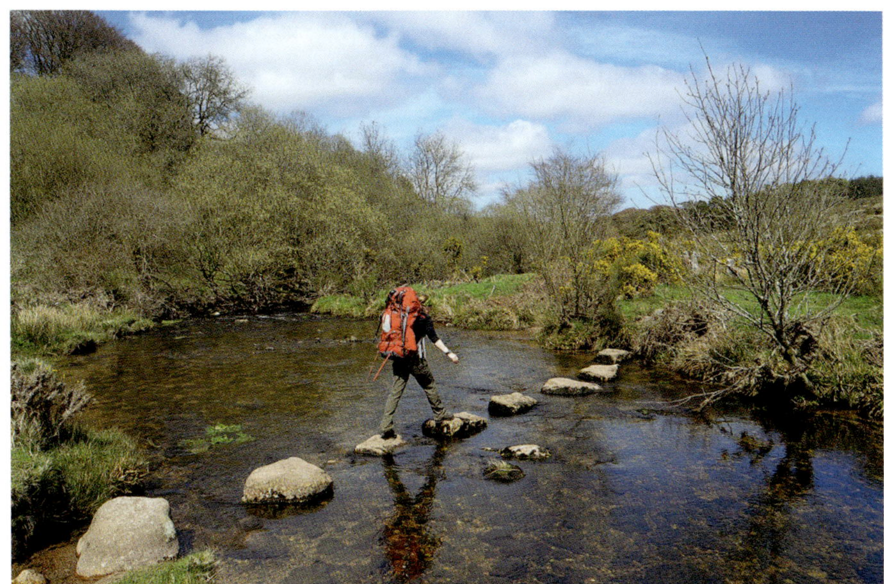

The stepping-stones over the Swincombe at Sherberton.

Resisting the attraction of re-walking the Monk's Path in the other direction, we did at least think it best to now make a turn. With nothing nearly so certain as a medieval stone marker to head for next, we decided to follow Devonport Leat towards the tin mining remains at Whiteworks. From here, we struck out over the southern edge of Royal Hill, making for a double river crossing near Sherberton. Once two fine sets of stepping-stones had been negotiated, we climbed close to, but not over, Bellever Tor, before pottering down through shady woodland to Postbridge.

I'll have to admit, that after sitting and eating an ice-cream on a welcome bench, it was less than easy to saddle up again. Rarely has the climb up a hill as low as Broad Down felt like such hard work. Mind you, as the sun fell slowly towards the horizon, I wouldn't have swapped our campsite, tight on the bank of the East Dart River, for many other spots.

Homer might have felt at home next morning as dawn appeared with rosy-fingered glow. Not that I felt much like a Greek hero, with legs still stiff from the previous two days moorland rambling.

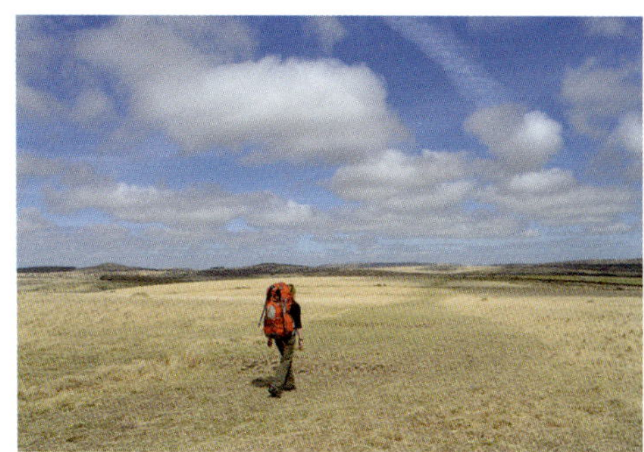

Heading out along a popular route from Whiteworks.

Approaching Sittaford Tor.

Fortunately, by the time Sittaford Tor rose into view over the edge of Winney's Down, everything seemed to be working properly again. The sun was out, the air was still and clear and we had the moor to ourselves. Reaching Whitehorse Hill, and finally rising above 600m again, we looked out at a sheet of white cloud stretched below us in every direction. While we had sunshine, the rest of the county was probably muttering curses about another dull Devon day.

Making our way across the short, boggy stretch to Hangingstone Hill, I recalled the old Kenyan joke about how to spot a drunk driver – it'll be the one travelling in a straight line. You'd certainly have to be pretty inebriated to try a direct route across this impressively rutted collection of peat outcrops and soft, sludgy brown pools, no matter how close the two high points seem to be.

And then, as we loitered again, munching a little further through a home-made loaf and enjoying the sunlit landscape ahead, we revelled in the pleasurable uncertainty that had stamped such a distinctive mark on our journey. Despite numerous self-propelled journeys each year, we rarely set out without pretty clear destinations and objectives. It's all too easy then to work diligently, and perhaps rather blindly, to meet them. Forced this time to pause at almost every new rise or valley opening, to ponder on the next stage of our route, much more time was spent in actually looking at what lay around us. With all this meditative scrutiny I'm sure came a greater appreciation, and enjoyment, of the complexity and just plain beauty of what Dartmoor has to offer. We certainly embraced the flexibility. At one point we'd turned right for no reason other than the sky in that direction was bluer. On another occasion, a developing route idea was abandoned to leave a pair of blond-maned ponies alone with their very new foal.

Mind you, despite the lack of planning, we still had very real goals, they just didn't happen to be physical ones. Peaks and passes where replaced by the purity and simplicity of movement and discovery.

Following a descent from Hangingstone, we met our last choice – a brief plod up Steeperton Tor, the short climb up the other side of the gorge towards Oke Tor, or

a downhill route running alongside the fledgling Taw. I'd like to say that we chose the river because we'd not followed it before. Truth is our legs were tired, and this gentle descent looked much easier than the familiar uphill options. It was worth it though, and we dawdled constructively along the bank before bursting out into that surprisingly broad open area between Oke Tor and Cosdon Hill.

Back in Belstone, heaving my rucksack into the back of the van, I realised our hard-pressed 'tin tent' had formed the only fixed physical destination during our walk. Had this mattered?

I started with a quote from Major Tillman, and can't help another springing to mind here at the finish. This almost non-stop traveller was once asked, what was the best way to have an adventure. His answer? 'Pull on a good pair of boots and walk out the door.'

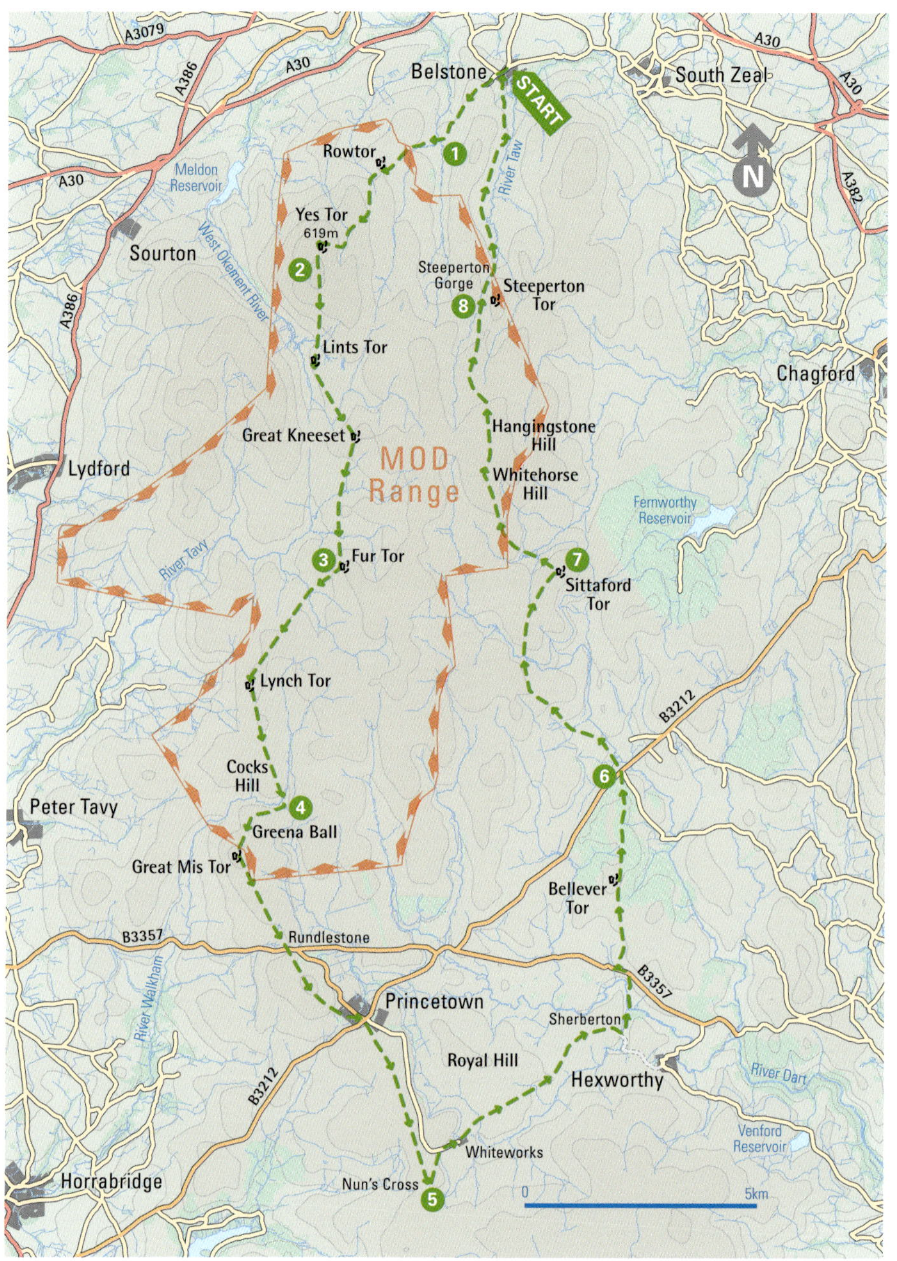

A3079
A386
A30
A30
A30
Belstone
START
South Zeal
A382
N
Meldon
Reservoir
Rowtor
1
River Taw
Sourton
West Okement River
Yes Tor
619m
2
Steeperton
Gorge
Steeperton
Tor
8
Chagford
Lints Tor
A386
Great Kneeset
MOD
Range
Hangingstone
Hill
Lydford
River Tavy
Whitehorse
Hill
Fernworthy
Reservoir
Fur Tor
3
7
Sittaford
Tor
B3212
Lynch Tor
Cocks
Hill
Peter Tavy
4
Greena Ball
6
Great Mis Tor
Bellever
Tor
B3357
Rundlestone
B3357
River Walkham
Princetown
Sherberton
River Dart
River Walkham
B3212
Royal Hill
Hexworthy
Horrabridge
Whiteworks
Venford
Reservoir
Nun's Cross
5
0
5km

START Walk into the village, passing the green on the right to head out onto the moor, following a good track to Cullever Steps.

1 Cross the East Okement River and climb to find the track that skirts Rowtor and West Mill Tor. Then climb to Yes Tor, before taking the broad ridge S to High Willhays.

2 Continue south from High Willhays, dropping to visit Lints Tor before continuing up the West Okement valley to skirt Great Kneeset, Little Kneeset and Fur Tor, passing the latter fairly close to the west.

3 Drop downhill to cross Fur Tor Brook and the infant Tavy, before climbing gently to Lynch Tor, from there heading almost south to Cocks Hill, before continuing to drop to the Walkham Valley (we camped here).

4 Climb a little west of south to cross Greena Ball and climb to Great Mis Tor. From here taking the right of way through Rundlestone and on to Princetown, where a good track leads on from the square to Nun's Cross.

5 Head north-east to locate the Devonport Leat, following it upstream to find Whiteworks, and a good, marked route across high ground to the south of Royal Hill and on to cross the river at Sherberton. Follow a marked path to cross the B3357, passing close to Bellever Tor on the way to Postbridge.

6 Just before the car park, take a track left off the road, heading out to cross Broad Down before dropping to the East Dart River (our second camp), where a crossing can be made at various points before climbing to find a wall that leads to Sittaford Tor.

7 Follow another wall NW to drop, and then climb, to Whitehorse Hill, continuing north over Hangingstone Hill to find a good track that heads north to a ford, below (and to the west) of Steeperton.

8 Drop down Steeperton Gorge to follow dry ground to the west of the Taw, finding a good track that heads back to Belstone.

Watern Tor, during our Perambulation.

30 Dartmoor Perambulation

Start / Finish	South Zeal car park SX 652 934 (50.7248, -3.9113)
Distance	82km / 51 miles
Ascent	1,535m
Time	2 – 4 days

'Et inde liealiter usque ad parvam hogam que vocateur para Hundetorre.'

Many of the paths and tracks that criss-cross Dartmoor are ancient in origin, with a number probably dating back to the earliest days of farming in the Neolithic period, possibly even before that. It has long been suggested that prehistoric features such as stone circles, stone rows and even burial mounds were as much navigation aids as foci for ritual, providing very visible marker points in the landscape for prehistoric travellers.

Route guides must have existed from an early date too, even if the first were almost certainly learnt by word of mouth, to be recited as the journey took place. These routes are long gone of course, and written or printed route guides don't appear until much more recently, the earliest dating from books and maps printed in the eighteenth and nineteenth centuries. There is however one pretty dramatic exception. And not only is this route guide fairly old, it also results in what can only be described as a very long Dartmoor tramp.

The story starts with Henry III making a very generous gift to his cousin Richard, Earl of Cornwall. Like all forests, the Forest of Dartmoor was an area of valuable hunting ground, and Henry was almost immediately in dispute with four local landowners about the extent of his lavish present. A survey was needed.

Approaching Cosdon, with Ernestorre, on the High Willhays ridge, off to the right.

Heading south from Cosdon, with Hound Tor and Thurlestone visible up ahead.

It's known today as the Perambulation, and in the year 1240, the Sheriff of Devon moved fast to comply with Henry's command. The royal instruction, inscribed on vellum, required 'twelve good knights of the country' to visit the forest and establish the exact line of the boundary.

Despite having taken place quite a while ago, more than just the existence of this surprising property assessment is known. All twelve knights involved (Henry obviously anticipated trouble with those landowners) are named. We even have the date, July 24th, when the survey commenced. Amazingly, a detailed description of the route taken by Hugo Bellay, Guy Breteville and their fellow surveyors also survives. Very useful to anyone interested in Dartmoor history, anyone familiar with medieval Latin that is.

Fortunately for Susannah and me, the manuscript has been translated, although disagreement still lingers around the identity of some of the waymarks. It's easy to agree that *Hundetorre* must be Hound Tor for example, the northern one that is, and few will argue that *Eylesburghe* is now Eylsbarrow, but what of *Ysfother* or *Turbarium de Alberysheved*, neither of which name appears on any modern map?

In the end, and despite some doubts over a landmark or two, there's reasonable consensus regarding the general route. To a large extent, even 800 years later, it's still there, fossilized in the land use history of the area, and over significant stretches of the journey around the moor, the route still follows this division between the forest and adjoining parishes, marked by a dotted line on OS 1:25,000 maps.

Back in the summer of 1240, those dozen knights aimed first for *Cossedone*, or Cosdon. Planning our re-enactment this was pretty convenient, as the hill fills a fairly hefty chunk of the view from our house. So, after a short drive, and rather late in the morning, we started out, climbing first to the remains of the beacon at the top of this broad mound.

From here, peering into the October sunlight ahead, we could already make out the next two ancient waymarks. Far off to the right, at possibly the highest point on the moor, sat *Ernestorre*, almost the last forest boundary on our circumnavigation. I

Thurlestone.

say possibly the highest point, because this is one of the medieval locations around which debate still wafts, but we'll come back to that... in a couple of days.

We stopped for lunch in the lee of Hound Tor, the northern and admittedly less imposing of the two granite outcrops sharing this name on the moor. Then on to Thurlestone. Although very close to Watern Tor, it's this more northerly outcrop that forms the old marker. Like an overblown 1950s American car wing, the exuberant granite shark's fin is hard to miss.

With a name this large, *Wotesbrokelakesfote* should be easy to find too, and the *fote*, or foot, of a stream known today as Hew Lake is simple to locate, where it meets the North Teign River. All well and good, but for at least a few hundred years, a stone known as the Manga Rock, has formed the corner of Gidleigh parish, thereby marking the edge of Dartmoor too. This stone may also have been the boundary in 1240. The debate about that still rumbles on.

Anyway, Susannah and I decided to find the rock: a rounded granite lump lying on a broad open slope amidst quite a few other rounded granite lumps. At least, once located, the letters GP, chiselled into a flank, confirmed its identity.

Manga Rock.

Long Stone, on Shovel Down.

The Heath Stone, inscribed with text in 1974.

Our first night, on the edge of what was known in the thirteenth century as the Turbarium de Alberysheved.

Onward then to a much more obvious stone marker: Long Stone, sat tall and proud on Shovel Down. Should you ever decide to give this route a go yourself, I suggest you cross the Teign close to the wall by the river junction, keeping tight alongside this boundary on your way east. We followed that dotted parish boundary on our map. It looked like a more direct route. All I can say is, I wish we'd taken our canoe.

Once we'd peered up in admiration at Long Stone, legs still soaked to the knee, we turned south once more.

Now one of the problems with using an old route description is that things can change, and at some point, between 1240 and today, someone had quite thoughtlessly built a reservoir across our path. To be fair, as evening began to fall, this actually made for a quite pleasant wander around the wooded edge. Eventually reaching the Heath Stone, vandalised in the 1970s, we moved on a little way to Hurston Ridge, camping for our first night, not far from the vague edge of Metheral Marsh, or the mysterious *Turbarium de Alberysheved*.

Dawn arrived in classic Dartmoor style; slowly, and without any real evidence that a sunrise had actually taken place. Packed up, we trudged uphill to the Bronze Age barrow of *Furnum Regis*, where, pushing my own skills in Latin translation to their very limits, I knew we'd arrived at King's Oven. Nothing in the vicinity looked warm enough to merit the name, mind you, but as we topped the rise and looked down on the Warren House Inn and Walla Brook Head, the sun did try to make amends, adding a gentle glow to the outlook.

Turning to their route notes, the 1240 surveyors would now have been invited to continue *sic in longum Wallebroke usque cadit in Dertam*, or along the course of the river. Hmm…

We were about to go off-piste.

Now I could blame the dense commercial plantation, which today stretches for quite some distance along the near riverbank, but in reality, a walk along this narrow

Left: looking down on the Warren House Inn and Walla Brook Head.

Right: working our way along the Walla Brook valley.

and deep-sided valley would always be tough. It's at this point that I'm going to mention that Susannah and I are far from the first walkers in recent years to have given this Dartmoor Perambulation a go. In fact, quite a few have made the rounds. And while this confession might be made at just this moment to avoid being falsely accused of claiming a 'first', in reality I'm mentioning it now only to point out that almost everyone else seems to have made the same route decision here.

On the day, this meant a slight swerve to the left, which would take us along good paths, and a section of road, to our next destination, the meeting of the Walla Brook with the East Dart. We salved any sense of guilt, by reminding ourselves that this deviation actually increased the distance. Besides, we argued, would mounted knights really have stuck tight by the river?

In the end, dropping downhill at the north end of Corndon Ridge, we did follow the stream for two or three kilometres to the confluence, fighting our way through thick undergrowth, and discovering some of the prettiest bits of Dartmoor we've

Walla Brook.

Crossing the West Dart.

seen. Judging by the tangled vegetation, including some very dense gorse (yes, it was quite prickly), I suspect very few people do the same.

A very pleasant riverside saunter took us on to Dartmeet. Gazing down from the high stone viaduct carrying the B3357, I wondered whether the fragmentary clapper bridge below had carried those knights 800 years before.

A stiffish climb, and a drop past Huccaby, found the West Dart, and a string of worn stepping-stones. Fortunately, following prolonged wet weather, these still stood clear of the water.

Ironically, crossing the narrow outfall, or foot, of O Brook proved more of a challenge, and we were thankful for a fallen tree that formed a natural bridge to the rough path on the far bank. As at many other points on this journey, I did wonder how mounted knights would have fared here. Did these eminent soldier-surveyors ride local ponies, or even (no, surely not) dismount and actually walk?

I'll admit we were growing a little tired by this point, and the slog up the stream edge to Dry Lake was a slight effort. Things didn't improve much, with some pretty rough going before the stone-festooned summit of Ryder's Hill. The incredibly marshy upland stretch to the head of Western Wella Brook was only slightly better, and by the time we'd struggled down through the extensive swathe of distorted tinner's refuse bounding the stream, the confluence with the Erme was met with some relief. Tent up in the dark, and dinner eaten, we were soon asleep.

It was dark when we emerged again, the light only beginning to reappear as we crossed the river and slogged, once more, uphill. Not an easy start to a morning, but more than compensated for by the views from Eastern White Barrow. As we made for *Grymsgrove*, or Erme Head, joining the Abbott's Way as we went, the sun emerged fully at last.

Arriving at the head of the Erme, and while wandering about in this remote spot in search of the next marker, I pondered on the fact that the job must have been much easier in 1240. While the knights may well have considered themselves above the need to engage directly in the hunt, there would have been a healthy retinue to call on; knights just didn't travel without at least one page or squire, probably both, to cater for their every need. Yet even this probably large team of eagle-eyed assistants may not have been required.

Like many of the boundary features on the route, this stone (marked, just to confuse things a little further, with an A for Arme) not only defined the edge of the forest, but also the parish alongside. Back then, and in a way that's hard for us to imagine today, the parish was very important indeed, and the exact limit or extent of the area was often a cause for friction with its neighbours. As a result, along with other officials, most parishes would appoint a 'meresman', a local topography expert, whose job it was to know those bounds. As they travelled from one parish to another, it's highly likely the knights, and their impressive entourage, would have employed these specialists to identify the key boundary markers, picking up a new one as each new boundary was met. Susannah and I just wandered about a bit until we reached the correct spot.

Camp two, by the Erme.

As we made for Grymsgrove, or Erme Head, joining the Abbott's Way as we went, the sun emerged fully at last.

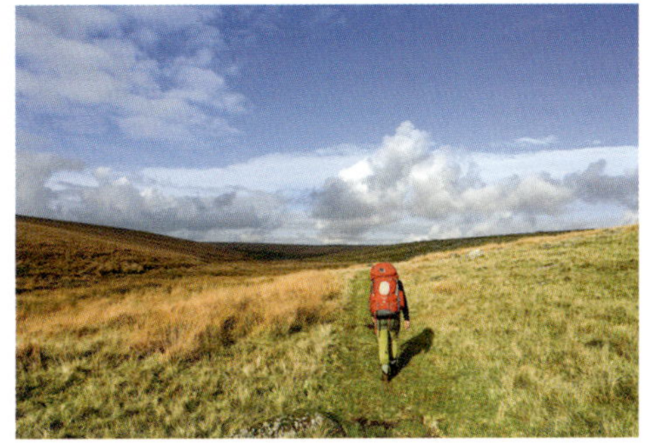

Heading up the upper Erme valley at the southern edge of the route.

Eylesbarrow.

South Hessary.

Left: looking south to the sea from close to North Hessary Tor.

Right: Great Mis Tor.

On a good path at last, we soon had *Eylesbarrow*, Siward's, or Nun's Cross and both South and North Hessary Tors under our belts. Cresting the rise beneath the imposing telecommunications mast near Princetown, we gazed out at Great Mis Tor, and a red flag!

Now I've written quite a few Dartmoor walking accounts, and with every one I add a small box informing readers that much of the high moor is in fact an Army firing range. I've done the same in the Safety section of this book, where, before setting out, I suggest prospective walkers check that it's not in use. The thing is, I very rarely do this myself. Yes, back in the 1970s and 80s, the range was often active, but today, and with shrinking numbers, the Army seems busier elsewhere. I am up on the high moor frequently, right through the year, and I see a red flag flying only very occasionally. Yet there it was.

Tired, the sun heading for the horizon, and with just 20km to go (right through the range), we plodded on, facing the unsavoury fact that we would soon have

to throw in the towel. Dropping into a slight dip, the tor was hidden for a while. Climbing out the other side, wondering how best to reach home, I looked up again, blinked a few times to be sure, before checking with Susannah.

'Can you still see that flag?'

She gazed up towards the granite outcrop and its flagpole. 'No, it's gone.'

Our pace lengthened again. Brushing with the tor, we dropped beyond to pitch our tent on the banks of the Walkham.

Sometimes, a day just works perfectly. Our third on the moor was a fine example.

Rising, the mist was thick, and moisture hung like tiny jewels from every blade of grass as we climbed to White Barrow. Walking on a bearing, visibility still no more

The view north along our route from Great Mis Tor.

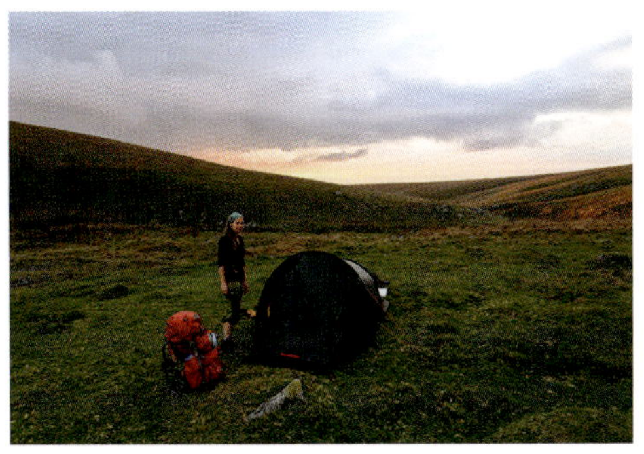

Evening three, on the banks of the Walkham.

Lynch Tor, appearing out of the mist.

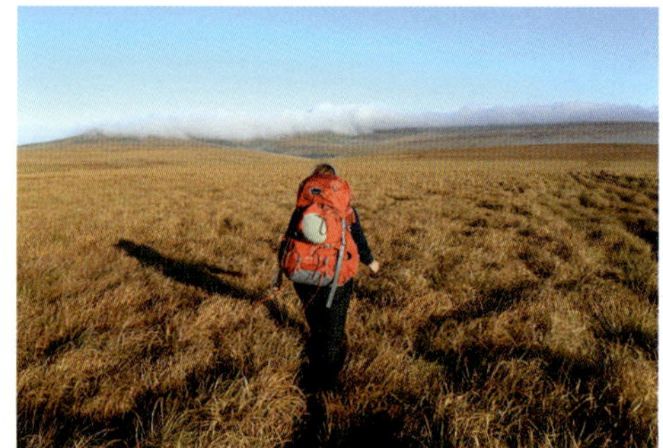

Heading towards the Tavy.

Sandy Ford on the West Okement River.

than a couple of hundred yards, Lynch Tor, and Limsboro Cairn, emerged from the pearly shroud as the sun burnt through.

A mist bow arced across our lumpy lack of a path, leading our way to the meeting of Rattle Brook and the Tavy. Even managing to throw my boots, not to the far side of the river as intended before wading across, but straight in, didn't seem to matter.

Rattle Brook Head, *la Westsolle*, or Stenga Tor and the steep drop to another stream crossing, this time the West Okement, all met under a stunning blue October sky. Even the climb to the very top of Dartmoor, legs really aching now, was glorious.

Aware of the *Ernestorre* debate, we visited both contenders for this lofty medieval waymark, High Willhays and Yes Tor. Erne, from the Norse *Örn*, was the Old English name for an Eagle, but sadly no large raptors perched at either outcrop to give the game away.

Last stop, the position of the long-demolished chapel of St Michael at Halstock. The site is reputed to be lost, and maybe it is, but a glance at an early description of the

Belstone Common, with Cosdon, near the start of our perambulation, lit yellow up ahead.

setting – 'by a ford' and 'with a spring' – and the perusal of couple of aerial photos, gave us somewhere to visit. It might even be the spot.

Climbing over the northern edge of Belstone Common to find our red van, the sun setting at our backs, we felt we'd achieved something. Now to send a report to the palace, letting HRH know that his forest is still there.

With this walk, and considering the account just given, I've decided to dispense with the style of route description presented elsewhere. Instead, here's the route in the form of a list of waymarks. It provides the names used in the Latin document from 1240, and the destinations as you can find them printed on 1:25,000 OS sheets today. Start with the first, and work your way round.

The route is marked up on the accompanying map as well, although only at a very small scale. I've given a number to indicate the site of each marker. With the account given above, the rest is up to you.

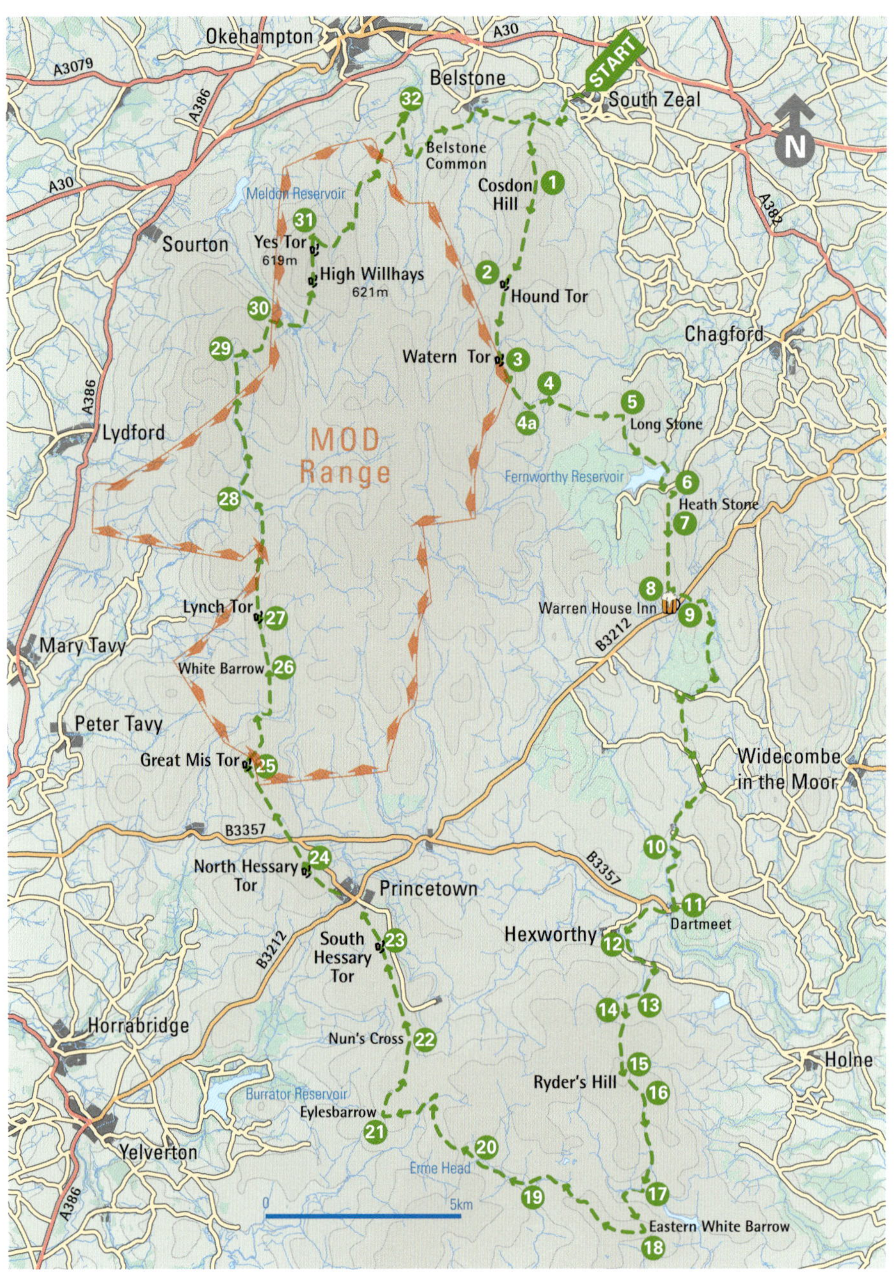

Okehampton
A3079
A386
A30
Belstone
START
South Zeal
A382
Belstone
Common
32
Cosdon
Hill
1
Meldon Reservoir
Sourton
31
Yes Tor
619m
2
High Willhays
621m
Hound Tor
Chagford
30
Watern Tor
3
29
4
5
Long Stone
Lydford
4a
MOD
Range
Fernworthy Reservoir
6
Heath Stone
28
7
Mary Tavy
Lynch Tor
27
8
Warren House Inn
9
B3212
White Barrow
26
Peter Tavy
Widecombe
in the Moor
Great Mis Tor
25
B3357
10
B3357
24
North Hessary
Tor
11
Dartmeet
Princetown
Hexworthy
12
B3212
South
Hessary
Tor
23
Horrabridge
Holne
14
13
Nun's Cross
22
Ryder's Hill
15
Burrator Reservoir
16
Eylesbarrow
21
20
Yelverton
Erme Head
A386
19
17
0   5km
Eastern White Barrow
18
N

1	*Cossedonne*	Cosdon	SX 636 915
2	*Hundetorre*	Hound Tor	SX 629 890
3	*Thurlestone*	Thurlestone (close to Watern Tor)	SX 629 869
4	*Wotesbrokelakesfote*	Hew Lake Foot	SX 636 859
4a	(or possibly Manga Rock)		SX 6361 8579
5	*Heighestone*	Long Stone (on Shovel Down)	SX 660 857
6	*Langestone*	The Heath Stone	SX 672 837
7	*Turbary de Alberysheved*	Metheral Marsh (or the head of the Metheral)	
			SX 671 830
8	*Furnum Regis*	Kings Oven (the cairn)	SX 672 813
9	*Wallebrokeshede*	Walla Brook Head	SX 675 810
10	Along the river to the confluence with the East Dart		SX 672 747
11	*Avenam*	Dartmeet	SX 672 732
12	*Okesbrokesfote*	O Brook confluence	SX 663 724
13	*la Dryworke*	Dry Lakes' tin streams	SX 661 710
14	*Dryefeld*	The gulley south from Dry Lake	SX 661 706
15	*Battyshull*	Ryder's Hill	SX 660 691
16	*Wester Wellabroke*	Western Wella Brook Head	SX 664 683
17	Down the river to Avon		SX 664 662
18	*Ester Whyteburghe*	Eastern White Barrow	SX 665 652
19	*la Redlake*	Red Lake Foot	SX 636 662
20	*Grymsgrove*	Erme Head (Arme Head stone)	SX 62058 67274
21	*Elysburghe*	Eylesbarrow	SX 600 686
22	*Crucem Sywardi*	Siward's or Nun's Cross	SX 604 699
23	*Ysfother*	South Hessary Tor	SX 598 723
24	*Aliam* (another) *Ysfother*	North Hessary Tor	SX 578 743
25	*Mystor*	Great Mis Tor	SX 562 770
26	*Mewburghe*	White Barrow	SX 568 793
27	*Lullingesfote*	Limsboro Cairn	SX 566 805
28	*Rakernesbrokysfote*	Rattle Brook Foot	SX 561 837
29	Up Rattle Brook to stone on west side of stream		SX 559 868
30	*la Westsolle*	Stenga Tor	SX 568 880
31	*Ernestorre*	Yes Tor	SX 581 902
32	*Capelle Sancti Michaelis de Halgestocke*		
		Halstock Chapel	SX 6052 9336

Bibliography

Here is a brief, select list of the many publications and websites used in the writing of this book:

Dartmoor Atlas of Antiquities, Jeremy Butler, Vols 1-4, Devon Books 1991-1994, ISBN 0861147003, 0861148894, 0861148665 and 0861148119

Dartmoor, Richard Worth, 1953, reprinted by David and Charles 1988, ISBN 0715351486

Dartmoor Stone, Stephen Woods, Devon Books 1988, ISBN 086114841

Guide to Dartmoor, William Crossing, 1912, reprinted by Peninsula Press 1990, ISBN 1872640168

The Dartmoor Reaves, Andrew Fleming, Batsford 1988, ISBN 0713456663

www.dartmoor.gov.uk

These three are also recommended reading for any Dartmoor walker:

Dartmoor 365, John Hayward, Curlew Publications 1991, ISBN 9780951403723

Mountain and Moorland Navigation, Kevin Walker, Pesda Press 2016, ISBN 978190609556

Outdoor First Aid, Katherine Willis, Pesda Press 2013, ISBN 9781906095352

Last, but not least, I also want to mention TGO, or The Great Outdoors. Over the years, similar versions of many of the walking routes in this book have appeared under my name in this fine magazine. Without the encouragement resulting from their use of my work, I doubt this book would have been written.

Index of Place Names